America's
Printed & Painted Fabrics
1600 - 1900

America's Printed & Painted Fabrics 1600-1900

by Florence H. Pettit

All the Ways There are to Print Upon Textiles
A Most Complete History of World Fabric Prints
All About the Printers and Patterns of America
& Other Things That Went On from 1600 to 1900

*with over 150 photographs and
six color plates
Twenty-six drawings by the author*

HASTINGS HOUSE · PUBLISHERS
New York

To: Robert

CONTENTS

I · HOW DO THEY PRINT A FABRIC?

II · FABRIC DECORATION BEFORE AMERICA

III · JAMESTOWN COLONY TO THE REVOLUTION, 1607-1775

IV · FROM THE REVOLUTION TO 1900

LIST OF ILLUSTRATIONS

ACKNOWLEDGMENTS

To my husband, Robert M. Pettit, who took almost half the pictures and made the prints of them, my loving thanks.

To three very special people who have helped me during several years of work, my gratitude:

> Miss Alice B. Beer, Curator of Textiles of the Cooper-Hewitt Museum of Design, Smithsonian Institution, N. Y. C. (formerly Cooper Union Museum), without whose encouragement and advice this would never have become a book,
>
> Miss Jean Mailey, Associate Curator in charge of the Textile Study Room of the Metropolitan Museum of Art, N. Y. C., and
>
> Mr. D. Graeme Keith, Curator of Decorative Arts of the M. H. DeYoung Museum, San Francisco.

And my thanks to some extraordinarily helpful and knowledgeable people:

> Mrs. Elsie McGarvey, Curator of Costume and Textiles of the Philadelphia Museum of Art,
>
> Mr. John Cummings, Curator of the Bucks County Historical Society, Doylestown, Pennsylvania,
>
> Mr. Peter H. Blair, Advertising Manager of the Cranston Print Works Company, N. Y. C.,
>
> Miss Marion A. Conant, Librarian of the Historical Society of Dedham, Massachusetts,
>
> Miss Janet MacFarlane of the Farmer's Museum, Cooperstown, New York,
>
> Miss Charlotte M. Wiggin, Curator of the Litchfield Historical Society, Litchfield, Connecticut,
>
> Mr. Albert Hise, Curator of the Massillon Museum, Massillon, Ohio,
>
> Miss Catherine Fennelly, Editor, Old Sturbridge Village, Sturbridge, Massachusetts,
>
> Miss Elizabeth Boyden, Assistant Curator of the Pocumtuck Valley Memorial Association, Old Deerfield, Massachusetts,
>
> Miss Rose T. Briggs, Curator of the Plymouth Antiquarian Society, Plymouth, Massachusetts, and
>
> Mr. Clifford P. Monahan, Director of the Rhode Island Historical Society, Providence.

PREFACE

The historian wants to make his story accurate for the experts, but he hopes to keep it lively for the laymen; he wants history lovers to find it significant and history ignorers to find it interesting. He can hardly expect history haters to read it at all. So, this book was not written *especially* for anyone, but simply for everyone who wants to know what the first American printed fabrics were, a little about their heritage, how they were made, and what else went on at the time.

Many books with titles such as *Two Decades of Textiles* or *A Textile History* illustrate only woven fabrics; they show no prints, and the text (by omission) does not even acknowledge their existence. In the lexicon of some experts printing is a secondary thing that can be done to make a fabric decorative; the view is also sometimes taken that *American* printed fabrics occupy a very small and obscure niche in history.

In this volume we leave those experts to their view and take our own look at the hundreds of artists, artisans, inventors and tradesmen who made up a part of the colorful heritage of America. We think you will agree that the story turns out to be a rather lively one — it is brought together here from many almost-lost sources — and much of it is animated with a peculiarly American verve. Printed fabrics, especially those made by hand, have a variety and an intrinsic charm about them that cannot be rivalled by the cloth that emerges from the measured mechanics of the loom.

The story needs some background since American colonists did not spring from the soil of New England fully clothed in linsey-woolsey or calicoes. So, first we shall explore how *all* textile printing is done, then review briefly the early fabrics of the world, and then tell the American story starting with the Jamestown colony and ending at the turn of the 19th century. The tale is told with many pictures and not so many words about American printed and painted fabrics. We learn about the people who used and wore the prints and especially about the enterprising people who made them.

America's
Printed & Painted Fabrics
1600 - 1900

Fig. 1. A Textile Printer's Trade Card, 17th century, from *The Chintz Book*, by MacIver Percival, N. Y.: Frederick A. Stokes Co., Inc., 1923

I

How Do They Print a Fabric?

THE BASIC METHODS

Pᴿɪɴᴛᴇᴅ fabrics have certain distinctive characteristics because of the way they are made and the fabrics pictured in this book will seem to take on a whole range of personalities and styles, once we know how they were done — and where, and for what use. Experts can date and place fabrics within inches because they recognize something about the printing method and the design style — even though they cannot always tell exactly how patterns were printed. Clearly defined qualities tell many things about prints, and usually make them look consistently as they should, but they can be fakes, too; prints have sometimes imitated woven patterns, they have also been made to look like patchwork, like wallpaper, like rush matting and like embroidery. They have added flavor to history by being — on occasion — forbidden to be worn, illegal to be sold, and so thin that women had to invent pantaloons to wear under them. And once printed calicoes rescued New England from a financial depression.

The fabric printer wants to accomplish one or more of these purposes: to impart color to cloth, to remove color from cloth, to enable the cloth to receive color, or to enable cloth to resist color. He has many ways of working and uses a variety of tools and materials, some of which are familiar to us even though the names of the four basic methods may sound technical and unfamiliar. They are: direct, discharge, mordant dyeing and resist printing. After we define these briefly, we shall take a look at the techniques used by printers to accomplish them. The four are called *printing* methods, but they also include painting, dyeing and bleaching.

1. DIRECT PRINTING

This is when color is applied directly to the cloth by painting or printing it on; it is the oldest and simplest method and may be done in three ways (these are sometimes referred to as *chemical* colors, but can be any one of a variety of pigments and dyes):

(1) *Painting* is when the color is put on the cloth by hand, usually freehand from a brush or painted through a stencil; it can be done also with fingers, sticks, feathers and daubers.

Fig 2. Canvas, hand painted — Peru. Courtesy of the Cooper-Hewitt Museum of Design, Smithsonian Institution

Fig. 3. Printed linen, Russia, 18th century; block printed on heavy, natural color linen in black and red-orange pigments. Courtesy of the Cooper-Hewitt Museum of Design, Smithsonian Institution

(2) *Relief printing* is when the parts of a block or plate that are to print are cut so that they stand up in relief from the non-printing background areas of the block and are inked or coated with dye and pressed onto the cloth to print. This is block printing (and the seldom-used relief roller-printing) and has a bold, direct look to it, usually without extremely fine detail or fine lines.

(3) *Intaglio printing* is when the design is cut *into* the block or plate; the name comes from the Italian verb "intagliare," meaning to carve or engrave. The cut plate is inked, the flat surface is wiped clean, then printed and when the engraved plate is pressed into the cloth, the color is "pulled out" of the incised lines or areas onto the cloth. This can be done by wood engraving (end-grain cutting in hard wood), copper or brass plates, or incised copper or metal rollers. It has a feeling of delicacy and detail impossible to achieve in block printing, but can also have large solid areas of color where many finely incised lines give up their color in one solid spot.

Fig. 4. Copper-plate print on linen, c. 1786, France, Toile de Jouy "L'Amérique à la France." Courtesy of the Smithsonian Institution

The twentieth century — not covered in this volume — makes use of two more methods of direct printing: a stencil process called silk-screen printing and lithography, or offset-lithography, printing.

Color is not the only thing that can be printed directly on cloth; wax, pastes, chemicals, lacquers and bleaches may be applied this way, too; they are described later.

2. DISCHARGE PRINTING

This is a process of *removing* color from cloth after it has been dyed. Chemicals with a bleaching action are printed on dyed cloth, then it is processed so that the dye comes out, or is "discharged," where the bleach was printed. This gives a white or undyed pattern on a dyed ground; it has much the same appearance as a resist print. Commercial printers today use the discharge method often; it has been done in many forms since the early days of printing and can be combined with other methods of multiple color printing.

Fig. 5. Dark blue sheer cotton woven with a pattern-stripe, discharge pattern in white; Arnold Print Works, c. 1870. Courtesy of the Museum of the Rhode Island School of Design

Fig. 6. Cotton, resist-dyed with various mordants and madder; from north India, c. 1300 (found in Fostat, Egypt). Courtesy of the Cooper-Hewitt Museum of Design, Smithsonian Institution

3. MORDANT DYEING

This is really a form of direct printing, but because it is rather special we list it as another basic method; colors applied in this way are called *raised* colors. Mordants are chemicals with two properties: (1) they are "fixers" of color, and (2) they make cloth receptive to dye. Some fabrics can't be dyed or printed at all without first using a mordant. One or more of these substances are printed on the cloth in a pattern, then the cloth is dipped into dye. Only the *receptive* printed parts will soak up the dye (or "raise" it) and become permanently colored; colors will wash out of every other part. Sometimes the whole cloth is treated with a mordant first, then printed with a dye. Different chemical mordants will cause the cloth to turn different colors in the same dye pot, and this magical process has been discovered, rediscovered and used all through the history of printed fabrics. Many substances serve as mordants, including the many forms of metallic oxides, tartaric, acetic and sulfuric acids, and lime in various forms.

4. RESIST PRINTING OR DYEING

This is mostly a hand process and consists of a sealing-off, or coating, of the cloth so that it will *resist* dye color in a pattern; these are sometimes called *dipped* colors. Starch pastes or waxy stuffs are hand painted or printed from blocks on the white cloth in a pattern, then the cloth is dipped into dye, fixed, and the paste or wax is washed or melted out or scraped off. The pattern is thus left as white cloth where the paste or resist medium was applied, and the rest of the cloth is colored. Repeated wax-paintings and dye-baths may follow. Javanese batiks are masterpieces of resist printing (wax-painting and dyeing) in many colors. In early America the so-called blue resists were simple paste-printed and indigo-dyed patterns. Cloth also may be sealed off by being tied tightly in patterns with waxed string, or is sometimes tied around pebbles or pegs, then dyed; this resist method is called tie-dyeing. The distinctive look of a resist print is its lack of sharp precision, and in the case of wax-painting, the crackles in the wax occasionally take the dye and show clearly. Some very early Java batiks were done so carefully and painted and dyed so many times that they are precise and wonderfully detailed. (See also Fig. 13.)

The four basic printing methods: direct, discharge, mordant dyeing, and resist printing are used sometimes alone, sometimes in combination in accordance with whatever method will work best on the cloth fibres. Cotton and linens can be printed without mordants, but are sometimes treated with tannic acid first; wool and silk almost always require mordants, though wools are seldom printed. In the early days trial and error was the way to discover printing secrets; now fibre technology and dye chemistry are of utmost importance to the industry. Most of the processes are an effort to make colors *fast* — a

Fig. 7.   Egyptian wax-printed and dyed cotton, c. 13th century.
Courtesy, Museum of Fine Arts, Boston

problem that has been the fabric printer's biggest headache for thousands of years. The ancient printer used all sorts of substances, juices, and liquids — among them cow dung and his own urine — to fix colors. It seems safe to conclude that some things were tried in true desperation! The dyer's skill was regarded as a sort of magic; he himself had no idea what made it work. In the Holy Land the dyer's skill was held in such high regard that the workers were freed of a requirement to have "clean hands" for certain ceremonies and for eating. Through the years knowledge of dyeing increased and by 1900 it had become a fairly exact science. Even today, however, when synthetic dyes are controlled from start to finish by the scientist, colors sometimes fade or run. And some venerable cloth fragments dyed centuries ago and now owned by museums still magically retain their bright color.

*   *   *

HAND PRINTING PROCESSES

Designs may be applied to cloth by hand or by machine in several ways. The first and most-used method of hand printing was block printing — today the most-used process is silk-screen printing. Seldom-used methods are stencil, batik, tie-dyeing, and painting. Since the invention of roller-printing about 1785 most fabrics have been printed by power presses with metal rollers, which originally printed three or four colors and now as many as sixteen. We describe all these methods here briefly as an introduction to descriptions accompanying each photograph.

1. HAND BLOCK PRINTING

This is a process of applying colors onto cloth, bark fibres, skins, etc., from an inked block into which a design has been cut. This is the oldest, slowest, and in many ways the finest method of fabric printing. Many primitive methods of decorating by pressing natural forms into clay, then using the hardened clay with dye to print, or by pressing carved wood forms onto cloth, skins and grass-weavings are the origins of the block print. South Sea island and Hawaiian tapa cloths are handsome examples of primitive block prints. For these, a pounded-out sheet of inner tree bark was printed with carved wooden blocks dipped in vegetable dyes or juices. The long-lasting fibrous sheets served as all-purpose cloth for household and decorative uses.

American Indians printed small block patterns on some of their baskets, using carved turnips dipped in dye or juices.

Blocks for fabric printing may be solid wood, solid metal, metal fastened to wood, felt glued to wood or combinations of these. The color can be

ig. 9. Printed tapa cloth from he Fiji Islands in two shades of rown. Courtesy of the Smith-onian Institution

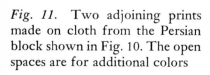

Fig. 10. Wood printing block, Ispahan, Persia, 17th century. Size of printing surface is 5″ x 7⅜″; thickness is 1¾″. Courtesy of the Museum of Art, Rhode Island School of Design

Fig. 11. Two adjoining prints made on cloth from the Persian block shown in Fig. 10. The open spaces are for additional colors

anything from berry juices to a mixture of dye and paste (gum tragacanth or similar thickener); in our century the color is sometimes an oil-base ink and and the block is carved linoleum.

The procedure is briefly this: the pattern is planned on the designer's drawing table. He may make his design any size from a very small hand-size unit up to a dimension of from 15 to 18 inches — not much larger. The block may be rectangular or square, or it may be cut to follow the contour of the design unit; the printing surface must be absolutely flat, but the back can have a handle carved into it, or attached to it. The design may be drawn directly on the wood, or it may be transferred by tracing it from a drawing (in reverse) on the block. The design is then carved with a knife and curved gouges so that only the design itself is left standing. All background or non-printing parts are cut away to a depth of about $\frac{1}{16}$″ or more so that the design stands up in relief, and the dye or color is applied only to the elevated parts. Each color to be printed must have a separate block and each must be planned and keyed to fit with the others so that all colors will print in register. Small metal pins called "pitch pins" are driven into the four corners of the block (or at least two corners) in the same position, and these are used to register the colors in a multi-color design. The small pins receive the dye or ink along with the design and the printer sets the second and succeeding blocks on the cloth so that the pin-dots coincide with those from previous blocks. These little register dots can sometimes be seen on hand blocked fabrics. Register may also be achieved by marking off the fabric in advance of printing. Sometimes fine line parts of the design are made in metal. Strips of brass, copper, or iron are shaped into the design, then driven on edge into the wooden block and leveled so that their thin top edges take the dye and print onto the cloth as a durable but delicate part of the pattern — often the outline. This is called a *coppered* block and was commonly used in colonial days to print embroidery and braid patterns. Sometimes straight nails or metal pegs are driven into the block, leveled, and inked to print a small pattern of many dots; this is called "picotage," from the French word for *prick*: "picoter," and the English sometimes called these "Pinned Grounds" or "Piqué Work."[94] Because wood or metal will not hold large amounts of dye, felt was sometimes glued into areas of the design — usually outlined with wood — and this took up more dye and printed it better.

When dye or a dye and paste mixture are used, the block is pressed onto a dye-soaked felt pad, then pressed by hand onto the cloth laid out on a padded table. The dye will print quickly upon contact so this does not require much pressure, and blocks may have a handle or inset hand-holds carved into the back. If ink is used it is rolled onto the cut surface of the block with a gelatine or rubber brayer, then the inked block is hammered against the cloth with a rubber or wooden mallet because more pressure is required (heavy and slightly rough cloth like Belgian linen requires more pressure in printing than organdy or lawn). The inking and pressing or pounding are repeated for each impression of each color until the whole length is printed. This is direct relief printing in its simplest form.

A dry textile is used when printing with dyes, but for oil inks cloth is sometimes moistened before printing. Then it may be steamed to fix the colors, stretched, and dried. As mentioned before, an already dyed fabric may be block-printed with bleaching agents to discharge the color in a pattern; it may be printed with wax or paste, then dyed as a resist pattern, or mordants may be printed before dyeing to produce different colors in one dye bath — all from a relief block.

Direct block printing gives well-defined colors, but pressure and position may vary, or the amount of dye will differ from print to print so that the pattern has some unevenness and hence an unmistakable distinction. The hand-cutting of the block, the slow, careful printing, and its subtly variegated and imprecise look make hand-blocked prints uniquely beautiful. In an attempt to speed up printing, a complicated device called the Perrotine press was invented in 1834 in France by M. Perrot. It printed three or four colors from small blocks attached to a flat-sided post moving on an axis, but it proved to be ungainly and was soon abandoned. Attempts to mechanize the process by mechanically routing out the blocks and arranging overhead carriers for them during printing were tried but never proved to be an improvement. So-called "India" prints done by hand in many colors from wooden and coppered blocks in Europe were the first famous block prints produced in quantity and some of them also had some colors painted in by hand. French and English 18th century block prints now seen in museums are among the most beautiful and valuable fabrics printed by the block method; England still produces some yardage of hand-blocked linens. The English, French, Indian, and other European methods all used dyes — the ink method was first used with engraved plates, but for fabric printing it is primarily a 20th century development. To the confusion of the buyer some old English hand-blocked designs have been reproduced on engraved copper rollers and are turned out in quantity by machine. They are labelled "English block prints," which suggests hand printing, but they are not done by hand at all, so, caveat emptor!

2. STENCILING

The process of applying colors by hand through openings cut in parchment, paper, or metal stencils is a very ancient but now little-used method of fabric decoration. The design is drawn, then traced onto the stencil material and the areas of the pattern to be colored are cut away, leaving parts of the stencil where the cloth must be shielded from the color. Small ties must be left to hold the stencil together and these appear as spaces between units on the cloth and give the design its characteristic look. A separate stencil must be cut for each color in a design, and dye or color is simply painted on through the openings. Early Japanese stencils are probably the masterpieces of the art, and were used also as a guide for painting on resist wax or paste. Oriental craftsmen sometimes cut two identical paper stencils, and glued hair or silk threads between them to hold the whole together and act as ties. Combinations of hand painting and stencil dyeing achieved very detailed patterns.

Early American stenciled fabrics are rare because there were comparatively few of them; they were made at home and were not produced commercially. The stenciled counterpanes and coverlets can be identified by the small spaces dividing parts of the design and by the barely perceptible fact that color is sometimes more intense around the edges of a shape where it touched the edge of the stencil. It is difficult to distinguish between some early block prints and stencil prints. Some museums and historical societies have in their collections a few charming examples of coverlets, and there are to be found many of those Victorian delicacies called "theorem paintings." These were done on velvet or satin, made partly with stencils, then framed for the parlor walls.

Twentieth century silk-screen printing — the method by which most hand-printed fabrics are now done — is nothing more than a refinement of

Fig. 12. Quilt made by Frances Newbury of Gales Ferry, Connecticut, c. 1850; stenciled in red and green. Courtesy of the Lyman Allyn Museum, New London, Connecticut

Oriental stencil printing. The stencil is now a plastic or lacquer film instead of paper and it is stuck to a fine silk which holds the stencil together and eliminates the ties. The color is pushed across the silk-screen stencil with a rubber squeegee instead of being brushed on; this has developed into a very precise method, but has great flexibility and is used in many ways for fabric printing and also for fine art prints called *serigraphs*.

3. BATIK

This is technically not a printing process, but rather a painstaking method of dyeing cloth in a pattern after painting it with wax. It was done originally in the Orient, particularly in Java, and has been revived briefly at various times in other countries and is probably the original resist printing. The design is drawn or traced lightly on the cloth or followed from a drawing that can be seen through a fine cotton or silk. Hot liquid beeswax is trailed on from a tool called a "tjanting." This is a small metal cup on a handle, with a hollow copper tube running to the tip and serving as the applicator of the liquid wax.

Fig. 13.   Detail of the corner of a Javanese batik c. 1780, printed on fine cotton and used as a sarong. Courtesy, Metropolitan Museum of Art

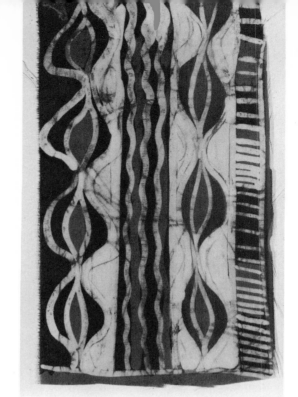

Fig. 14. Small contemporary batik on silk with "trailed" wax (undyed) design on a background dyed gold and green; made by artist Berni Gorski

The cup is dipped into the pot of melted wax and refilled as needed for more "drawing." Large areas that must be protected to resist the dye may be painted with a brush dipped into the hot wax. The wax cools and hardens and thus makes the painted parts resistant to the subsequent cool dye bath. To add more colors, the first wax is left on if needed, or melted off after the first dyeing, then more protective wax painting, dyeing, wax removal, and final washing follow. The wax can be cracked purposely, or may crack slightly in handling, and when dye penetrates the cloth through these tiny cracks, the batik takes on its characteristic crackled look. The Javanese also did block prints, using wax printed from the block on the cloth instead of painting it on. Such blocks were called "tjaps" and the fabrics were called "tjap batiks"; they were done more rapidly and could thus be produced in greater quantity.

Batiks are rarely done today except as fine art hangings on silk or very fine cotton, and are seen occasionally in contemporary art exhibitions; some have been commissioned as church hangings. They enjoyed a short revival during the art nouveau period about 1900, and are now sometimes imitated in roller-prints, deceptively called "batiks."

4. SELDOM-USED HAND PROCESSES

The process of tie-and-dye, the name of which almost explains itself, and already mentioned under resist printing, is familiar to many from school days. Portions of a piece of cloth are gathered up and tied tightly with waxed string, then part or all of the cloth is dipped into dye which cannot penetrate the tied portions. Early Peruvians tied pebbles into the cloth with waxed string in regular patterns which resulted in small white circles on a dyed background. In India, tie-and-dye was called *bhandana work*, from the Hindu word "bhanda," meaning to tie. The method is still used in India and the Orient, sometimes in fine, complicated designs done by tying the cloth around a pattern of pegs or pins set into a board, using sheer cottons and silks for clothing and scarves. The Japanese did carefully controlled tie-and-dye and combined it with stenciling and embroidery on silks for robes. On paper they achieved a similar effect by multiple folding and dipping the edges into dye.

Painting with a brush and dye or oil colors on fabrics is distinguished mainly by its variety over the years. It probably reached its height of excellence in the "toiles peintes" of India early in the 17th century, in which the whole design of a very large panel was sometimes painted, resist-painted, dyed with mordants, and also painted with dyes. North American Plains Indians made some handsome paintings on animal hides by incising or burning the drawing and adding the painting by hand with earth and vegetable colors.

Painting by hand on fabrics is done on an almost negligible scale in the 20th century; textile dyes or oil colors are sometimes used to decorate clothing and accessories — on two widely disparate scenes: the primary school grades and in the ateliers of haute couture.

Fig. 15. Cotton printed by tie-and-dye method in dark red on white cloth. Peru, c. 1400. Courtesy of the Cooper-Hewitt Museum of Design, Smithsonian Institution

Fig. 16. Small tied square of wool cloth which has been tied and dyed once and is now ready for a second dyeing. Prepared by artist Berni Gorski

Fig. 17. Silk scarf tie-and-dye design in mauve on white showing a simple and typical pattern. Prepared by artist Berni Gorski

Fig. 18. Dakota woman and Assiniboin girl wearing painted hides as robes, from a painting by Carl Bodmer. Courtesy of the Smithsonian Institution

MACHINE PRINTING PROCESSES

The need for more and more printed cloth led to a desire for faster, more uniform printing methods and culminated in the invention of machines for printing. The swift changes of fashion, a market expanded by the population growth, and better and better dyes kept the presses going, once they had started. This all came about through these steps in the broad chronology of fabric printing: first, clay tablets or rollers were used, then hand-cut wooden blocks, then metal parts were added to the blocks to give precision of detail and strength so that blocks would not break down with repeated use. Metal blocks were used briefly, mainly for printing hot wax. The Perrotine press was developed to print four blocks at a time; then, finally, metal hand-engraved plates of copper or brass were made and printed in large presses, before copper-roller printing came to be used almost universally.

1. COPPER-PLATE PRINTING

This method of textile printing began about 1750 and lasted until about 1830; it cannot be called accurately a *machine* method, but we describe it here because a heavy iron press was indispensable in achieving the pressure required to print. The process was, however, essentially a hand operation and never became completely mechanized.

The method grew out of the discovery that small, hand-engraved plates like artists' etchings could be printed with ordinary printer's ink on the same presses that were used for relief printing of broadsides on paper from type and woodcuts. The engraved copper plate was fastened to the flat bed of the press, face up, inked, then wiped clean so that only the engraved lines held ink. The cloth was placed on the plate, a padding — probably of felt — was put in place, the upper metal plate was moved into position, a geared lever was used to apply pressure, and the color was "lifted out" of the lines onto the piece of fabric by the intaglio method described earlier. It was at first used in America for printing embroidery patterns on cotton, and later for commemorative kerchiefs, maps, and religious broadsides on white satin intended to be kept as souvenirs or framed as pictures.

A special press was later developed in England called a "rolling press," or "star-wheel" press, which was operated by a large winch that the printer turned by using both his arms and feet, and it had two large rollers whose mangle-like pressure squeezed the cloth against a copper plate.[100] This, or a similar, press made it possible to use much larger plates — from 18″ to 36″ across, and instead of printer's ink, a dye and paste mixture was perfected. In 1752 in Ireland the first color-fast dye-and-paste printing was done on a continuous length of cloth. This marked the true beginning of copper-plate textiles.

Fig. 19. Copper-plate toile de Jouy, France by Huet, c. 1786, entitled "La Liberté Americaine," in red. Courtesy of the Smithsonian Institution

In 1803 in Scotland Robert Kirkwood invented a still better press that involved two parts: the "D" roller and a registering device called a "ratchet" which greatly improved all subsequent copper-plate printing.[100] This made it possible to move the cloth along when the flat side of the "D" roller came around, thus accurately spacing the next position of the print on a piece of cloth from 10 to 14 yards long. The pictorial, finely detailed prints are of the class generally called "toiles" and, as already mentioned, most copper-plate prints were done in one color — black, purple, dark blue, or red.

In the beginning the method was regarded as a great improvement over block printing because of the greater size of the plates, the design detail possible, and the partially mechanized printing. But by 1830 the slow and rather cumbersome process was found to have its own limitations, and it soon became obsolete. It was said, ". . . it can be counted as one of the earliest casualities of the industrial revolution and was driven out of existence by the demands for faster and cheaper production."[100]

2. ROLLER PRINTING

The next step in the search for speed and efficiency was to form the flat copper plate into a seamless cylinder and to use it as a roller for printing. This was, at last, a much faster way to print fabrics that were by 1780 available in great quantities from India and were beginning to come from American mills. Again the character of the designs changed because patterns were limited in size to the circumference of the roller — about 16″.

The roller-printing mechanism first patented by a Scotsman, Thomas Bell, in 1785 to print six colors at one time was first powered by water, then by steam. It was essentially the same as modern presses, though present-day machines will print as many as sixteen colors at one time and are electrical marvels of speed and precision.

Bell's patent does not mean that he was the first to invent the use of the printing roller, as Oberkampf at Jouy in France and others claim to have used rollers slightly earlier than his patent. Even earlier, wallpaper had been printed from wooden and wood and metal rollers. And, as we know, pre-Christian printers had used rollers by hand long before; it took several centuries to go back to it and discover that the roller provided — if not the best — at least the fastest way to print.

Wood-block prints began to go out of style, and with the advent of roller printing were soon almost abandoned. Blocks numbering in the thousands must have provided fuel for many bonfires, because blocks of any real age are now rare.

For direct roller printing in simplest terms, a copper roller is engraved with a design, inked, and rolled against the cloth which pulls the dye out of

Fig. 20. Calico Printing in 1835, from an engraving in *The History of Cotton Manufacture*, by E. Baines, London, 1835

the engraved portions and is thus printed by the intaglio method. The designer of a roller print must plan his pattern so that it repeats exactly and neatly fills the circumference of the printing roller — of about 15″ or 16″. This means that when you look at the finished cloth, you will see the same design repeated down the length, with a unit reappearing every 15 inches. If the fabric is a stripe running the length of the cloth, you will, of course, see nothing at all but a continuous stripe, but it will have been printed from a new inking-wiping-printing sequence every 15 inches. The design must also fill the length of the roller — which is the width of the cloth — and can be from 36″ to 52″ or more. At first rollers were engraved by hand and skilled engravers were the prized employees of the early print works. Then rollers for small pattern designs were made by being pressed or indented in a measured repeat by hardened steel patterns or "mill" rollers. Later, and at present, rollers are made by a pantographic process photographically and the design is etched into the roller to the proper depth by acids. The finest line or detail can be printed from a finely etched roller, but also large solid areas of color can be printed from parts that have been textured with parallel lines to hold the dye and paste mixture, which distributes itself evenly on the cloth in one solid spot.

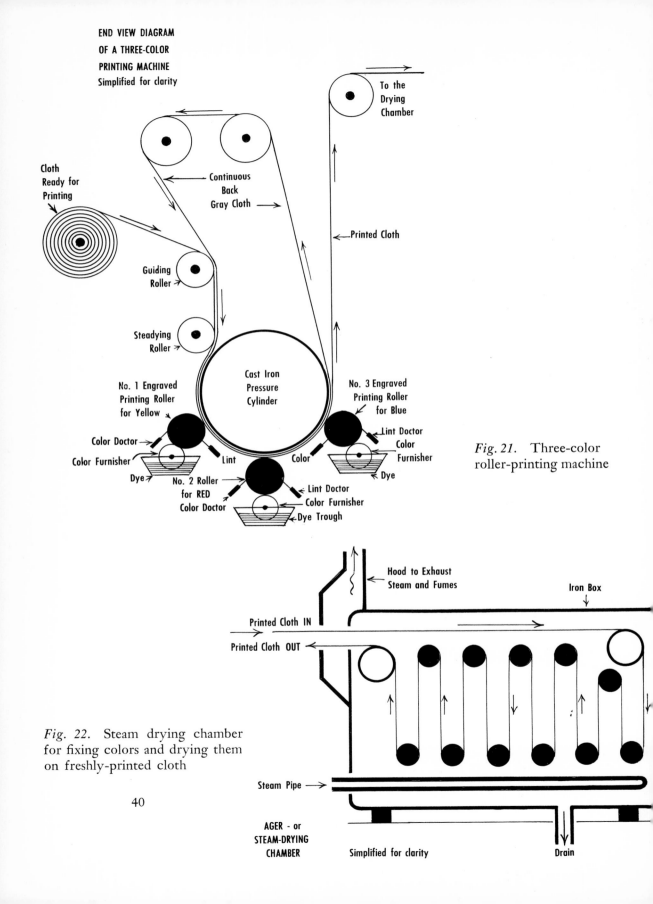

END VIEW DIAGRAM OF A THREE-COLOR PRINTING MACHINE
Simplified for clarity

Cloth Ready for Printing

Continuous Back Gray Cloth

To the Drying Chamber

Printed Cloth

Guiding Roller

Steadying Roller

Cast Iron Pressure Cylinder

No. 1 Engraved Printing Roller for Yellow

No. 3 Engraved Printing Roller for Blue

Color Doctor

Color Furnisher

Dye

Lint

Color

Lint Doctor

Color Furnisher

Dye

No. 2 Roller for RED
Color Doctor

Lint Doctor

Color Furnisher

Dye Trough

Fig. 21. Three-color roller-printing machine

Fig. 22. Steam drying chamber for fixing colors and drying them on freshly-printed cloth

40

Hood to Exhaust Steam and Fumes

Iron Box

Printed Cloth IN

Printed Cloth OUT

Steam Pipe

AGER - or STEAM-DRYING CHAMBER

Simplified for clarity

Drain

The roller-printing machine consists of five basic parts as shown in Figure 21; these are:

1. A large, padded cylinder around which the cloth rolls — this is the pressure cylinder and holds the fresh cloth against the printing roller.
2. The engraved copper roller bearing the design for *one* color.
3. Two scraping knives for each color roller — the "cleaning doctor" for for wiping excess ink off the roller *before* each impression, and the "lint doctor" for scraping lint off the roller *after* each impression.
4. The inking roller, which is half immersed in the ink trough and rolls against the printing roller, depositing ink in the engraved depressions of the printing roller.
5. The ink trough containing the dye-and-paste mixture, or other special printing substances for variations of direct printing such as mordants, discharge chemicals, etc. *Paste* — usually gum tragacanth, gum arabic or gum senegal or a similar synthetic — is used with most dyes and other media simply as a thickener for liquids, so that they will roll on and off the plates more evenly than a water-like liquid. (*Dye*, when thickened, is referred to as "*ink*.")

A multi-color press has only one padded pressure cylinder and this is surrounded by the color rollers that print. Each color must have a separate engraved roller with its own set of scrapers, ink roller, and ink trough. Only the printing rollers are motor-driven; the others operate by friction from them. Colors are applied to the cloth in a sequence more rapid than the eye can follow, usually starting with the lightest color and proceeding to the dark. The fabric rolls off the press completely printed and goes directly on to the steaming and drying operations — or stretching (tentering), polishing, shrinking, or whatever is required.

The speed and precision of a modern press are remarkable; it is even possible to print directly on both sides of a fabric in perfect register in what is called a "duplex" printer so that the color and design are exactly the same on both sides. The discharge method — discovered and used by early printers — is still in common use by machine printing and produces a pattern that also looks the same on both sides of the cloth. The resist process is primarily a hand method and is seldom done by machine.

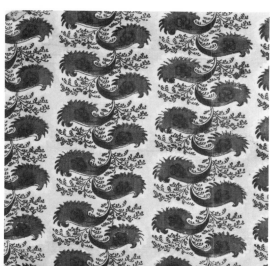

Fig. 23. A small-patterned roller print on sheer cotton in three colors done about 1860 by the Arnold Print Works, North Adams, Mass. Courtesy of the Museum of Art, Rhode Island School of Design

3. PRINTING OTHER SUBSTANCES

Since the early 19th century, in addition to direct, discharge, and mordant printing, presses have been used to give various other effects to fabrics. Cotton and synthetics can be printed with substances that will shrink the fabric in stripes or patterns, resulting in crêpes, plissés, matelassés, etc. Cloth may also be printed with a sticky adhesive, then run through a blower where thousands of tiny cotton, rayon, or wool fibres are blown about and stick to the fabric where it was printed. This results in a velvety-looking surface where the adhesive was printed and produces a "flocked" fabric.

Hollow printing rollers with the design cut out like a roller-stencil are filled with lacquer and rolled against the cloth; metallic colors are often printed this way because metallic inks are thick and dry too quickly to go through a conventional roller press.

Fig. 24. Two swatches, probably from a French sample book, of matelassés used as examples by the Arnold Print Works at North Adams, Mass. Courtesy of the Museum of Art, Rhode Island School of Design

Fig. 25. Felt printed with metallic sil ink (lacquer) from a hollow stencil-ro on a press. Made about 1870 by the A old Print Works, North Adams, M Courtesy of the Museum of Art, Rh Island School of Design

Fig. 26. A French warp-printed taffeta chiné with characteristic diffused outlines

4. WARP-PRINTING OR DYEING

One other process with ancient origins can be described either as a printing process or as a weaving process — it is called warp-printing. It was originally done by hand (and still is in some countries) but can be done by roller presses, too. Knowing some of the essentials of weaving will make the method more understandable. Weaving is simply the interlacing of two groups of threads: (1) The warp threads, stretched in measured spacing on a frame or loom, and (2) the weft threads, wound on a shuttle (a slender spool) and drawn under and over, under and over the warp threads from left to right, then right to left until a fabric is woven. In warp-printing the threads that are to be stretched on the loom are first wound on a "warp beam" frame, carefully measured off in accordance with the pattern, and on that are tied off with fibre cords, to be tie-dyed in a measured design, or printed as if they were a fabric, painted by hand, or rolled past printing rollers on a machine. Then they are strung on the loom and woven with a plain-colored or white weft thread. This gives a diffuse or indistinct pattern because only half of the threads are printed; it may be familiar to you as cretonne. In India since ancient days a warp-dyed fabric has been called an "ikat"; in Japan it is a "kasuri," and on French silks it is a "chiné" or "flammé."

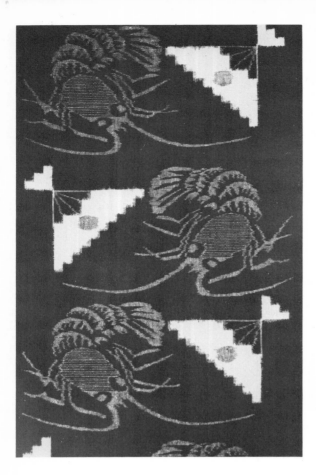

Fig. 27. Japanese double kasuri in deep blue and white, 19th century. Courtesy, collection of Betty Willis

Once you have seen one of these fabrics you will recognize the others readily. If threads for *both* the warp and weft are pattern-dyed before being woven, the resultant fabric is called a warp-and-weft print, or a *double* ikat or kasuri. The design will still have an indistinct edge, but the center will be purely colored, or clearly white, where both threads cross (either dyed or undyed).

5. LITHOGRAPHY

Another development is the lithographic printing process invented in 1796 by Aloys Senefelder, who published a book on his discovery in 1818. The original method made use of smoothly polished stones of fine, white European limestone in a size of about 14″ x 18″ and about 4″ thick. These were used by artists to make prints on paper by drawing on the stone with an oily crayon or by painting with a liquid called "tusche"; only the oily marks held the ink for printing. The drawing was done entirely by hand on the stone, then the print was made from it in a hand-operated press that exerted considerable pressure to transfer the ink to the wet paper. The stones could be ground down with pumice and used again after the previous design had been erased. Lithography was used for prints like the Currier and Ives series, the Hudson River prints, magazine illustrations, etc., often printed in one color — black — and tinted by hand with water colors. Artists still use stone, but for most other printing stone has been replaced by a much cheaper, thin, flexible metal plate — usually zinc or aluminum — on which a photographically-transferred image is etched by chemicals. The plate is then fastened around the drum of a roller-printing press which prints with extreme speed and accuracy. Both the artists' stone and the metal plates print with oil-base inks combined with a wet surface on the principle that oil and water do not mix. Lithographic printing on cloth is limited to a few specialties such as bookbinding cloth, towels, handkerchiefs, maps on cloth, etc., but is extensively used in a still newer version called *offset* lithography on paper by which the image prints first on a rubber "blanket," then offsets onto paper. No other processes are used in combination with lithography.

6. SPRAY-PAINTING AND DRUM-PRINTING

Two other contemporary machine methods should be mentioned here to complete the roster, since both involve cloth of one kind or another. Spray-painting is done in a manner that the name suggests, usually through stencils for fibre rugs, awnings, display hangings, or just to coat fabrics like canvas and oilcloth. Drum-printing is similar to warp-printing but is a uniquely complicated method by which warp threads are wound on a huge drum about 18 feet in diameter and thus printed for special uses such as patterned machine rug weaving.

CONCLUSION

We have now reviewed the methods and principal techniques used to print and paint fabrics, but the story is only half-told without its history — more about where and when fabrics were printed and less about how they were done. Let us take a look at the history from the human side and from earliest times, for this will then give us the whole background for all American printing.

Fig. 28. Cylindrical pottery printing stamps from Colombia, S. A., about 3″ long. Possibly used for border patterns on cloth, possibly to apply dye to man's skin. Courtesy of Museum of the American Indian, Heye Foundation

II

Fabric Decoration Before America

A COMPLETE HISTORY OF WORLD FABRIC PRINTS

THE first type of cloth a man ever made was probably a rough matting of grasses and twigs, crisscrossed and tied. Soon after that he must have discovered that other softer fibres could be harvested, dried and twisted together, and woven by hand to make the first real cloth. He then fashioned a frame on which to stretch his strings or grasses, and so the first weaving was done on the first loom. We wonder where this might have happened . . India perhaps, or Egypt, China, Mexico or Peru?

In the lands of antiquity most of the cloth that was made became rags and tatters long ago, then dust, then finally nothing. Our gleanings that cloth, and especially patterned cloth, did exist must come from enduring relics in temples and tombs, and sometimes only from reports of the church or from stories of travelers and warriors — preserved and retold through the years.

Artisans of the most ancient civilizations began to color cloth with dyes and patterns almost as soon as they learned to weave it. By the year 3000 B.C., patterned clothing had replaced primitive man's printed or chalked symbols on his own sun-tanned skin.

The early tribal chieftain's identifying markings had become, by 3500 B.C. in Phoenicia, a bright purple robe dyed with Tyrian purple. This is one of the oldest known dyestuffs and was made by extracting color from a species of shellfish — a secret process that brought riches to Phoenicia from the many peoples who wanted this brilliant purple. It became the color of authority, worn by emperors and kings.

Indigo, a blue dye made from the leaves of the plant *Indigofera*, was known in India by the year 3000 B.C., too. It is probably the most important dyestuff ever known and was the only blue dye used for almost 5000 years. Your own New England great-great-great-grandmother may have had a barrel of indigo brewing in her dooryard; she used it to dye the homespun threads for her loom from which she made striped and checked cloth for her home and clothing.

Before the Christian era, farmers in Egypt cultivated fields of yellow crocus to reap the saffron for yellow dye. Bright reds for the dyepot came from an insect that yielded kermes, and from the root of the herb, madder. Artisans also ground up a variety of stones and minerals and cooked barks and leaves to get more colors for their designs. So, man has made his fabrics colorful almost as long as he has made history.

Without a shred of cloth to prove it we know that 3000 years before Christ, silk was woven and dyed in China, and that cotton fabric was woven and colored in India. A thousand years later, Egyptian tomb paintings show costumes stamped with patterns; in Peru, clay cylinders with designs pressed into them were used with dye to make border patterns. Native Mexicans, Peruvians and some other western Indians did printing and dyeing of cloth. These prehistoric Americans are even said to have known a process for giving a high glaze to fabrics — possibly by rubbing it with smooth stones. Fine linens and cottons actually remain in Egyptian mummy cases found in our own time, and records show that linen decorated with Egyptian symbols was found in tombs of 1500 B.C. and earlier. In Java, wax-painted batiks dyed in many colors in that incredibly laborious process were found in a temple of 1200 B.C.

An early version of almost every method of fabric printing now known was done somewhere in the world by ancient craftsmen. By the term "fabric printing" we mean all methods by which pigments or dyes were applied to cloth. In Egypt, India, Mexico, Peru, Java, and in China and Japan there was some form of stamping, painting, block printing, stenciling, tie-dyeing, batik, or simple roller-printing.

During the period of conquest and travel of the 500 years before Christ, reports tell us the story of fabrics in many lands. In 450 B.C. the Greek historian, Herodotus, wrote of India, "The people possess likewise a kind of plant, which instead of fruit, produces wool of a firmer and better quality than that of sheep; of this the Indians make their clothes." In 327 B.C. Alexander the Great brought back to Greece "India prints that rivaled the sunlight and resisted washing." Another Greek traveler reported than Indians wore "flowered garments made of the finest muslins." Pliny's *Natural History* written in A.D. 61 describes Egyptian chintzes under "painting":

"They also paint clothing in Egypt in a manner extraordinarily marvelous. After they have finished the cloth white, they line it not with colors, but with mordants that absorb colors. When this is done, it is not apparent on the cloth; but when the cloth is dipped in the dye-pot, after a moment it comes

Fig. 29. Block-printed linen in black on undyed ground; found in Fostat, dated c. 1300. Courtesy, Cooper-Hewitt Museum of Design, Smithsonian Institution

out painted. And the strangest part is that although there is only one color in the pot, that color produces several on the cloth, varying according to the quality of the mordant it receives. Nor can it afterward be washed out. So the dye-pot, that would undoubtedly blend the colors together, if it received them already painted, selects from them one single color and paints while it boils. And the dyed cloths are firmer than if they were not dyed."[32] We recognize this as a detailed description of mordant-dyeing almost exactly as it has been "discovered" several times since.

From the beginning of the Christian era until about A.D. 1300 weaving, dyeing, and printing continued to develop in both eastern and western worlds. In a variety of distinctive styles of design craftsmen were using hand processes that have changed very little throughout the 4000 years of their history. Each country had its own characteristic methods and motifs, and with the advent of wars and conquests, trade routes were opened and some designs changed hands and were modified and adapted by other nations.

The oldest existing remains of ancient fabrics bearing designs known to us today came mostly from three places: Fostat, the harbor town of old Cairo in Egypt, Bokhara in Central Asia, and Calicut in India. The burial grounds of Akhim in Panopolis, Upper Egypt, yield examples of fabrics of A.D. 300.

The Copts, early Egyptian Christians, though known principally for their weaving, were skilled in block-printing and used a resist method; Coptic decorative arts are preserved in several special museums and collections today. Three of the cities that gave us fabric treasures also gave us the names of three fabrics: "fustian" (an early cotton and linen cloth) was named for Fostat, "buckram" after the city of Bokhara, and "calico" from Calicut. The Hindu word "chint" meaning *variegated*, gives us our seven-hundred-year-old word "chintz."

A very old East Indian superstition grows out of the Indian arts of weaving, dyeing, and decorating cloth. It was believed that if a favorite child was clothed in a garment of many colors no evil spirit could harm him because attention would be diverted from the beauty of his person to the beauty of his garments. In the East, Mohammed forbade the making of the likeness of any living thing, and this led to the development of geometric decoration in all Moslem arts. This influence has been felt in the design of textile patterns in many countries.

Antiquarians tell us that dyed or painted cottons, probably Indian, were known to Europeans in the late 15th century — perhaps much earlier. They may have been known in England as early as A.D. 700, as Adam Bede wrote in his *Life of St. Cuthbert*: ". . the synod of Cloveshoe forbade priests to wear clothes dyed with Indian colors." This is an early incident of prints being forbidden — this time for religious reasons; others occurred later. Printed cotton was found in the grave of St. Caesarius, Bishop of Arles, in 542.

The history of cotton growing and of cultivation of flax for linen, and their spinning and weaving, has guided the history of fabric printing because these fabrics have been much more used for decorating and printing than silks. The term "printed cotton" has been used to mean sometimes pure cotton, sometimes a mixture of cotton and linen, or especially in early times, pure flax linen. Silks historically have been dyed in the thread, or after being woven into cloth; they have been woven into many kinds of decorative patterns and textures, or have been embroidered, but seldom printed. It is uncertain whether it was Egypt or India that produced the first cotton thread and wove fish nets, then fabrics of many sorts. Egyptians are supposed to have invented the pre-shrinking process. The Greeks began to grow cotton in the year A.D. 100 and were the first Europeans to produce it; they, too, used the cord for fish nets. Cotton spinning and weaving traveled as an industry to Spain, thence to the Netherlands and finally in 1250 to England. France, Holland, and Belgium had long produced flax for linens. By 1100 fabric printing had been done in a small way by hand in many parts of Europe — having followed surely the path of the spinning and weaving industries.

In the year 1200 in Europe printing was most highly developed in the monasteries along the Rhine river. The monks produced printed linens and some silks by hand-blocking and these Rhenish fabrics rival any block-printing that has been done since. They used black, dark blue, and red pigments and some that resemble gold and silver. They also used resist printing; many of their designs were imitations or adaptations of woven patterns such as bro-

Fig. 30. Natural linen fragment, block-printed in dark gray — possibly originally a pigment containing metal of some sort but probably not silver; 13th century Germany. Courtesy, Cooper-Hewitt Museum of Design, Smithsonian Institution

cades and damasks. Motifs were often stylized animals and birds in roundels of leaf and flower forms. Their patterns show a simplicity and strength of design still much admired by fabric designers. As there is always difficulty in identifying very old examples, there has been some question recently as to the authenticity of some museum examples.

Perhaps the oldest, and surely one of the most amusing and informative how-to-do-it books ever written, is Cennino Cennini's *Treatise on Painting, or Book of the Arts*, written in Italy about 1380.[12] Cennini tells everything the artist needed to know from how to make his own charcoal for sketching to how to make a plaster cast of his own body! Of interest to us is his detailed description of printing on linen from carved wooden blocks — proof that the craft was known in Italy, although no known printed fabrics of that period remain. His formula for oil colors mixed with varnish, and his method of inking the block and then rubbing the back of the cloth to print, is almost the same as the process still in use.

Eighteenth century explorers found examples of primitive block-printing in the Samoan islands. These and the early Hawaiian prints — tapa cloths — are handsome fibre fabrics that made a tough, long-lasting fabric of many uses.

Fabric Decoration Before America • 51

China and Japan give us an oriental chapter of the fabric-printing story, but since textiles from both of these countries were almost all silks (except the roughest peasant cottons) they were almost never printed from blocks or plates. They were decorated in many other ways and have their own distinctive beauty and richness. The art of printing from wood blocks was supposedly invented in China about A.D. 500 — other evidence notwithstanding — but was used only to print on paper or other similar materials. Between 600 and 1300 Chinese silks, dyed, woven, and embroidered, reached a peak of beauty and sumptuousness, and China had a thriving trade in raw silk and woven fabrics. Cotton was known earlier, but was not cultivated until 1360 and cottons were used only as household and utility fabrics. The oldest known stencils are Chinese; however, they were not used to decorate cloth, but were used with charcoal as pin-pricked patterns for frescoes. Jesuit priests introduced engraving on copper into China in the early 19th century but the method did not prove to be agreeable to Chinese craftsmen. Beautifully dyed silks and embroideries are the fabrics for which China is famous. Country women in China do cotton weaving on small hand looms and often on the same farms where cotton is grown, carded, and spun. These country fabrics are about 18″ wide and are printed or stenciled in simple designs with a resist paste made of ashes or flour mixed with gum or glue. They are then dyed black or indigo blue. Markets sometimes sell them with the paste still on; the buyer completes

Fig. 31. Plain cotton with design applied by resist-stencil and dyed dark blue; reddish color added by hand painting. Japanese, 19th century. Courtesy, the Metropolitan Museum of Art; Purchase, 1965, Rogers Fund

the process by washing the paste out of his own fabric and so reveals the pattern in white.

The Japanese adopted very early both the silk industry and the art of printing on paper with wooden blocks and have achieved beautiful results in both arts. The introduction of Buddhism in A.D. 552 brought about a flowering of all the arts and Japanese silks and embroideries came to rival those of China. Records from the seventh century in Japan tell of fabrics painted by hand in gold; later they were stenciled with lacquer and then dusted with gold powder. The Japanese made stenciling an art of their own and used it as commonly as block printing was used in western countries.

The Japanese also knew batik as it was done in Java, and they called it "rokechi." By 1400 stenciling and tie-dyeing, called "shibori," were used in combination with embroidery for the magnificent silk robes worn by the actors in Nō dramas. Stencils were cut from tough, flexible parchment paper or from the bark of the mulberry tree and were so delicate that two stencils were glued together with hair or silk ties, as mentioned before. By 1680, Kyoto was the center of dyeing as well as of weaving and other crafts. Cotton and silk were resist-dyed in all sorts of patterns for kimonos and robes. Crests and insignia were popular motifs, and tie-dyeing and shading with dyes were highly developed textile arts.

Two types of 18th century Japanese fabrics that are still made and used represent gracious customs: the "furoshiki," stencil-decorated cloths for carrying packages, and "fukusa," painted and embroidered silk pieces made for wrapping important gifts.

Also typically Japanese are the still made weft-patterned fabrics called "kasuri" as shown in Fig. 27. The unique, softly blurred quality of the design, usually done in one color — black or blue — is unmistakable and is caused by the weft-printed or warp-and-weft-printed threads barely "missing" the outlines of the design where the colors change.

Oriental fabrics provide us with many distinctive motifs: dragons, fish, clouds, bamboo, chrysanthemums, costumed figures, and calligraphy, but they have had very little direct influence on the style of western textiles. The 17th and 18th century "chinoiseries" used Chinese motifs in copper plate and copper roller prints, but the fabrics still retain their English or French character and could never be mistaken for an oriental fabric.

Between 1300 and 1600 more and more elaborate weaving and embroidery came into use in many parts of the western world and printing came to be used less and less as a method of decorating fabrics. During these years the art of producing fine tapestries, brocades, damasks, silks, satins, velvets, and embroideries was at its height. This was the period that produced the real treasures in woven fabrics when artisans of the textile guilds worked hours, days, and weeks to make one beautiful woven or embroidered fabric by hand. As textile-making skills and methods improved, they themselves became popular subjects in the religious art of the Middle Ages. Many pictures show the Virgin Mary spinning or practicing other textile arts. A 16th century pictorial tapestry in Rheims cathedral shows the Virgin at work on a small hand loom weaving a narrow fabric with a floral pattern.

Almost no examples remain of significant printing done during this time; when fabrics were printed they were often an imitation of the appearance of more costly woven textiles, designs were based on woven patterns, and fabric printing as an art with its own qualities was literally lost. Almost 300 years elapsed before printed textiles were thought of again as anything but a cheaper imitation of patterned weaving.

In the early 1600's the men who were to become the founders of the East India trading companies could not have realized what would happen when their ships landed with a new kind of cargo — painted cotton panels from India. Englishmen as well as many traders on the continent soon discovered that the market for these new and colorful small-patterned chintzes and panels called "palampores" was such that there was to be an awakening of the whole printed fabric trade — which had been dormant for three centuries. The story of India painted cottons thus becomes important since they had a great and lasting effect on 17th century world trade as well as on all subsequent printed fabric design.

There is a romantic story of how the India trade began which says that a British ship captured a Portuguese vessel laden with India-patterned cottons and that the colorful cargo created a furor and led directly to the founding of the East India Company in England in 1600. Another version of the story is that in a complicated import-export maneuver involving a search for markets for British woolen goods in Asia, traders brought back a few India-painted cottons early in the 17th century. East India trading companies were founded between 1600 and 1700 by Portugal, Holland, England, France, Sweden, and Denmark. Spices and many other commodities were involved, but as soon as the companies were established, careful records were kept, and we have the books of the British traders to tell us of their dealings with India in the cotton trade.

It is probable that the whole matter of India-figured textiles and their influence on floral patterns of the western world is plagued by more universally-held misconceptions than any other segment of the story of decorative design and its "foreign" influences. Experts on the subject of India cottons are not exactly in disagreement, but various versions of the story differ and are vague on so many points that it is hard to formulate a concise story. Two people who have spent decades studying India cottons agree on most points; the two are Mrs. Gerard Brett of the Royal Ontario Museum in Toronto, and Mr. John Irwin, head of the Indian Section of the Victoria and Albert Museum in London.

Mr. Irwin says, "The first India cottons came to England as 'token' parcels on heavily-laden spice ships. They were intended as something special for the Directors, or as bribery items rather than commodities. Everybody *seized* upon them."[77] This last point is one upon which there is universal agreement!

The India fabric shown in Fig. 32 (and in detail in Fig. 33) is said by Alice B. Beer, curator of textiles of the Cooper-Hewitt Museum of Design, to be "the most important Indian textile in the museum." A similar example is owned by the Victoria and Albert Museum in London. Miss Jean Mailey, assistant curator of textiles at the Metropolitan Museum of Art, describes the textile shown as follows: [74]

"Section of a painted and dyed bed-curtain in rich reds, aubergine (eggplant), soft yellow-green, tans, browns and light blue. An Indian export made at Pondicherry on the Coromandel coast in the late 17th century, it came from Ashburnham Place in Sussex, England, and is representative of the first and finest type of Indian export cottons to be popular in England and (later) in America. (The pattern is repeated across the width of the fabric in a 40″ horizontal design, but there is no vertical repeat.) The 'print' is made by a complicated succession of processes: first, a pouncing-on of the design, then resist-painting, then resist and mordant dyeing, and finally some direct hand painting. Although the designs of these early India cottons are the same as later European-made prints, their effect is of hand painting in rich colors due to the many hand operations, and the care with which they were done. The later 18th century European prints were done by blocks and lack the color and variety of detail of their earlier eastern prototypes."

Miss Mailey also writes, "The reverberations created in Europe in the 17th century and later by the exotic imports of these trading companies was profound. Among the most far-reaching of these were the Indian muslins, silks and, above all, the painted and dyed calicoes which, about 1670, became the rage for hangings, bed-fittings, dresses, dressing gowns, mantles, waistcoats, and hat-coverings."[78]

It is easy to gain the impression that the early India cottons *in the original form* were the pieces that became "the rage" — and here is the point at which one misconception comes about. However, Mrs. Brett's more specific description of the chronology of what happened to the prints gives a slightly different, and more accurate, view of the story. She says, "Since native India chintz designs found little favor in Europe, they were first modified to suit European taste, and replaced by designs in pattern-books and sent to India for the India chintz painters to 'adapt.' "[97] This is now the generally accepted story of what happened between 1600 and 1670 when the vogue became current in Europe.

Mr. John Irwin says, "... starting in the 1640's the patterns were specifically commissioned according to orders from London. Indians used mor-

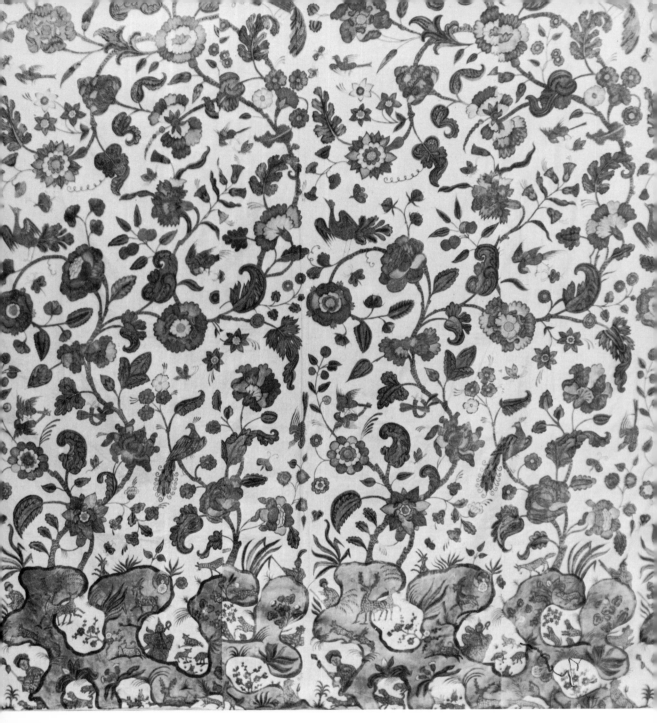

Fig. 32. 17th century hand-painted India cotton panel made at Pondi-cherry on the Coromandel coast. Courtesy, Cooper-Hewitt Museum of Design, Smithsonian Institution

dant dyeing and preferred a *reserved* pattern [light] against a colored ground. The English buyers persuaded them to change the designs to a reserved *ground* with colored patterns. Then they [the British] prepared patterns and sent them out for the Indians to copy."[77] An interesting letter in the records of the East India Trading Company dated November 27, 1643, shows that one trader wanted to supply the British market with fabrics that would suit the taste of the times. He wrote to his factor (agent) in Surat, India, "Those quilts which hereafter you shall send, we desire may be with more white ground and the flowers and branch to be in colors in the middle of the quilt as the painter pleases, whereas now most part of your quilts come with sad red grounds which are not so well accepted here, and therefore, let them be equally sorted to please all buyers."[96]

In 1689 an Englishman in India wrote, "Chintzes are here painted according to musters [representative specimens] which are given to the painters, which they imitate completely and extremely well, for their character is so stupid that they cannot imagine anything by themselves but can only imitate something so that it has a complete likeness."[79]

The practice of sending designs for the Indian craftsmen to follow was also used later by other countries and continued up to about 1775, and thus, design elements that appear to be English, French, Italian, or Chinese (via

Fig. 33. Border detail of the 17th century hand-painted India cotton shown in Fig. 32, showing animals and a figure of Chinese feeling

Europe) actually *are* from those countries. Many instances of direct copying from identifiable sources are known — the copying of a well-known series of English flower engravings is documented, and the slight Indian changes are interesting and amusing. The artisans copied the flowers and leaves quite faithfully, but took the bouquets out of the vases and tied them with a ribbon bow.

The original palampores had great brilliance and beauty and the processes of mordants, resists, and painting seem to us very complicated, but were done beautifully by the native artisans. Various names were given to the painted panels and their variations: "toiles peintes," "indiennes" (which came to mean the French copies), "pintados," "chittes," and just "callicoes." The cottons with smaller floral designs were usually called "chints," or chintz, and were used for clothing also. All the names seem to be interchangeable in usage.

"In 1632 King Charles was curious to see whether India prints could be done on wool. He sent some pieces and asked to have them 'painted' in India in the manner of the chintz. The experiment fell through, but later a factor wrote to the King that painting could 'not be done on colored cloth, but on white cloth only, and that in pieces not above 4 or 5 yards at the most, which is stained after the form of the fine paintings of Masulipatam and put into so many dye vats as there are several colors, that part of it which must not take the dye being covered with a kind of earth; the rest which is uncovered takes the color of the dye whereunto it is put.' "[96] One may hope that the King understood!

Mr. John Irwin enlightens us about another misconception about India "prints"; he says, "The flowering Tree of Life cannot be proven to be either Indian or Persian art. It probably originated in England where it was fashionable in Elizabeth's time, about 1585. Some Gothic tapestries with curled, scroll-like leaves are nearer to the leaf-treatment of the palampore designs than anything in Indian traditions. Even the chinoiserie influence probably came via Europe . . . Because of the exhorbitant prices charged [in England] for authentic Chinese and Japanese articles [screens, carvings, furniture], British artists were encouraged to emulate the style. Another form of sample pattern used in India was the pattern-book in common use among embroiderers and lace-makers, many of them originating in Italy or copied from Italian sources."[77] It is possible to find in early India cottons such alien elements as oak leaves and flowers that never grew in India, but came straight from the notebooks of European artists.

The brief compendium of professional opinion on page 62 should serve to lay to rest some of the popular misconceptions about India chintzes.

Fig. 34. *Opposite page:* Painted cotton, India, 18th century. A delicate floral design in red, yellow, blue, green (by over-painting yellow and blue) with violet and black for stems. Courtesy, Cooper-Hewitt Museum of Design, Smithsonian Institution

Fig. 35. Large cotton palampore, used as hanging or coverlet, India, c. 1775 from Madras. Painted, resist-dyed and mordant-dyed in shades of red, blue, green, eggplant, yellow with brownish-purple outlines on undyed ground. Courtesy, Cooper-Hewitt Museum of Design, Smithsonian Institution

Fig. 36. Detail of the right border of the panel on opposite page

Fig. 37. Detail of base of the tree in the panel on opposite page

1. The early India "prints" were not printed, but dyed and painted. Much later European imitations and variations *were* printed from blocks.
2. The first few palampores (of which almost none remain) were of eastern origin, but soon the Indian craftsmen did *no* original designs at all.
3. The "Tree of Life" is not Indian and not Persian, but is a combination of early European motifs, modified by eastern artisans.
4. It was *not* the first India cottons that "flooded the markets" but the later commissioned imports. The original palampores were so expensive that almost nobody could have afforded to buy them.
5. The cheap, so-called India prints on the market in the 20th century bear no resemblance whatever to the designs that revived the art and influenced the course of printed fabrics. A flowered kitchen apron might be more like them than the India print bedspread.

The colorful Indian hangings made use of motifs as varied as Nature herself, were regarded as curiosities and luxuries, and had an oddly appealing foreign look to European eyes accustomed to damasks, velvets, and heavy tapestries. The fine Indian cotton fabric was in itself a novelty — the only familiar cotton or linen fabrics of the time were plain household linens woven in France, Holland, and Germany.[96] The market for all kinds of India cotton grew apace between 1630 and 1700 and they met with delighted acceptance from fashionable Europeans. It is well to remind ourselves that this is exactly the time when the first colonists were arriving in America, so they too could have seen and acquired some India cottons in Europe.

In his diary of September 5, 1633, Samuel Pepys says, "Creed, my wife, and I to Cornhill, and after many tryalls bought my wife a chintz, that is, a painted Indian callicoe for to line her new study which is very pretty." We can conclude that "many tryalls" meant that there was a wealth of prints from which to choose. Men of fashion wore dressing gowns made of printed India cottons, and had waistcoats and "small clothes" (trousers) made of them too. Dressing gowns were not only for bedroom use but were worn as a light jacket or coat and were seen in the streets of London on the most fashionable dandies. A French engraving of 1780 shows an elegant, bewigged Frenchman in a summer suit made entirely of indiennes. A favorite dressing gown was the *banyan* — a style also affected by American colonists. Women loved the sheer, delicate cottons and in France, Madame de Pompadour furnished a whole apartment at Bellevue with indiennes; their adoption as a style was overwhelming.

Two types of silks were exported from India, but in nothing like the quantity of printed cottons. These were "patolas," or double ikats, and "culgars," silks decorated by tie-and-dye patterns and used for saris.

By 1700 the flood of India cottons to western ports had depressed prices of European goods to a point where an embargo was finally put on their importation into England. In France, manufacturers of silk, velvet, and tapestries claimed their business was ruined, and in 1687 the importation of India fabrics was forbidden. The same law also prohibited the *copying* of Indian fabrics, so we know that in France there must have been a newly-established cotton-printing industry reproducing India designs and profiting from their immense popularity. An English law was in effect from 1720 to 1736 forbidding the *wearing* of printed calicoes! It must have been a thankless task to try to enforce that one. All the laws had very little effect on India cottons — or perhaps served to make them loved even more. The trade decreased temporarily, but the laws were not stringently enforced and the public appetite for the chintzes and calicoes continued well into the 18th century.

In imitation of the costly hand-painted and dyed India cottons, Europeans began to make less expensive prints by using dyes with wooden blocks, or

Fig. 38. Block-printed cotton made in Nantes, France, about 1790; white ground with natural-size flower sprays in soft red on a lavender picotage background. Courtesy, Cooper-Hewitt Museum of Design, Smithsonian Institution

Fig. 39. Block-printed cotton from Alsace, France, c. 1799. Large scale flowering branches printed in deep purple, red, green, blue, and yellow on white ground. Flowers are of Oriental inspiration. Courtesy, Cooper-Hewitt Museum of Design, Smithsonian Institution

blocks with steel pins, and they sometimes painted one or two additional colors. Some were printed entirely from blocks in all-over floral designs with leaf and flower forms derived from India chintzes. Small-figured designs made it possible for middle-class and peasant women to dress in fashion at small cost. The European printers soon acquired considerable skill, and the fabrics began to be used also for furnishings.

The pervasive influence of Indian cottons in their many variations on western decorative design was profound. The combination of Indian artisans' skillful technique with their eastern interpretation of English, French, Italian,

64 • Fragment of painted and mordant-dyed cotton; India, Coromandel Coast, ca. 1725 Width 22″; colors, red, pink, yellowish-brown and brown-black. One of the original early floral designs of the type that served as design inspiration for centuries Courtesy, Cooper-Hewitt Museum of Design, Smithsonian Institution

and Oriental styles came finally to have a style of its own that is still called "Indian." It provides a rich legacy for designers who could hardly carry on without it. Almost every bit of our printed cloth, embroidery, rugs, wallpapers, and other objects that bear floral and leaf decoration has a foundation in India-painted cottons of the 17th century.

The first print works were established in England in 1676 at West Ham by William Sherwin, who patented his invention for "A way for printing broad calicoes and Scotch cloth with a double-necked rolling press which is the only true way of East Indian printing and staining goods."[26] It is believed by some that this was a patent for the first copper-plate printing in England, because a "rolling press" was a copper-plate press.

A refugee from the French edict of 1687 — a cotton printer named Cabannes — was reported to have fled France and gone to settle in Richmond where he started the "first" British printing of textiles, in 1690. Crayford is sometimes called the mecca of English printing, its industry dating from 1700. Anyway, it is certain that India cottons, because of their popularity all over Europe, were responsible for the establishment of a whole new fabric-printing industry, especially in France, England, Ireland, Switzerland, and Holland. Our very early colonial American printers came from these establishments — many of them were English or Scottish — and all had learned to make (or copy) designs, cut wood blocks, print, and finish fabrics by all the methods then known.

By 1690 the French edict was no longer enforced and enterprising artisans saw the promise of a new industry with a wide market for its products. The prohibition against French printed cottons was removed in 1759. This is indeed the world's good fortune, for about 1760 at Jouy, just outside Versailles, one of the first and most famous print works started producing what became the best-known prints in the western world — the "toiles de Jouy." The name is so familiar that we take it to be a proper noun describing a specific print; it actually means "fabrics from Jouy."

The first prints produced by Christophe Oberkampf at Jouy were printed from hand-cut wooden blocks and the designs were done in several colors (polychrome) — fruits and flowers growing from one sturdy, winding stem in the style of some Indian chintzes. He also produced many small-patterned floral "sprig" designs with tiny motifs on pastel backgrounds. These were printed over and over in many variations for twenty or thirty years; they sold cheaply and were used by the working class for their clothing and gave the company its first financial success. At one time Oberkampf had 10,000 different block-printed designs requiring about 30,000 separate blocks of a size that could be grasped by hand.

He introduced dotted designs — also of Indian origin — using metal pins to make the printing surface in a picotage design; he also used felt-filled areas

English block print on natural cotton ca. 1780 in three browns, two reds and light • 65 blue. Fragment 28″ x 33″; spread eagle is 16″ from top of wing to tail; large flower 7″ x 8″. A type of imported English textile used in fine colonial homes and much admired and imitated by the first American printers. Courtesy, Cooper-Hewitt Museum of Design, Smithsonian Institution

for more solid color-printing. Jean Baptiste Huet was Oberkampf's chief designer and engraver and was an artisan of great taste and skill; he also made designs for the Reveillon wallpaper factory — another newly-established industry in Europe. The cottons used at Jouy came mostly from India and the factory became one of the best customers of the East India Company for plain cottons and linens.

The print works at Jouy began using copper plates for one-color fabrics about 1770, though the process was invented in Ireland earlier and had been developed primarily in England. The Jouy prints changed greatly in character when the plate method was introduced; scale and style became distinctive to the intaglio method. Because of the new technique of cutting fine lines into copper plates with a sharp cutting tool called a "burin," and because of the large plate size now possible, the designs became very different. Large, decorative floral units, stripes, and classical panels for cushions, screens, and chairbacks appeared, then pastoral and illustrative scenic prints and historic and patriotic events were pictured. French and English printers engraved plates showing scenes from American history and buyers in America liked the textiles depicting George Washington and Benjamin Franklin as classical heroes.

From Jouy came scenic prints such as those picturing balloon ascensions — the aeronautic experiments of the day — as important as a twentieth century rocket launching. In the 18th century such events were great social occasions, too, and the prints recorded fashions of the day. Whole story-telling fabrics such as "Paul et Virginie" and other bucolic scenes became the romantic recorders of styles and customs.

Designers found that the finely-engraved lines on copper made it possible to do shading and to approach realistic illustration never before satisfactory with wood-block printing. In some ways the artisans were carried away by their new opportunities and produced some designs that now may seem unsuited to fabric decoration, but they are amusing and charming, nevertheless. Many European copper-plate prints are regarded as the most distinctive and beautiful of all the toiles, and have been widely copied. Copper-plate printing was finally found to be slow and difficult and was abandoned about 1830. English printers (unlike artisans in most other countries) continued to use wood blocks for their finest furnishing fabrics and these continue into the 20th century.

About 1800 Oberkampf began using metal rollers — the idea was brought back from Lancashire by his brother Frédéric. Some experts credit Jouy with being the first large print works to make successful commercial use of copper rollers for producing fabrics in many colors. Again, the scale and style of designs changed. Not long before this time a method had been discovered by which indigo could be mixed with orpiment (arsenic trisulphide) and gum

ig. 40. Block-printed cotton from Jouy, France, c. 1775. All-over pattern of large-scale flowers on branching stems, printed in red, green, yellow, [b]ue, and purple on a white ground. Courtesy, Cooper-Hewitt Museum of [D]esign, Smithsonian Institution

thickeners so that its oxidization and thickening were delayed long enough to allow it to be printed directly from blocks and plates for blue on white designs. But indigo was still troublesome stuff and in 1806 Oberkampf offered a prize of 1200 francs for the perfecting of an indigo that could be printed.[98] After copper-plate and copper-roller printing came into use at Jouy the factory continued for a while to use wood blocks for several favorite designs, but this became a diminishing part of the business and was finally abandoned for the "more modern" method.

The name *toiles de Jouy* was eventually given to the whole class of copper-plate and copper-roller prints, especially scenic prints, whether they were actually made at Jouy or not. One book on English chintzes describes a fabric as an "English pastoral toile de Jouy with landscape effect." Other French print works flourished at Lyons, Montpellier, Mulhouse, Bordeaux, and Nantes, but none of their fabrics rivalled the excellence of those from Jouy, and many were merely copies. Oberkampf's immense technical skill and the good taste of Huet are generally credited with giving Jouy prints their excellence.

In 1810 at Jouy a chemist invented the first fast-color green dye; this was an important event for the dyeing and printing trades because up to then all greens had been made by painting or printing yellow and blue together. Experts are able to date many fabrics by this circumstance. As late as 1815 the problem of printing indigo blue from a block or plate was still not solved.[98] Other technical improvements also came from Jouy, and their fabrics — no matter how great the volume of production — were noted for fine quality. When a Jouy print was stamped along the edge "Bon Teint," it meant that the color was really *fast*.

The French prints gradually lost the primary Indian design influence and began to follow the styles of the French court starting with the Louis XVI neo-classic style, then Rousseau's back-to-nature themes, historic scenes, Directoire styles, and finally Empire; Oberkampf received the Legion of Honor from the Emperor Napoleon himself. Ladies and gentlemen of the court visited the Jouy factory and loved to be taken around to see the work in progress. With the eclipse of the fortunes of the Empire, Jouy gradually declined and after the death of Oberkampf in 1815 the print works closed, after 83 years in business. The designs from the Jouy atelier are still being reproduced and used with admiration and a special sort of affection. In America, both French and English toiles were used in rich southern colonial homes, and are now often called by Americans "colonial prints."

In England during the late Jacobean period of the 17th century, wood-block prints with blue or black dyes on a natural background were done because it was forbidden by law to import any other dyes at the time, and Germany held most of the secrets of European dyeing.

41. Design typical of the style of copper-plate prints, although this one is ⸳ibly a one-color French block-print made to imitate an English copper-plate in ⸳ut 1765. Courtesy, Smithsonian Institution

By 1700 the English dye industry had progressed and was flourishing, so the beautiful polychrome wood-block prints similar to the early Jouy prints were also done in Britain. Wood-block printing has continued there, and to many people the term "wood-block print" means an English chintz; floral chintzes are England's forte. The so-called oldest firm of block printers in England (1790), Messrs. Stead, McAlpin & Co., are still in business.

There were print works developing all over Europe and both mechanical and technical knowledge were increasing. By 1750 the prints of England, Switzerland, and Holland were said to rival the "prints" of India. European craftsmen experimented through the years with vegetable dyes and eventually found the chemicals and processes to fix the colors, as well as discovering many chemical dyes. The only known bleach until about 1774 was the sun, until in England, Scheele discovered the use of chlorine. The primary washing agent had always been plain cold water — often in the form of a running stream or river. More efficient man-made water systems were devised, and fabrics were washed with soap. The glossy finish on chintz originated, or originated again, in Holland and gives us the name of our shiny fabric known as "Holland Cloth," used for window shades. In the latter part of the 18th century glazing was done by hand in England with smooth flint (agate) stones set into wooden blocks with handles. Glazing is now done by metal rollers and wax or lacquers.

England gave us many important inventions in the fabric trades: Arkwright's machine for spinning cotton in 1769, and Hargreaves' spinning jenny in 1770 — a device that spun several threads at one time. Samuel Crompton's "mule jenny" patented in 1779 was a cross between the two earlier inventions and could draw, spin, and wind many threads. The power loom was invented in 1785 by Edmund Cartwright, and this was the most important of all because it meant that there was far less dependence on imported cotton goods when factories could use water power and finally steam to operate their own weaving looms.

Scotsman Thomas Bell's 1785 patent on roller-printing machinery, also used at Jouy, meant the end of most hand-printing, but it meant the beginning of the whole new industry of machine-printing. Most colonial printers had knowledge of the hand methods, and when the engraved rollers and machinery came to America, craftsmen were imported from Europe to use them and to train new artisans.

The Peel family of Bury, Lancashire, made a fortune with their cotton manufacturing and calico printing works from about 1770 to 1850. Robert Peel, his son, and his grandson — the first Sir Robert Peel — established the business and founded the family that later became famous in British government. Many printed calicoes from the Peel works were exported to the American colonies and the first print works in America took some of their style cues from the Peel and Yates sample books. Small-patterned calicoes were the natural result of improved roller printing and colonial women used many yards of the prints from Bury for their dresses.

In Italy a Swiss artisan named Michele Speich, who was highly skilled in block-printing, started working near Genoa around 1787 and several other Italian printers began making the large, floral-printed cottons called "mezzari." The designs were based on India palampores, but instead of being painted they were printed in many colors from as many as 80 small wood blocks on one piece. The mezzaro (Fig. 113) once owned by the American printer, John Hewson, is a fine example of the style and quality of the prints. They are sometimes referred to as "scarves," but they are about 90″ square, made of two pieces of fine cotton sewn together down the middle, the same as prints used for coverlets. Italian women of the early 19th century did sometimes wear the mezzari as country garb, making of them a hood and wrap-around robe — more like a banyan than a bandanna. The Speich factory ceased operating in 1850 and the original hand-printed mezzari are now museum pieces.

Fig. 44. Curtain, block-printed in red, blues, violets, yellow, and green; wide border of chinoiserie design is printed in one piece with body of curtain. Printed at Bannister Hall near Preston, England, 1806. Courtesy, Cooper-Hewitt Museum of Design, Smithsonian Institution

Between 1825 and 1880 more synthetic dyes were discovered and developed to replace the old vegetable and earth colors. Aniline purple, alizarine, and a coal tar product that replaced indigo came into use; they could be closely controlled in production and gradually became more reliable.

Roller printing made use of the new dyes and better machines, but progress had the effect of standardizing fabric designs — in both dress goods and furnishing fabrics. There were no copyright laws and the designs became pawns in a kind of game of copying, sales competitions, and quick style changes, so that the elements of decorative invention and good taste were all but lost. This sameness and perfection, as might be expected, finally brought about a reaction from at least a few designers, and the most influential of these was an Englishman, William Morris. He was a multi-talented designer and a successful cotton printer, among other things. He had several clearly-stated theories about the simplification of design and the use of color, and his fabrics and wallpapers were the undisputed forerunners of what came to be called "modern design." His style was much admired and quickly followed in America, and he became one of a group that included Louis Comfort Tiffany and others who became the mentors of Art Nouveau which influenced fabric, wallpaper, and all decorative design around 1900.

* * *

Following are two charts of dates and events that provide a review of world fabric printing and of European printing during the time of America's colonization. These happenings represent the family tree of New World printed fabrics.

A Date Chart — Early Fabrics, Dyes and Printing

3500 B.C.	PHOENICIA	Phoenicians of Tyre discovered the earliest dye — Tyrian purple made from a species of shellfish
3000 B.C.	CHINA	Silk was woven
3000 B.C.	INDIA	Indigo, one of the oldest and most important of dyestuffs, was used at this date; it came to replace *woad*, a less "fast" blue dye. Indigo was the only blue dye used up to the 20th century
3000 B.C.	INDIA	Cotton fabrics were found in a tomb at Mohenjo Daro
2500 B.C.	CORYCUS	Cilicia (Egypt) was the center of the crocus-growing industry for saffron yellow dye
2100 B.C.	EGYPT	Tomb paintings showed costumes stamped with orderly designs
2000 B.C.	PERU	Clay cylinders were used to print border patterns
1500 B.C.	MEXICO & PERU	These countries practiced tie-and-dye, batik, block- and small roller printing; they also perfected a finish that glazed cotton fabrics
1594 B.C.	THEBES	A patterned red and blue fabric was found
1466 B.C.	EGYPT	Linen was found in the tomb of Thotmes IV decorated with Egyptian symbols
1200 B.C.	JAVA	Batiks (wax-painted and dyed cloth) were found in a temple

450 B.C.	INDIA	The Greek historian, Herodotus, wrote of an Indian plant "that produced wool — and of this, Indians make their clothes."
327 B.C.	GREECE	Alexander the Great (356-323) brought back Indian painted fabrics that "rivaled sunlight and resisted washing."
300 B.C.	INDIA	A Greek traveler reported that Indians wore "flowered garments made of the finest muslins."
1 A.D.	EGYPT	Pliny described in detail the Egyptian method of printing with small blocks on fabrics
100 - 200 A.D.	GREECE	The Greeks were the first to grow cotton in Europe; they carded and spun cord to make fish nets
300 A.D.	EGYPTO-ROMAN	Fabrics of bold design were printed with wooden blocks
500	EGYPT	Some of the earliest examples of printed textiles were found in the burial grounds of Akhim in Panoplis, upper Egypt
600	CHINA	The art of printing from wooden blocks was employed for printing texts on paper. Later, Japan borrowed the art from China
542	FRANCE	Printed cotton was found in the grave of St. Caesarius, Bishop of Arles
552	JAPAN	Buddhism brought about a flowering of Japanese arts
600	ARABIA	Mohammed forbade the making of any likeness of living things; this was responsible for the development of geometric design
900 - 1300	CHINA	Most glorious period of its art; silk was cultivated, dyed, woven and embroidered
1100	EUROPE	Fabric printing had been done on varying scales in many countries
1200	GERMANY	Monks in Rhenish towns did block printing on fabrics; this may have preceded printing on paper in Europe
1250	ENGLAND	Cotton spinning was introduced; it came from Egypt or India to Spain, thence to the Netherlands, and finally to England
1300	ITALY	Cennini's *Treatise on the Arts* described in detail the art of printing on linen from blocks
1300 - 1600	EUROPE	With the increasing skill of weavers, the era of tapestries, damasks, silks, and embroideries was at its height. Fabric printing began to decline and was done very little for the next 300 years

(Date charts are also at the end of Sections III and IV)

"FIRST" EUROPEAN PRINTERS AND PRINT WORKS

1576	ENGLAND	First English print works established at West Ham by William Sherwin[26] believed by some to be copper-plate printing with ink
1578	HOLLAND	Two merchants of Amsterdam and a Turk founded the first European print works where they claimed to be printing in eight colors "in the Indian manner."[26]
1686	GERMANY	Etienne Dutrite and others established themselves as cotton printers in Berlin[26]
1689	SWITZERLAND	Manufacture of Indiennes started at Neuchâtel[27]
1690	ENGLAND	A French refugee, Cabannes, set up the first printworks at Richmond[26]
1691	SWITZERLAND	Fazy, Micheli, and Vasserot set up a factory at Geneva[26]
1746	FRANCE	Cloth printing was begun at Mulhouse
1752	IRELAND	The first copper-plate printing using dye-and-paste was done by Francis Nixon at the Drumconda Works near Dublin

1760	FRANCE	Christophe Oberkampf started his print works at Jouy near Versaille
1761	ENGLAND	The earliest *dated* English print was recorded by "R. Jones at Ol Ford."[14]
1770	ENGLAND	Robert Peel started his print works at Bury, Lancashire
1771	SCOTLAND	First cotton printing works were set up at Glasgow[45]

CONCLUSION

We have reviewed all the textile printing methods and techniques, and their history prior to colonization of America, if briefly. Wood-block printing of fabrics has almost disappeared and copper-plate engraving for textiles has ceased to exist; with these two methods went some of the most distinctive and charming patterns in fabric history. Dyes have been perfected to the point where the use of hand-painted wax and indigo dyeing are no more than a memory. The painstaking handwork of early artisans is an almost lost tradition and exists now only on an infinitesimal scale of craftsmen-turned-artists in an industrial society.

Printing of all kinds has been influenced greatly by the progressive steps in cotton manufacturing, as it is the most-printed fabric. Flax culture and linen-making and the refinements of cotton growing, carding, spinning, and weaving gave us many kinds of cloth by the time America was colonized, and trade with England and the world brought silks to early America. Some of the commonest kinds of cloth used in the colonies have entirely disappeared: linsey-woolsey, perpetuana, darnick, camlet, and kidderminster. Others have proven to be very long-lived: calico, chintz, damask, serge, satin, and velvet. There are now more than 200 kinds of cloth in common use, and new ones like vinyl and mylar are appearing on the scene. Most of us would recognize a surprising number of textiles: batiste, bouclé, burlap, chambray, denim, flannelette, gingham, hopsacking, jersey, muslin, piqué, shantung, taffeta, velour, and whipcord, to skip through the alphabet.

All fabric printing and dyeing throughout the world, and especially European printing during colonial times, had an influence on styles and taught American printers their methods. The entire design of cotton-producing machinery was brought to Rhode Island in the brain of an Englishman, Samuel Slater, called the Father of American Manufactures. And Francis Cabot Lowell "remembered" the design of the power loom. It is indeed a pity that there is so little left of the products of what was once an important industry in our colonies. Early settlers had many uses for their fabrics and little reason to save them, so we find their story in what can only be called *shreds*, and these make a puzzle that is difficult to put together. Let us now examine the fabrics Americans have made and decorated from earliest times to the turn of the century, and see if we can make something of the pieces.

III

Jamestown Colony to the Revolution, 1607 to 1775

1. AMERICA'S HISTORICAL BACKGROUND

THIS volume purports to cover the three hundred years from 1600 to 1900, but the year 1607, when the Jamestown colony was founded in Virginia, is the true date of the beginning of the white man's America. We cannot search out details of the fabric story, or even understand the circumstances of its development, without first looking at the facts of life of the early colonists in a setting that may not be too well remembered from previous studies.

The social, political, and economic life of colonial America was British, so we must begin with England. In 1497, Henry VII had sent John Cabot on two expeditions, and on the basis of his explorations of the North American shores, had laid broad claim to the areas north of Spanish Florida and Mexico. Spain controlled most of what seemed to be the most valuable lands then known: Mexico and Peru on one continent and Germany, Austria, Flanders, and part of Italy on another; Portugal held parts of the African coast and all of Brazil. Explorers from Portugal, Italy, Spain, and France continued to make voyages and draw up maps of the American continent for the next hundred years, but only small and scattered settlements were attempted. Henry VIII did not seek to secure the British claims, and Queen Elizabeth's enterprise was to send Sir Francis Drake around the world, mainly to advance British trade. When the Queen died in 1603 her country held not one clear mandate, colony, or protectorate outside the British Isles anywhere in the world.

ENGLISH · 1620   ENGLISH · 1620   ENGLISH · 1666   ENGLISH · 1666

Between 1500 and 1600 life for the common man in rural England had become increasingly toilsome and unrewarding under the remnants of a feudal system in a largely agricultural country. London was an overcrowded city of 100,000 with royal palaces on one hand and on the other, death, disease, dirt, robbery, violence, hangings for minor thefts, poverty, and every kind of political oppression. Under Henry VIII, lands and monasteries of the Roman Catholic Church were confiscated, thus removing the only semblance of charity for the poor; the citizens were in turmoil and currency became worthless.

Among the first people to revolt outwardly against these circumstances were the Puritans who thought the Church of England — then a part of the State — had become immoral and unprincipled. Another group of Puritans, called Separatists, wanted to establish their own church. These groups grew in strength and under James I the Puritans acquired enough seats in Parliament to begin to make demands of the king on both social and religious matters. The king finally vowed to make the Puritans conform, or "to harry them out of the land."

King James believed America to be rich with gold, and was quick to give approval and a land grant — more than what is now the State of Virginia — to a group of merchants called the London Company when they formed an investment company to send colonists abroad. They set up a form of government and council with the requirement that the Church of England was to be the religion of the new colony and that English laws were to prevail — the name became the Virginia Company. The first expedition in 1606 sent three shiploads of men (no women and children) with supposedly enough supplies for a year. The sea voyage took more than two months on vessels that consisted mainly of a deck and a hold partly filled with ballast sand. Passengers slept and did their own cooking in the hold — which had a headroom of five feet. The food was awful and sickness and death sailed with them. Fifteen died en route and the remaining 105 men landed in Jamestown hoping to find wealth and make their fortunes.

PURITAN · 1650

PURITAN · 1650

A fort and rough settlement were begun and later ships brought women and families, and soon there were dwellings and the beginnings of farming and business. This was a struggling, even though a comparatively wealthy, colony from the beginning, but in 1622 they suffered fearful losses in an Indian massacre. The original company eventually ran out of money and the investment was not successful. When King James died in 1625, Charles I chose to transfer the government to the House of Burgesses in Jamestown and by 1642 the colony was progressive and fairly prosperous under English governors sent by the crown. The Virginia colony finally became one of the richest and had some of the largest estates and plantations in the New World — thanks largely to wealth gained from tobacco crops. From the beginning it was of a different character than any of the other original colonies.

The best-known ship in America's early history — the *Mayflower* — landed at Plymouth, Massachusetts, in December, 1620, with a very different kind of colonist. The ship carried 102 people — 18 of them were women — and all were Separatists, the most strict sect of Puritans. They came in sombre dress as religious refugees from James' England and were in no sense adventurers or in search of profit, but sought only a haven of freedom. The first winter was so severe that half of the colonists died within five months, and the wilderness almost won the battle against this small group — but not quite. In 1625, more Puritans sailed into Cape Ann, Massachusetts, and some of these went on to make a settlement at Salem. Five years later, during the reign of Charles I, the largest number of Puritans began to arrive in Massachusetts and eleven ships brought almost 1000 people. They were fairly well off and were able to finance the enterprise themselves; they unswervingly pursued their religious tenets and when a few Quakers appeared among them the newcomers were persecuted, some were hung, and the remainder were driven out of the community. Perhaps the Golden Rule went overboard during the perilous voyage. Others arriving at about this time were Church of England members and some of them settled in Connecticut.

In England there was political upheaval under Cromwell, Charles II, and James II, before a stabilization came under William and Mary in 1689. During all this time, migration to America was increasing. Puritans and many others came to the New World; Puritan opponents called "Cavaliers" came to Virginia, Church of England members continued to come, and a Congregational church was set up as the first Protestant cooperative. Between 1600 and 1770 about 750,000 people came to America seeking a new life. More than half of them had means enough to pay the cost of passage and to set up a new society. Life on the east coast was laborious and the climate was rigorous, but by 1650 good crops, growing business, hard work, and ingenuity gradually brought a modest prosperity. The colonies came to vary widely in their attitudes toward religion and, although we may think of colonists seeking and finding religious freedom, intolerance persisted until long after the Revolution.

Whatever the circumstances of the first several years of the American colonies, there were constant hardships, wars with the Indians (fought by unheard-of new rules), wars with the Spanish, wars with the French, and every kind of social, economic, and religious problem. In 1619, a Dutch ship brought to Jamestown the first African Negroes and sold them as slaves — they had been taken from a Spanish slave ship. The colonies varied in many ways — the Dutch came to New Amsterdam (New York), the Germans to Pennsylvania, the Dutch and Swedes to Delaware, the Catholics to Maryland, and the British "Lords-Proprietors" to North and South Carolina. The blood of every American ran in the veins of these people, and this turbulent (and in this case, brief) factual background is the one against which America began to be a nation.

Historians Charles and Mary Beard describe the realities of the migration and of the settlement of America thus:

"Occupation of the territory claimed by England in America, building the "New England" in the wilderness, required the transfer of thousands upon thousands of men and women from the Old World to the New World. This meant a resettlement on an enormous scale. Trading corporations and proprietors alike confronted that problem. They had titles to great areas of land, they could buy ships, tools, stock, seeds, and other things necessary to starting agriculture on the virgin continent. But empty lands in America were in themselves worth no more to their nominal owners than lands on the moon. Money in their hands was in itself just so much dead metal. Stock, tools, implements in storage were equally inert.

"Only labor could put the material, capital, and vacant lands to use. Only able-bodied men and women possessing many skills and crafts, many arts and sciences, could produce the food, clothing, shelter, and other necessities of a civilized social order, could build prosperous and self-sustaining societies in the territory claimed by England.

Fig. 46. Table-type tape loom, 18″ x 26″, on which colonial women wove by hand tapes and ribbons of all kinds for their clothing. Courtesy, Smithsonian Institution

"But trading corporations and proprietors, even aided by the English government, could not simply commandeer farmers, mechanics, artisans, and managers for colonial adventures. In the nature of things, most of the men and women for the undertaking had to be persons who were willing, even eager, to cross the sea. They had to be volunteers moved by one reason or many reasons to tear up their roots in the Old World and brave the perils and toil of transplanting themselves across the wide ocean into the lonely territory claimed by the English Crown. The bulk of white men and women who came to North America between the founding of Jamestown in Virginia in 1607 and the eve of the American revolt against Great Britain came voluntarily. Even those who indentured, or bound themselves by contract to labor for a term of years as servants, in order to pay their passage, were, in the main, volunteers.

"It is true that many white laborers were kidnapped in England for shipment to the American colonies and that Negroes were dragged out of Africa for that purpose by slave traders. Forced migration of laborers was undoubtedly extensive. Yet the overwhelming majority of immigrants came to America of their own choice."[7]

This historical background is given here with a definite purpose — to remind ourselves that a colonist had for his first several years in America only one goal: to keep himself alive, housed, fed, and clothed in a demanding new life. Settlers came with great hopes but also with great fears, and with very little in the way of worldly possessions. The first sea-trunks can hardly have been expected to hold anything but necessities and people had to depend on what they knew, and on their own two hands, to make a start. Reliance on England was at first necessary, and was finally enforced by the mother country. It was quite a few years before it was recognized by either the colonists or the kings of England that the new generations of Americans gradually were moving toward independence.

Since few examples of 17th century textiles remain except those of European origin, we must reconstruct what the first American chapters of the fabric story really were. A few treasured India chintzes surely found their way to American harbors very early — and more came as shipping increased. Old New England wills bequeathed "figured cloathes" to a son or daughter, and these undoubtedly came from Europe. In a pioneer society there could be no thoughts of luxuries or decoration and the few bright bits of cloth were treasured.

Dense forests provided wood for homes and the simple, necessary furniture and then came the homemade spinning wheel and the loom. Cloth was then, and always has been, indispensable. The first cloth — in fact *all* the cloth — woven in the colonies for some time was a household necessity and it was rough and utilitarian in character. Household linens and warm clothing had to be made and until these needs were met it was unthinkable to spend time on decorative things. Knitting and embroidery were probably the next domestic arts of the colonies, after spinning and weaving — and most of the knitting was probably of socks and stockings.

One authority says, "American textiles of 1645 owe their utilitarian character to the primitive surroundings in which they were evolved and they reflect as well the economic conditions under which they were developed."[37]

When we think of pioneer America we must remember that along the east coast and among the colonies close by, but inland, the quality of life varied widely from the beginning. The colonies could be divided very broadly into three types, and these determined many qualities of style: 1. The Puritans and Separatists were people of strong convictions but were financially poor

Fig. 47. "Primitive Cotton Factory in Alabama." A family enterprise, out of doors; woman at left is carding cotton, woman at loom weaving, girl in foreground winding yarn for a warp, woman at right is "plying" yarn (twisting two threads together) that has been spun on the spinning wheel behind her. It is possible that they are actually working with wool, as the hanks on top of the loom look very heavy for cotton. Courtesy, Smithsonian Institution

and they came mostly to Massachusetts, Connecticut, and Rhode Island from England and Holland. 2. Wealthy families came to Virginia, Georgia, and the Carolinas, and were largely English and French, They brought wealth and also found the most productive and wealth-producing agriculture in tobacco, rice, and later indigo and cotton. 3. The Dutch first colonized New York and were thrifty, well-to-do merchant colonists, though the area was later taken over completely by England. Other Dutch, German, and English settled in Pennsylvania and Delaware.

The whole character of areas colonized by people of various European backgrounds established distinctive qualities for each region that can be sensed even in the 20th century. How else could we have the merchants of New York City, the thrifty Germans of Pennsylvania, the gentlemen and belles of Virginia, and the proper Bostonians of Massachusetts?

The American story has to be divided also by dates: (1) from the early settlements to 1688, when England began to be aware that America represented a broader destiny than was at first thought by the proprietary companies, and (2) from 1689 to 1776, when trade grew and foreign markets for American resources were developed. The colonists began to be "settlers" and were no longer "pioneers." The leading political thinkers (radicals) saw the time coming when English influence and control had to be thrown off. Some of the eastern colonies (Connecticut, for one) had more people within its boundaries than the colony was able to support by its own agriculture and commerce, so the need grew for inter-colony trade.

One historian says that the founding of Philadelphia in 1682 marked the close of the pioneer period of American settlement. The gap (not only geographical) between pioneer New England and the rich plantations of Virginia had been closed by the English occupation of New Amsterdam.[9] The image of a new nation began to emerge.

QUAKER - 1680

QUAKER - 1680

In the South riches came from agriculture, but in New England agriculture was carried on by small farms and they produced little more than enough to support themselves. Some of the Dutch in New York held thousands of acres in only a few estates, but the Dutch in America were merchants and shippers. From Pennsylvania north, families had to make things for themselves or go without; both men and women became skilled in many trades and arts and made their own necessities, tools, machines, and gadgets. Home industries flourished simply because many people could not afford to buy imported goods.

Practically all manufactured goods from steel knives to fine silks came from England, and she held a monopoly for more than 150 years on American trade. Things made or grown elsewhere had to go to England first, then be brought over on British ships with duty, freight charges, and commissions added to the price. The first exports from America — tobacco, rice, pitch, and indigo — could be sold only to English buyers because independent trade with all other countries was strictly prohibited. Resentment against British duties on imports and the British trade monopoly were the chief grievances that led to the Revolution.

One letter that gives us a picture of an Englishman's view of the colonists was written to the British Board of Trade by Lord Cornbury, Governor of the Province of New York, in 1705:

"I hope I may be pardoned if I declare my opinion to be that all these colloneys which are twigs belonging to the manufacturing tree of England, ought to be kept entirely dependent upon and subservient to England, and that can never be if they are suffered to go on in the notion that they have that, as they are Englishmen, so they may set up their same manufactures here as people may do in England; for the consequences will be, if once they can see they can cloathe themselves, not only comfortably, but handsomely too, without the help of England, they, who are not fond of submitting to government, would soon think of putting in execution designs they had long harboured in their breasts. This will not seem strange when you consider what sort of people this country is inhabited by."[3]

Lord Cornbury's long-winded opinion undoubtedly echoed the thoughts of most Britons, and by 1776 everybody knew what sort of people he meant.

In 1699, the colonists were forbidden to export woolen goods anywhere — not even to other colonies — and this was in spite of many governors having encouraged its production. In 1732, the export of hats (a thriving trade) was forbidden and, in 1750, the setting up of iron mills was outlawed. Many other laws were enacted to bar colonial trade, culminating in the Stamp Act of 1765, a far-reaching tax levy which resulted in the first open revolt in the colonies. The House of Burgesses in Virginia was one of the first colonial governing bodies to pass laws in defiance of increasing British pressures, and other colonies soon followed its example, up to 1775 and the Revolution.

2. AMERICA'S FABRICS

This story so far shows why printed fabrics used by colonists were almost all imported from England and later via England from France and India through the importing companies. It also shows why some of the early examples of American printing came from modest, one-man enterprises or even from home industries. We must rely largely on colonial newspaper advertisements to tell us that the fabric trades did actually start at an early date in America.

One authority says, "As a field of research in the history of printed cottons, America is barren soil. Not only has the material itself disappeared — and quantities must have been imported — but, aside from scattered references in wills, inventories, and commercial histories of the cotton industry, there is little other than occasional newspaper ads to suggest the possible source and type of 'calicoes' used by our colonial forebears to dress their women and curtain their four-posters."[14]

And another says: "The 17th century craftsmen in America were men who had been trained in a mediaeval shop tradition. Their influence persisted in the work of the 18th century. Many American craftsmen followed the contemporary English style closely and had the books of the English architects and designers, but there was inevitably a lag between the English and American styles, and in the rural districts the older tradition of shop practice was extremely tenacious."[11] Also, it was said that "American craftsmanship developed steadily and consistently from the earliest days up to the Revolution in the Northern colonies, and there was a good deal more of it in the South than is generally supposed. Most of the early craftsmen were English and the culture of colonial America was basically English, though a variety of other nationalities was represented ...Scotch, Welsh, Irish, Dutch, German, Swedish, and French and all these affected the English influence a good deal."[11]

Dyers were among the first tradesmen to set up and advertise their business establishments in the colonies, and later, when England was discouraging the American textile industry, the town dyer was not stopped from plying his trade. He often did bleaching and cleaning of fabrics and was thus regarded as the provider of a town service rather than as a practicing craftsman. Nevertheless, dyers worked constantly to improve their colors, to make them permanent, and to concoct more colors from the plants and chemicals obtainable. However, when they advertised that they printed something in "the latest style," they meant *English* (or sometimes French), and this persisted for many years.

It is interesting to mention that "when cottons and muslins were first introduced, printed in England (c. 1700), it sometimes happened that they were sold with the intention to deceive, but they were detected because *the smell was not the same*; they had not the smell of the East. This difficulty was gotten over by the use of *vitivert* or *kus-kus*, the rhizome of an Indian grass. There was a well-known sachet still sold in 1917 in England called mousseleine sachet."[95]

Before we deplore America's "barren soil in the research in the history of printed cottons" let us put some dates in order. The East India painted cottons that are acknowledged to have revived the whole craft were first seen in any number in England in 1631, in France in 1658, and by 1675 a French craftsman was said to be working in Châtellerault imitating the "chittes." The first English patents were granted in 1619, but the (supposedly) first print works were not established until 1676. Henri Clouzot, a scholar of textiles, says that by 1720 the painted cottons of England, Switzerland, and Holland rivalled the chittes of India, thanks to the exodus of French printers after the prohibitive edict of 1687. So, in summary, the American colonists were barely off the ships and on their feet on new ground when printing began *anywhere* in Europe. Thus it seems really quite remarkable that America's first advertising printer, George Leason, began printing "all sorts of Linnens" in Boston as early as 1712.

Most Americans were facing the hard facts of life in the early days, and by the time the colonies could progress independently of England, roller-printing had been invented and soon was utilized to set up the fabric-printing industry. It is true that few examples remain — due to two basic facts: cloth has an extremely useful character long after its original purpose has been served — as rags for utilitarian chores, and, secondly, it is the prime material for paper-making. Colonial newspapers had many advertisements for clean rags wanted for paper-making.

THE
New-England Courant.

"*PAPER MILL. Whereas some Gentlemen design to set up a Paper Mill in New England, if a supply can be had to carry on the business; These are therefore to give Notice that James Franklin, Printer in Queen Street, Boston, buys Linen Rags, either coarse or fine, at a Peny a Pound.*"[17]

Fig. 48

VIRGINIAN · 1725

Since it is our purpose to explore what *did* exist, and now that we have reviewed all the factors influencing what does *not* exist, let us begin to look at what is known. Many of the hand-printed and painted fabrics of the American colonies are charming, ingenious, and decorative. They tell us a lot about the people who made them — such as the mother who made and carefully decorated a sewing case for her daughter and the craftsman who painted an eagle on a soldier's marching cape.

3. THE FIRST COLONIAL FABRICS
AND THE SIX "FIRST" PRINTERS

The first American newspaper, the *Boston News-Letter*, was not founded until 1704 — a hundred years after Jamestown. Public notices in America's first hundred years were lettered by hand and stuck up in the town squares for the citizens to read; if we had records of these announcements we indeed would have a living history of colonial life. Two from Virginia, dated about 1660, are so expressive that they could hardly be improved upon by a fiction writer:

> "*Every Person neglecting to appear at the Days of Exercising the Militia shall be fined 100 pounds of tobacco.*"

> "*For the better taking alarms upon the approach of Indians, the frequent shooting of guns at Drinkings is prohibited.*"

In New England, the towns early set up records of births, deaths, wills, and estate inventories and it is from some of these that we learn what household effects and clothing were owned by colonists, and fabrics are mentioned fairly often. One sad tale of colonial superstition is that of the execution in 1656 of Mrs. Anne Hibbins as a witch in Boston. She is said to have been the sister of a Massachusetts governor and widow of a Boston merchant with Court connections, but her influential family could not save her life from the witch-hunters. The inventory of her estate is one of the earliest to mention fabrics; it listed "Five painted Callicoe curtains and Vallients." These might have been India painted cottons used as bed hangings or curtains and valances. Several such inventories and wills show that cloth of all kinds was treasured and willed to heirs. Colonists may have brought along a few treasures, but British ships brought more and more cargo for sale and this included India chintz, plain cotton, possibly linens and surely velvets, brocades and other fabrics of European manufacture.

Colonists made their own looms and spinning wheels and began to spin linen thread and weave and make their own household cloth, along with handspun thick woolens for clothing needed in the severely cold winters. There may have been a few pioneer printers who set up work in small shops or at home, but 17th century American prints have disappeared entirely. Any decorative fabrics were apt to have been of English origin or imported by England from the East and shipped to the colonies.

In 1640, the Massachusetts court issued orders that flax should be grown and that young boys and girls should be taught to spin it into linen thread. Bounties were offered for linen grown, spun, and woven in the colony.[22] By 1650, spinning classes were formed in many Massachusetts communities and every family was *required* to spin a certain amount or be fined.[21] In Virginia, flax grew wild and the growing season was much longer; spinning classes were set up for children as young as seven and eight. Cotton was never used as a material for these homespun industries, only flax and wool; cotton was difficult to spin by hand, and had no strength for use as a warp on the loom. Some cotton was imported from the West Indies in the 17th century, but England's prohibitive policies as well as a scarcity of money and labor prevented development of the cotton industry for another hundred years.[5] Cotton, if used at all, was limited to mixtures of linen warps and wool for linsey-woolsey, and for rag carpets. Even in England no *all-cotton* fabrics were made until about 1770, when the Arkwright and Hargreave inventions perfected cotton-spinning.[22]

It is interesting to read the descriptions of clothing and fabrics left in wills because so many of the names are unknown to us, and the color names sound oddly romantic. About 1670, one clothing legacy listed: "philmot, gridolin, puce, grain colour, Kendall Green, Lincoln Green, watchet blue, barry, milly, tuly, stammel red, Bristol red and sad colour."[21] Later, at about the time of the Revolution, we read of colors whose names are clearly meaningful: "Congress Brown, Federal Blue and Independence Green."[21]

The homespun era was not so well known among the wealthy planters in Virginia, except among the plantation workers' families. As early as 1660 the landowners were ordering rich and fancy dress from England and France and the governor finally issued a "Sumptuary Edict" which said, ". . no silke stuffe in garments or in peaces (except for whoods and scarfes), nor silver or gold lace, nor bone lace of silke or threads, nor ribbinds wrought with gold or silver in them."[24] These same Maryland and Virginia planters paid most of their bills in pounds of tobacco, and one gentleman's tailor bill in 1643 read this way:[24]

"To making a suit with buttins to it	80 lbs.
1 ell canvas	30 "
for dimothy linings	30 "
for belly pieces	40 "
for hooks and eies	10 "
for stiffinin for a collor	10 "

In contrast to the well-decorated southerner, the Massachusetts Puritans from 1640 to 1660 wore only black, brown, or gray heavy wool clothing, gray or green woolen socks, white linen collars and cuffs, and the ladies wore white aprons. The Puritan wife undoubtedly spun, wove, dyed, and sewed together every inch of her family's drab outfit.

Shortly after 1700, newspaper advertisements began to give us a picture of the first American fabric printer. It is probable that he began working earlier in several places and was an established tradesman-artisan by the 18th century. Since we lack samples of his work, and since there were no newspapers to record his activities, we can only guess at this. As a matter of interest and because colonial newspapers are indispensable to our studies, here are the earliest newspapers and the dates covered in George F. Dow's book *Arts and Crafts in New England*, except for the New York papers. Most of these were weeklies at first and originally were printed on both sides of a sheet of handmade paper, about 8½″ x 13½″ in size.

Boston News-Letter	1704-1776
Boston Gazette	1720-1765
New England Courant	1721-1725
New York Gazette	1725
New England Journal	1726-1740
Boston Evening Post	1740-1764
New York Journal &	
Patriotic Register	1791

Between 1711 and 1765 advertisements from the *Boston Gazette* offer for sale fabrics from India, Germany, England, Scotland, Holland, and France, but not one word of any American fabrics — which were then only the homespun industries for local use.[17] However, during that era dyers and printers advertised that they would bleach and dye or print cloth brought to them, and this would have been linen homespuns. Before and during the Revolution "from Massachusetts to South Carolina the women of the colonies banded together in patriotic societies called The Daughters of Liberty, agreeing to wear only garments of homespun manufacture, and to drink no tea. In many New England towns they gathered together to spin, each bringing her own wheel. At one meeting 700 linen wheels were employed."[29] After the Revolution spinning bees continued to be held so that the advertising printers were kept well supplied with linen to be "stampt."

Between 1712 and 1824, there were *six* American fabric printers who claimed to be the "First Calico Printer" in America, and each had no reason to believe otherwise. The printer who first put his claim in public print must be declared winner of the distinction:

BOSTON NEWS-LETTER, April 23, 1712:

"This is to give notice that there is lately arriv'd here from England GEORGE LEASON who with THOMAS WEBBER of Boston, cloathier, have set up a Callendar Mill and Dye House in Cambridge Street, Boston, near the Bowling Green: where all Gentlemen, Merchants and others may have all sorts of Linnens, Callicoes, Stuffs or Silks Callendar'd; Prints all sorts of Linnens, Dyes and Scowers all sorts of Silks and other things, and makes Buckrames; and all on very reasonable Terms."[103]

The complete roster of self-styled "First Calico Printers" in America follows:

1. George Leason, Boston, 1712
2. John Hewson, Philadelphia, 1773
3. Herman Vandausen, East Greenwich, R. I., 1790
4. Zachariah Allen, Providence, 1790
5. Archibald Hamilton Rowan, Delaware, 1796
6. William Sprague, Cranston, R. I., 1825

In Boston, in 1715, one Francis Dewing advertised that "He likewise cuts neatly in Wood and Printeth Callicoes." One expert draws a lengthy conclusion from this ad. He says, "Housewives of Boston must have been familiar with hand-block printing, or Dewing's ad would not have been so worded. It is not at all impossible, in view of other activities he also practiced, that he may occasionally have cut blocks and sold them for women to do their own printing. A competent housekeeper would have sufficient knowledge of making the dyes it would be necessary to use. Printing on fabrics was a household craft and might be successfully pursued, as occasion demanded, by any woman who owned or could borrow the blocks. No doubt blocks were lent from one neighbor to another throughout whole communities, just as were the moulds for pewter spoons and platters."[25] This is not exactly fact and not exactly fiction; more possible than probable.

During the time that a few early printers were offering their services, colonial women were always on the lookout for the merchants' endless newspaper announcements of goods received by ship from England. Dressmakers needed all sorts of materials as well as trimmings, feathers, braids, buttons, and ribbons to keep in style as much as possible. India cottons continued to be received and were used for coverlets, hangings, and clothing.

Boston News-Letter, December 18, 1760:

"Hunt and Torrey have just imported from London, a Fine Assortment of Goods to be sold at their shop in Queen Street near the Prison in Boston, at the lowest prices for Cash or Treasurer's Notes. Rich black cloth and lead-coloured padusoys, damasks, sattins, lute-strings; persians; taffeties; grograins; alamodes; black silks and trimmings for cardinals and capuchines; muffs & tippets; broadcloths; Kerseys; ratteens; flowered serges; calimancoes; camblets; poplins; everlastings; bombazeens; hat and widow's crapes; oznabrigs; clear, spotted and flower'd lawns; checked cottons; fustians; dimothies; galloons; plain and figured ribbons of all sorts; garterings; nutmegs; cinnamon; mace, cloves; Bohea tea; looping and buttons for Hatts, &c. &c. &c.[17]

Beginning about 1700 figured lightweight cottons came to be used for a kind of dressing gown by men (particularly in the South) patterned on a loose oriental robe called a *banyan*, sometimes spelled banian or banjan — or called a nightgown or Indian robe. Men not only wore these nightgowns at home, but "sauntered abroad" in them. In the steamy heat of southern plantations where wigs, long wool coats, and tight knee breeches became insufferable, men wore a cotton cap and a banyan. These were reported to have struck visitors as "shocking clothes for gentlemen."[23] Elsewhere the banyans were sometimes made of brocaded silk or velvet, lined, and were sometimes reversible. In the South there was exceptional elegance at "gatherings," the races, and fairs. But at home the planters went in negligee costumes. *The London Magazine* reported in 1745: " 'Tis an odd sight, that except some of the Very Elevated Sort, few persons wear Perukes, so that you would imagine they were all sick or going to bed; Common People wear woolen and yarn caps, but the better ones wear Holland or Cotton. Thus they travel fifty miles from Home. It may be cooler for ought I know, but methinks 'tis very ridiculous."[24]

BANYAN · 1750

In the records is the life story of one banyan described as " . . a long, full banian of heavy cotton fabric figured with a palm-leaf design of many hues and lined with a soft sarcenet silk of bright orange hue spotted with white and green. On one cuff was sewed a bit of white linen inscribed in ink with these words: 'This Banyan was made in Canton in 1792 for Archelaus Brown by Chinese taylors. It was made by order of his son, Rufus Brown; Supercargo of the bark 'The Lively Nancy.' " The label goes on to describe how Mr. Brown, Sr. was believed lost in a shipwreck, but finally came home wearing the banyan — "his only remaining garment." The label concludes with the heart-rending phrase — "Which is Kept for Thankfulness."[23]

The first advertisement to tell us that the printer of a newspaper also had a fabric-printing business appeared in the *Boston Gazette* in 1720.

"*LINEN PRINTER. The printer hereof Prints Linnens, Calicoes, Silks &c. in good Figures, very lively and durable Colours, and without the offensive smell which commonly attends the Linnens printed here.*"[17]

And on August 14, 1753, the same newspaper had this news item:

"*SPINNING ON BOSTON COMMON. On Wednesday an excellent sermon was preached before the Society for Encouraging Industry and Employing the Poor by the Rev. Samuel Cooper, after which several Pounds, old Tenor was collected and in the afternoon near 300 spinners, some of them children of 7 or 8 years old and several of them Daughters of the best Families among us, with their Wheels at Work, sitting orderly in three rows, made a handsome appearance on the Common: — The Weavers with a Loom and one at work, on a Stage made for the Purpose, attended with Musick, preceeding the Society as they Walked in Procession to view the said Spinners. Several Thousand Spectators assembled on this Occasion.*"[17]

Fig. 49

4. OLD DEERFIELD, MASSACHUSETTS

Several wood blocks that may be among the oldest preserved in America are believed by one expert to be "rare and ancient."[37] Some are made entirely of wood for printing cloth designs and some are wood with metal inserts for stamping embroidery or braid patterns, and all are in the collection of Old Deerfield, a restored village in Massachusetts — a community that is of real historic interest.

The township of Deerfield was founded in 1673, after a tract of 8,000 acres had been bought from the Pocumtuck Indians for fourpence per acre. It was the northwest frontier and outpost settlement of New England for many years and its settlers bore the brunt of wars with the French and Canadians and several bloody Indian attacks; it was almost completely burned in 1703. Four years after the fire the community started rebuilding and, in 1797, Deerfield Academy opened in the building that now houses the Pocumtuck Valley Memorial Association's collection of early American objects and Indian relics. One exhibit is a heavy oak door with a tomahawk driven through it, and still in place. This makes for chilling speculation as to where the next blows might have fallen if a colonial musket had not been fired at the right moment — and on target.

In 1896, the village of Old Deerfield began reviving many old household industries and colonial trades and became a museum of charming homes restored and lived in by the participants of the project. It is now a serene village of exceedingly handsome wooden houses, all containing exhibits and furnishings of the period. The printer's house has a second-floor door through which heavy bundles of paper and equipment could be (still can be) hauled to a second-floor workroom.

The wood blocks shown are from a collection that includes quilts, children's clothing and bonnets, tools, tavern signs, and other pieces. One baby dress of sheer pink muslin is trimmed with intricate designs in fine white braid. The muslin was probably marked with blocks similar to those shown in Figs. 52 and 53 as a guide for the seamstress. On very thin fabrics a paper pattern stamped with similar blocks was sometimes tacked underneath and pulled off after the braid had been sewn on. The museum also owns a hand-printed quilt, probably stenciled, with fine quilting done around the outlines of the printed design of red and green geometric flowers and leaves.

Fig. 50. Calico printing block, 7¼″ x 10″, with wooden handles on the back. Heavily-grained pine with a simple design cut into the block so that it would print as a dark background with a white or light figure. May have been used as the center section of a kerchief. Courtesy, Memorial Hall Museum, Pocumtuck Valley Memorial Association, Deerfield, Mass.

Fig. 51. Similar calico printing block, 6″ x 10½″, with floral design. Same source as above.

Fig. 52. Pattern blocks for embroidery or braid-work. Brass strips shaped and set into the wood to print. The block shows traces of blue dye or ink. Probably nineteenth century. Courtesy, Memorial Hall Museum, Deerfield, Mass.

Fig. 53. Pattern blocks, similar to those shown in Fig. 52, and from the same source, Deerfield, Mass.

Fig. 54. Calico printing block, 6½″ x 11½″, with two handles on the back; this design was reproduced by the author in linoleum, printed on cotton and is shown in Fig. 55. The design was purposely *not* reversed so as to allow better comparison with the old block. Courtesy, Memorial Hall Museum, Deerfield, Mass.

Fig. 55. *Left:* Reproduced print on cotton made by the author from a linoleum block copied from the Old Deerfield original wood block.

Because no fabrics remain that were printed from the Deerfield blocks, the author has reproduced one of these (Fig. 54) cut in linoleum and has printed from it on sheer cotton to show more clearly what the pattern would have looked like (Fig. 55). It is a border pattern that might have been used to print around the edges of a coverlet, for bed hangings or curtains, or for edging a square silk bandanna. It is probable that the wood blocks were used with the simplest dyes compounded by housewives from juices of fruits and decoctions of flowers, leaves, and barks or roots. Colonists could obtain dyes from European traders, even in the earliest days, because dyes were valuable in trading with the Indians. The wood blocks shown may well be from the earliest days of the settlement, but the coppered blocks probably date from the nineteenth century revival of handcrafts.

5. SOME BOSTON PRINTERS

The names of only 14 pre-revolutionary colonial calico printers are known to us, and nine of these were in Boston — a fact that we learn from the first newspaper published in that city.

BOSTON GAZETTE, June 16/23, 1735:

"CALICO PRINTER — Francis Gray, Callicoe Printer from Holland; Prints all sorts of Callicoes of several colours to hold Washing, at his house in Roxbury near the Meeting House."[17]

BOSTON GAZETTE, December 22, 1747:

"STAMPED LINEN — These are to Inform the Publick, that I the Subscriber propose to come once more to Boston; if any Person or Persons have old sheets or Linnen to stamp, they are desired to leave them at the house of James Nichol in School Street, next door to the French Meeting House; and if they send them in Four Weeks from this Date, they shall have them in March next, without fail. As witness my Hand, Sarah Hunt."[17]

The other five printers were in Philadelphia and their names and advertisements are recorded in early Quaker City newspapers. In Boston, one of the first printers who managed to bring a printing press and type from England was James Franklin, who arrived in 1713. It is almost certain that his heavy equipment made the ocean voyage as a smuggled shipment or by dint of bribery of a ship's officer, as the English never would have permitted such business equipment to be taken out of Britain. Franklin founded one of the earliest newspapers, the *New England Courant* (See Fig. 48), and he, like

96 • French block print on cotton ca. 1780. Deep red, blue-green, lavender, brown, gra and yellow. Vertical repeat 21″; size of piece 23″ x 31″. The grayish-appearin area behind the designs is an extremely delicate picotage block design with hun dreds of tiny metal pins. Courtesy, Cooper-Hewitt Museum of Design, Smithsonia Institution

the owner of the *Boston Gazette*, printed, in addition to his newspaper, linens, calicoes, and silks.[37] His fabric printing must have been a separate enterprise, done by hand from blocks. But as early as 1716, copper-plate engraving was known in Boston and the press-size plates were printed with ink on satin or cotton for kerchiefs, mottoes, and prayers, as described in Section I. Yardage is not known to have been printed in America from large copper plates. When James Franklin died, his widow carried on the printing business and his two daughters helped as typesetters.

BOSTON NEWS-LETTER, May 11, 1749:

"*PLATE PRESS — A large Rolling Press for Printing off a Copper Plate to be Sold, Inquire of the Printer.*"[17]

The newspaper notices tell us many colorful details of the facts of life in the colonies that might otherwise be long forgotten.

BOSTON GAZETTE, September 15, 1760:

"*HANGING FOR ROOMS — Jane Savell acquaints her customers that since the Fire she is Removed to a Chamber at the Upper End of Milk Street, near the South Meeting House where she has got several pieces of beautiful painted Canvas Hangings for Rooms, some stone Pickled Pots and Jugs; a Quantity of pickled Cucumbers and Mangoes.*"[17]

BOSTON GAZETTE, May 26, 1761:

"*PAPER MILL — Wanted Rags of Linnen, cource and fine, old Sail-Cloth, Cotton or Checks, pretty clean and dry. Thos that will bring them to Mr. Alexander Boyce, on Mr. Gould's Wharf, near Mr. Hallowell's Shipyard, Boston . . . and as further encouragement to Indistry: They that will gather and bring the greatest Quantity of Rags between this Day and the 29th May, 1762, to any of the mentioned Places, shall receive a Premium of 12 Dollars and the second Quantity 8 Dollars and the third Quantity 4 Dollars.*"[17]

French block print on cotton (possibly linen), Nantes, 1790. Deep rose, pink, blue, gold and brown. Flower bouquets 7″ x 9″. A rather elaborate block print with a very French flavor. Courtesy, Cooper-Hewitt Museum of Design, Smithsonian Institution

In case we doubt that colonial calico was of much value, here is a sad little tale that makes it seem that in 1767 it was, in fact, most desirable.

New York Gazette or Weekly Post Boy, February 19, 1767:

"SHOP LIFTER. Monday last a Woman lifted a couple of Pieces of Callicoe off of Mr. Milligan's Shop Window, but a Negro happily seeing it, immediately gave intelligence thereof, Whereupon a Pursuit was made, the Woman overtaken, and the Callicoe found upon her; She was carried before an Alderman, who committed her to Jail; and 'tis said she is to have her Trial Today."[28]

— and yet another that accounts for the scarcity of samples of the work of the printers:

Boston Gazette, February 18, 1765:

"PAPER MILL — The Public are once more requested to save their linnen and cotton-and-linnen RAGS, all that is white and finer than Oznabrigs, two Coppers a pound will be given . . . Choice Press-Paper to be sold at Mr. Davis's abovementioned, and at the Mill at two Guineas per Groce."[17]

There are a number of references to the "home" printing of blocks, and to the fact that blocks were cut by professionals and sold to housewives so that they could do their own printing, and these are substantiated by at least one advertisement in Boston:

Boston News-Letter, May 13, 1773:

"To be Sold, very cheap for Cash, by the person who prints dark Callicoes, an excellent sett of Prints for the same. The person who has them to dispose of, would Instruct the Purchaser in the use of them if required. Enquire of the Printer."[17]

The "sett of Prints" means a set of blocks, and other references to "print cutters" indicate that the word *print* was often used to mean the *blocks* used for printing.

A famous and much-quoted instance of a woman printing her own fabric is described in Frances Little's book *Early American Textiles*. A fragment of the textile she refers to is owned by the Essex Institute in Salem, Mass., and another, shown in Fig. 56, is owned by the Metropolitan Museum of Art, but does not show the inscription. It is printed from a large plate of about 15"x28" in soft dark blue. The Little book says:

"The print that depicts scenes of agriculture and military life has an entertaining history. The lower half of the pattern, showing the campfire

Fig. 56. Printed cotton, American Haymakers and Camp Scenes. Plate-printed in blue about 1820 according to the Victoria and Albert Museum — mistakenly dated and attributed for many years. Courtesy, Metropolitan Museum of Art; Rogers Fund, 1913

scene, has long been [1931] in the collection of the Metropolitan Museum under the attribution of an American print, but with no further history to substantiate this claim. Another fragment lent to the Museum bears this inscription:

'Cloth spun, woven and printed by Elizabeth Pierce-Throop who was born in 1743 and died April 9, 1788 and is buried in Burying Place Hill Cemetery in Rehoboth, Mass. She married the second time Lieut. Jeremiah Wheeler.'

"There is also the epitaph: 'Her family did often share
    Her generous look and tender care
    Likewise her friends did also find
    A neighbor that was just and kind;
    She lived on earth greatly desired
    Greatly lamented when expired.'

"In the Essex Institute in Salem, Mass., shortly after, there was discovered the piece that combined both these features, with a harvesting scene in addition, thus establishing this print as one of American workmanship."[37]

The story really does not hang together very well, unfortunately. Almost anyone familiar with copper-plate printing would say that the print could never have been printed from a wood block, as most home-printed fabrics were supposed to have been done. Copper plates of large scale supposedly were not done in America, and a heavy iron press and considerable skill and strength were required to print them. It is hard to understand how gentle Elizabeth could have done it, or how such a story came to be. The Victoria and Albert Museum at first dated the fabric at about 1805 and later changed that to 1820. Both the Victoria and Albert Museum and the Essex Institute now call the whole thing a case of "documentary confusion." Since the story is so charming, it is really a pity to have it set straight.

However, it is possible that blocks *were* sold to women for printing at home, and they may have been loaned about the neighborhood, as were embroidery "stamps" and theorem stencils for painting.

6. EIGHTEENTH CENTURY ELEGANCE

From our vantage point after 300 elapsed years, American frontier settlements such as Jamestown and Deerfield seem to have disappeared rapidly, but the 100 years from 1600 to 1700 must have seemed very long to a lot of Americans. The frontier moved westward, and along the east coast, in the fast-growing cities, prosperity was not long in coming. In Boston, a cultured society with growing wealth was seen early in the 18th century and the first colleges, libraries, and newspapers were established in Massachusetts.

"The influence of the Royal Governor and his staff established a miniature court which closely aped the English dress and manners and rivalled English luxury. An English traveler named Bennet wrote of Boston in 1740, 'Both the ladies and gentlemen dress and appear as gay in common as courtiers in England on a coronation or birthday.' George Whitefield, the English religious leader, complained bitterly of the 'foolish virgins of New England covered all over with the pride of life' and of the jewels, patches, and gay apparel commonly worn. Account books, wills, and records attest to the great luxury and richness of dress which lasted throughout the century."[24]

In Philadelphia as early as 1726 the Quakers, through custom and denominational law, were pledged to simple, sober, and uniform dress; yet

100 • AMERICA'S PRINTED & PAINTED FABRICS

VIRGINIAN - 1740

even they felt the love of dress, which was so strongly crescent everywhere throughout the colonies in the early part of the 18th century. In 1726 the "Woman Ffriends" at a yearly meeting felt constrained to formulate a message to their fellow women Quakers. It said:

". . . and also that none of our Ffriends accustom themselves to wear the gowns with superfluous folds behind, but plain and decent, nor go without aprons, nor to wear superfluous gathers or plaits in their caps or pinners . . . neither to cut or lay their hair on their foreheads or temples.
And that Ffriends be careful to avoid wearing striped shoes or red and white heeled shoes or clogs or shoes trimmed with gaudy colors.
And also that no Ffriends use that irreverent practice of taking snuff or handing a snuff box to the other in Meeting.
And also that Ffriends do not accustom themselves to go with bare breasts or bare necks."[24]

In the South there had been elegance of dress from very early days. Clothes were ordered from England and France and, in 1747, when George Washington was 15, he sent these instructions to his tailor in England:

"Memorandum. To have my coat made by the following directions, to be made a Frock with a Lapel Breast. The Lapel to contain on each side six Button Holes & to be about 5 or 6 inches wide all the way equal, & to Turn as the Breast on the Coat does, to have it made very long Waisted and in length to come down to or below the bent of the knee, the Waist from the Armpit to the Fold to be exactly as long as or Longer than from Thence to the Bottom, not to have more than one Fold in the skirt and the top to be made just to turn in and Three Button Holes, the lapel at the top to turn as the Cape of the coat and Button to come parallel with the Button holes and the last Button Hole on the Breast to be right opposite the button on the hip."[24]

About twenty-five years later it was said: "To write a true account of dress during the years of the American Revolution seems a well-nigh impossible thing. Never was a poor historian confronted with more conflicting sources. In one letter you read of poverty, want, and privation — the next has a story of a great and gay ball. You read that the people of Boston died of the cold and inadequate food; the next sentence is the description of a theatrical entertainment in Faneuil Hall. It was a day of vast incongruities."[23]

At some date in the 18th century, and possibly even into the early 19th, it appears that a whole class of fabrics printed with large-scale indigo blue designs on white cloth existed in and around New York. They were unlike

VIRGINIAN - 1786

India chintzes and different from French and English textiles, too. There are very few fragments of them remaining among collectors and American museums today and the sources and dates of these blue and whites have become a puzzlement. Early advertisements sometimes mention blue prints, but many antiquarians believe these were printed elsewhere than in America. Museums, nevertheless, file them under the heading of "American." Reference material on them is scarce and scattered and it therefore seems important here and now to make what is (as far as can be ascertained) the first illustrated study of all aspects of what seem to be America's most interesting and unique fabrics.

7. BLUE RESIST PRINTS

The true identity of the so-called American blue resist prints on cotton is almost as mysterious as that of the Boston Strangler. Museum people are as eager to discuss them, but as reluctant to identify the subject, as would be a witness to one of the stranglings who protests that it was too dark to see the man's face. Everybody who is acquainted with them knows at least one way they *could* have been printed or dyed, but nobody is quite sure how they *were* done. Nobody knows for certain that they are American, but there is no very clear reason to think they came from anywhere else. Almost nobody has seen a block that might be supposed to have been used to print them, yet there is much evidence to suggest that they were printed from blocks. There were enough prints in the Eastern colonies sometime around the first half of the 18th century so that several museums now own examples of the same design. But one major museum that has the only examples of some rare early prints does not own one piece of blue resist believed to be American. Some people think they were commercially imported, like the English Staffordshire pottery called "American," made especially for export; some think the fabrics were brought home by colonial mariners as souvenirs, but nobody knows for sure from where. They are something like batiks, something like Japanese stencil prints, and something like Slovak and other folk art prints, but uniquely different from them all.

Quite a few people agree that they are charming, powerfully-designed, and very decorative in spite of — or perhaps because of — their simple and somewhat primitive appearance. They have a more forceful personality than many textiles and can be recognized easily as blue resists although nobody knows precisely how they were done, and many find the quality that makes the designs so distinctive rather puzzling. Sometimes the prints are one color — indigo blue on white — but more often they are done in two shades of blue, one a dark, true indigo and the other a lighter, medium-value of the same hue. The design is generally a figure of branches, flowers and leaves or birds with

Fig. 57. American blue resist print with birds and floral forms in two shades of blue on white. Courtesy, Metropolitan Museum of Art. Rogers Fund, 1940

flowers, seeds, and foliage in a bold pattern of meandering stems against a white background. The undyed background (called a "reserved ground") is seldom seen in other resist printed or indigo-dyed fabrics; most of them have white figures on a blue-dyed ground, as in Fig. 76. The designs lack sharp detail and are often characterized by their most unique feature: a pattern of small white dots running over the whole pattern of blues, providing the dotted details of drawing and adding a touch of delicacy within the bold shapes. The white dots, possibly printed with a resist medium from a block with metal pins, are used to delineate feathers and eyes of birds, petals of flowers, and the veining of leaves. White (or other) picotage dots are not at all uncommon, but the way they are used on the blue resists is distinctive. The whole effect seems slightly Chinese, but somehow is an almost impossible combination of folk art and baroque styles.

Unless there is an unknown exception in existence somewhere, the blue and whites were printed on a loosely-woven cotton or cotton and linen cloth, probably handspun, and the pattern is a continuous repeat of one design unit in an overall design. The units are quite large — often about 15″ x 18″ or more; the scale suggests that originally they must have been used exclusively as household furnishing fabrics and not as dress goods. They were never printed, however, like some coverlets with a center unit, other surrounding elements, and a border of a still different kind, in the manner of Indian palampores. If one could imagine a room in which these fabrics were used as bed-hangings or coverlets, it might be agreed that the blue and white prints would give their surroundings a strong and attractive character imparted by few textiles of any kind. (There is a bedspread in the Brooklyn Museum's Schenck House.)

An ill wind is known to have blown full in the face of this pleasant image when one museum curator said flatly, "I hate them!" Another person added a definitive comment when she said, "*Those* things!" Some people deplore the lack of careful drawing and dislike the uncommon boldness — qualities very different from the graceful curves and carefully-drawn, delicate forms of polychrome English and French floral prints based on Indian designs. The style of the blue and whites is unlike most other fabrics of the same date.

Antiquarians are understandably bothered by the fact that no prints of the kind have been found with printer's markings, names, or dates, so none can be documented in a scholarly way. Many of the fragments are said to have originated near New York and are roughly dated between 1700 and 1775, based partly on the style, confusing as it may be. Sometimes they are called "Hudson River" prints — meaning they might have been done in New York or New Jersey printing establishments. The idea that they were not made in America but were imported from Britain or by one of the East India companies is equally hard to substantiate. Extensive records of English and Dutch trading companies make no mention of orders for or shipments of prints described as blue and whites. The Albany (N.Y.) Institute of History and Art owns one blue and white print that carries along the end the British crown insignia, an excise record number, and the date 1766, printed in the same blue as the fabric.

The stamp could mean either that the cloth was printed in England intended for export to the colonies, or that it was printed elsewhere (India?) upon order of a British trading firm and intended to be a colonial export. Later in this study we suggest still another possibility. If the stamp is evidence of importation, it is the *lone* example representing true documentation we have at this time.

There are many advertisements in American colonial newspapers that mention "Linnens with true Blue and Whites," "China blues," and one printer offers for sale cloth "with very lively and durable Colors without the offensive smell which commonly attends the Linnens." Indigo vats were said to smell awful, and perhaps washing prints in streams was not enough! As late as 1824, the Cranston Print Works announced the beginning of its printing operation and advertised "new indigo blues"; another firm introduced something called a "Blue dip." It is interesting to note that the two words *blue* and *calico* were almost never associated, though seemingly most other kinds of early prints (except copper-plates) were called calicoes. The resist prints are called "porcelain blues," blue and whites or blue resists, but not *blue calicoes*; this fact alone makes them seem distinctive.

Fig. 58. American blue resist print with flower and leaf forms in two shades of blue on white. This is the same pattern as the piece owned by the Albany Institute of History and Art that bears a British crown stamp. Courtesy of Thomas D. and Constance R. Williams, Litchfield, Connecticut

The Boſton News-Letter.
And New-England *Chronicle*.

BOSTON NEWS-LETTER, 1761:
"The wife of John Haugen stamps linen china blue or deep blue or any colour that gentlemen and Ladies fancies."[37]

Fig. 59

It is because of two clearly opposing circumstances that the prints have come to be called *American*. First, there is no mention of them in the records of — or examples of them known in — other countries, and second, there are many colonial newspaper advertisements that *could* refer to them, and the fabrics do exist in United States museums only.

Being of uncertain origin and uncertain date, it follows that the method by which they were printed or pattern-dyed is uncertain also. The collections of the Cooper-Hewitt Museum of Design of the Smithsonian Institution in New York City (formerly Cooper Union Museum) have long been a mecca for students of world textiles. In May, 1956 the museum called together about 50 people — curators, museum directors, antiquarians, designers, technicians, and artists — to discuss the subject of American blue resist prints with the hope of solving the mystery of their origin and putting these fabrics into their proper historical niche. The discussions, examples, and color slides were interesting and informative and finally contributed greatly to an understanding of the problem, but offered no final clues to its solution. One impression drawn from the meeting was that museum curators and some others believed the technique of the blue and whites to be complicated and difficult. However, craftsmen who had done printing maintained that the process actually is not difficult and requires only very simple skills that in no way would be comparable to the requirements of making Java batiks, for instance. Indigo dyeing is a long, drawn-out process, but is only laborious and not difficult. It might be mentioned here that blue and white resist prints are done with wax or paste resists and blocks by the most primitive Senegalese craftsmen and by country craftsmen in Slovakia and elsewhere.

The museum's curators, Alice B. Beer and Jean Mailey, did produce for this conference a valuable 34-page study on the subject consisting of descriptions of resist printing and painting and indigo-dyeing excerpted from 10 books and other publications in English, French, and German and others from Switzerland, Japan, and America. It is from this study and other material that descriptions of the technique are summarized herein. (See special book list at end of Bibliography.)

Fig. 60. Fragment of early resist print with white figures on blue background; the motifs are in the style of Pennsylvania German prints. Courtesy of the Philadelphia Museum of Art

The prints are generally thought to have been produced by printing with a wax or paste resist by a relief method from blocks. The resist medium is apt to have been a hard-drying paste rather than beeswax or tallow, since the prints show no traces whatever of batik-like crackles and the whites are clearly white. After application and drying of the paste (twice if there were two blues), the fabrics were dyed in indigo in at least two — possibly many more — immersions to produce the two shades of blue, and the paste was removed by washing.

It should be noted here that there is a very good reason why indigo blue prints are (or were for years) always *resist* prints: *indigo will not work with mordants.* The fibres of cotton and linen soak up the indigo readily without any previous processing. This makes it impossible to print a mordant first to cause the cloth to take up the dye only where the mordant is, and to refuse it on all other parts, as with most other dyes. So, in order to produce a pattern, the cloth must be protected from the indigo by a resist paste or wax in order to keep the undyed areas white. It is important to understand the basic process; therefore, using an enlarged portion of the design from the fabric shown in Fig. 57, the author has prepared a series of progress drawings to explain the procedure more clearly than by words alone. The caption for each illustration in the series explains the steps; after a look at these, we shall review the various formulas and dyeing procedures and suggest several possible methods of printing. The square encloses a study area only, and does not represent a printing block.

Fig. 61. STEP 1: the first application of resist paste to all parts of the design that are to remain white: the entire background and the small dots and details. Shown as if the paste is a light gray color on white cloth, which it probably was

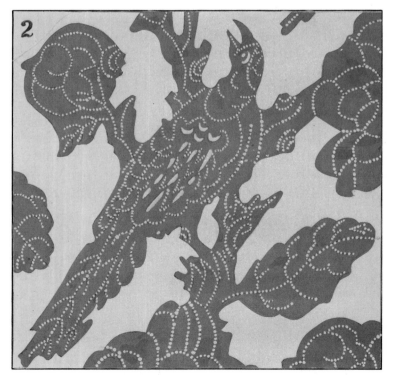

108 *Fig. 62.* STEP 2: Cloth after the first dye bath; whole design except parts reserved with paste is dyed light blue by short immersion in the indigo vat. Light gray represents the paste reserve, dark gray represents the light blue dye

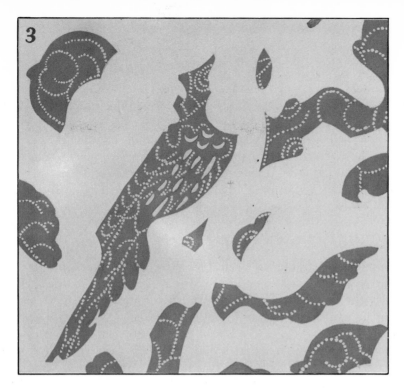

Fig. 63. STEP 3: Second application of resist paste to all parts that are to remain light blue. Unprotected parts — not covered with resist-paste — will receive more dye in the indigo vat until the color is deep blue

Fig. 64. STEP 4: Paste has been removed by washing and this is the finished print: light blue and deep blue on a white ground.

WAX AND PASTE RESISTS – INDIGO DYEING

The whole process of blue resist printing involves the use of two basic substances — the resist medium and the indigo dye. There are pages and pages of printed information and whole books about the techniques used for both of them, and we shall review here as briefly as possible some of that information in order to show that if a mystery exists about *technique* in America, it has not existed anywhere else in the world for hundreds of years; not in India, Egypt, Java, Japan, England, France, Germany, Switzerland, or Slovakia — to mention a few.

RESIST MEDIUMS – WAX AND PASTE

In India, the process of wax painting and dyeing as done in the early 18th century has been recorded in detail, and must be the same as the method used for centuries before that. The *wax* referred to is taken to mean either pure beeswax or tallow (animal fat). A letter written in 1741 by a Father Coeurdoux says,[5] "[In India] . . : as the blue is not painted on with a brush, but applied by dipping into a prepared indigo bath, the cloth must be gone over with wax everywhere [except] such places as are appropriate to blue or green. This wax may be put on with an iron pencil [Java tjanting?] as lightly as possible on one side only. The cloth . . is exposed to the sun . . . [so] that the wax only just melts sufficiently to penetrate to the other side." Then the writer explains that the cloth had to be rubbed with a round-bottom brass vessel to spread the soft wax through to the other side; then the cloth was "handed over to the Blue Dyer." After dyeing, the wax was removed by placing the cloth in boiling water.

Records show repeatedly, and it is generally conceded, that the Indian method of "painting" cloth was admired, sought after, and copied by most 17th and 18th century Europeans who first began printing cloth; it is always referred to as being done "in the Indian manner." So, although later European imitations were largely block printed, it seems safe to take this, or a variation of this, to be a basic primer of the method.

From a French book by R. Pfister we learn that "the ancients even in India did not know how to *print* indigo. One always proceeded by means of printing a reserve [of wax, for example], and then dyeing in a vat of indigo. When the fabric in open air has not the desired color, one has only to place it again in the vat to obtain a more intense blue. If, before this new immersion, one protects certain parts with wax, one thus obtains two different tones." In speaking of India again Pfister further says, " . . proceeds by hand painting after the outlines are traced by pouncing. In this piece . . . there has been a reserve of wax applied, or of starch, most often with a wood block." (Pouncing is a very old process of tapping a small cloth bag filled with powdered

Fig. 65. American blue resist print with flowering branches and leaves; leaves within leaves and flowers within flowers; two shades of blue on white. Courtesy, Cooper-Hewitt Museum of Design, Smithsonian Institution

charcoal or lampblack against the lines of a pricked stencil, thus transferring the finely dotted lines of the design through the holes onto the cloth. Subsequent painting or embroidery then follows the black dotted lines.)

From a German book by R. Forrer we learn that "The color blue at that time [1700] enjoyed especial popularity. Influenced by the Chinese porcelains introduced then commercially and the white-blue Delft faiences so akin [also called porcelains] these indigo prints were also called 'Porcelain prints.'" A little book of the year 1771 gives some instructions as to how the blue porcelain print is made and how the paste and ground impression — called the "covering over" — used in this process should be "cooked."

Three recipes for printing pastes are given, and, for better or for worse, here are the ingredients:

Recipe #1	Recipe #2	Recipe #3
white tobacco-pipe clay	cologne glue	water
alum	gum arabic	gum arabic
vitriol	starch	isinglass
6 egg whites	wax	brandy
starch	tallow	starch-flour
wax	pipe-clay	tallow
turpentine	alum	calf-gall
	vitriol	pipe-clay
	turpentine	

We have no way of knowing which formula worked best, but #3 certainly sounds the most delicious. They are pretty much the same, give or take a bit of brandy or turpentine. The book also says the cloth can be strewn with very fine sand in order to protect the material from getting damaged during the further steps of the procedure. We assume this acted as an effective stiffener, since mixing sand with some of the above formulas would surely result in cement.

A contemporary craftsman once took one of the above recipes that seemed to give the most specific amounts, and by translating "loths" into ounces, arrived at this:

> 1 pound of kaolin (white ceramic ball, or pipe-clay)
> 6 ounces of alum (probably a thickener)
> 3 ounces of vitriol (copperas or ferrous sulphate)
> 6 egg whites
> handful of corn starch
> 10-12 ounces of melted beeswax, stirred in
> 6 ounces of turpentine

Fig. 66. Blue and white resist print with many picotage dots, French, late 18th century. A very rare European blue and white in which there is a white background with blue figure, like the American prints. The design is subtly elegant and more refined than colonial patterns. Courtesy, Philadelphia Museum of Art

The opportunity to strew the sand on the cloth never presented itself since the mixture was a mess, and could not be applied to a printing block in any known way. Undoubtedly it was meant to be cooked, but since these directions were witheld, the secret is still preserved!

From Switzerland comes this information: "It was the Hugenots who brought us the secret of the *reserves*. The cloth was stretched on a printing table covered not with cloth, but with fine sand. With a brush the worker applied to all parts that should remain white a hot composition of wax or tallow and left free the parts he wished to make blue. The sand that was underneath kept the wax from spreading because it attached itself to that part. As soon as a section of the textile was waxed, the worker threw sand over it in order to fix the coating before it cooled. The sand also prevented the waxed parts from oiling the other parts when the cloth was folded. This cloth was then plunged into a vat of indigo, lukewarm or cold — never hot — so that the wax should not melt. After several dippings, it was taken out for removal of

Fig. 67. Hanging or large panel of white cotton printed in two shades of indigo by a resist technique, English, late 18th century. (There are no white picotage dots.) The fabric is 40″ wide, pieced, and appears to be printed from two blocks, each 15″ x 20″, in a repeat of 20″ x 30″. The Winterthur Museum in Delaware has an example of the same piece and a reproduction has been printed by Colonial Williamsburg. Courtesy, Cooper-Hewitt Museum of Design, Smithsonian Institution

the wax and to be dried. If one wished to obtain varied shades of blue, one covered with tallow, when dry, the parts that should remain pale blue, and re-immersed the cloth." It should be noted here that there is no mention of a block — but the wax was *painted* on.

A book printed in Paris in 1865 says, "... by means of blocks made for the purpose, one can cover every part one wishes to reserve; one scatters sand over that printing of reserve, and then one allows it to dry until it is hard as wood. Then this composition will resist the blue when the piece is plunged into the vat for seven to ten minutes ... the printing boards [blocks] should be of walnut and their engraving double the ordinary depth because this composition must be printed thicker, and charges the cloth more than ordinary printing." A much earlier reference says that "wood blocks were unsuitable for hot wax and had to be replaced by *metal* blocks made from a mixture of tin, lead, and pewter. A German book as early as 1686 includes a section called "How to make lead blocks for cotton printing.[99] Probably clay or plaster moulds would have been made from a carved wooden model, and the metal poured as in any casting process, to make the blocks from these low-melting-point metals.

In Japan, textile craftsmen used a resist paste for which a glutinous rice and rice bran were boiled, mashed, and kneaded together to make a paste to be applied to the cloth in one of three ways: (1) The paste was squeezed directly onto the fabric from a tube held like a crayon; skilled craftsmen could draw freehand with the paste, or sometimes used a rough sketch and could do very detailed and refined lines. Some Japanese cotton robes with multi-color designs, mostly stenciled, have parts of the design that look freehand or painted — these are probably the "squeezed-on" paste parts. (2) Using stencils — sometimes as many as 50 for one design — the paste was rubbed with a spatula into those parts of the fabric not covered by the stencil, through the openings. (3) A slightly thinned paste was poured directly onto the fabric where large areas were to be reserved, and guided with spoons or sticks to the margins of the drawing. (See Fig. 31)

The Slovaks have a good, short name for their resist paste — they call it "pap." One Slovak formula is:

> white painter' clay
> gum arabic
> acetate of lead
> lead sulphate
> blue stone (chalk?)
> salve (tallow?)
> alum

Fig. 68/69. Slovak printer distributed pap in the box-frame before placing pattern (block). *Right:* Placing pattern and printing cloth with pap. Note that the printer is placing the pitch pins on the cloth carefully where the design was measured off and marked in advance. From *Indigo Blue Print in Slovak Folk Art*, by Josef Vydra

This was to be diluted with water and boiled until a grayish pap was obtained. The Slovak book says, "Naturally, practically every dyer had his own secret formula for the composition and preparation of the pap. In printing, he uses a box-frame for spreading pap evenly on the pattern which he dips into the box and then presses onto the cloth, spread out on the press-table. The printed piece of cloth is then attached to poles at the ceiling and left to dry. Later it is dyed."

As you see, indigo prints in Slovak folk art are *all* white figures on a blue ground, and have been used for years for peasant skirts, aprons, scarves and table covers, and for the decorative cover of mattresses, which become part of the interior decoration of the house during the day. A few of their prints are done in two blues, and sometimes a yellow is added.

Fig. 70. Slovak bed stacked with mattresses covered with indigo print "feather-bed fabrics." From *Indigo Blue Print in Slovak Folk Art*, by Josef Vydra.

Fig. 71. Detail of Slovak indigo print feather-bed fabric with pear and grape ornament

Fig. 72. Detail of Slovak indigo print tablecloth border with wreath and rosette design

So much, then, for resist pastes and waxes around the world, and how they were applied; Java batiks have already been discussed. We have here shown in several of the excerpts from books, and from the Slovak photographs, the "evidence" we referred to in the beginning when we said that *blocks* were often used to apply resists.

INDIGO

Indigo, one of the world's oldest known, and long the most valuable of dyestuffs, had its origin in India (the word is Spanish for "India") and comes from the leaves of a rather graceful plant with yellow blossoms of the genus *indigofera*. It yields two or three crops a year and grows to about four or five feet in height in warm climates. It comes (or came) primarily from India,

INDIGO

Fig. 73

Java, and Guatemala and was first introduced into Europe about 1516. Up to the time its merits became known, *woad* was the plant used for blue dye, but indigo soon replaced the less satisfactory (and more fugitive) woad dye. About 1740, indigo seeds were introduced into South Carolina where it grew successfully, and by 1747 was exported to England and was sent to the northern colonies.[34] In 1771, England imported more than a million pounds from North Carolina, South Carolina, and Georgia, and indigo became one of the first profitable exports from the American colonies. It was used all over the world as the only blue dyestuff until as late as 1900. Only natural dyesuffs were used (mostly plant, some mineral) until in 1856, in England, Sir W. H. Perkin discovered the first aniline dye, *mauve*, a coal-tar product. In 1880, in Germany, the first successful synthetic blue was perfected from the same source and came into universal use thereafter.

Blue was a much-loved color and until 1810, when the first permanent green dye was discovered, indigo was used in various ways to combine with other yellow dyes to make green. Since it was the only substance known to make both blue and green colorings, it acquired tremendous value and was very profitable on world markets. Indigo became so valuable during the American Revolution that cubes and hunks "the size of a pigeon's egg" were used for money when paper currency became worthless.[7]

Considering the small yield of dye per plant, the laborious method of extracting the necessary glucose from the leaves, and the difficulty of making it into an effective dyestuff, it is remarkable that indigo ever came into use at all! To extract the substance called *indican* from the leaves, the freshly-harvested indigo plant is steeped in water to ferment for about nine to fourteen hours, then run off into "beating vats." Originally these had to be whipped up by hand with bamboo sticks, but later were stirred by a paddle-wheel or aerated by a blower. The precipitated indigo settled in the vats and the liquid was discarded. The indigo "mud" thus obtained was strained, boiled, and formed into bars and cut into three-inch cubes and dried. Natural indigoes at this point may have had as little as 20% or as much as 90% of the true coloring matter called *indigotine*, and buyers had to be very perceptive in recognizing the quality of dried indigo chunks.

Strange as it seems, the dried pieces of indigo, when ground to a powder for use, were *insoluble* in water and had to be reduced by chemicals such as lime and copperas, zinc powder or hydrosulphite in order to be used at all. This chemical reduction changed the substance into what dyers called "indigo white" — which was soluble in alkali, and that solution was finally called the "indigo vat." Any mental picture we may have of the dyer dipping his cloth into a pot of beautiful blue juice is entirely wrong. The liquid indigo was a clear yellow fluid. After cloth was immersed in it and brought out again into the air, the liquid in the fibres of the cloth oxidized and reconverted in a few minutes into first a yellowish-green, then green, and finally into indigo blue. Without exposure to the air where the process of oxidization could take place, the cloth could have been left forever in the indigo vat and, thus immersed, would never have shown a trace of blue. The vats were very odoriferous and lime had to be added constantly to maintain an alkaline mixture. An important part of the dyer's skill was a good sense of smell. Also, the dye "wore out" with use and new indigo had to be processed and added to the vats, or else the cloth had to be moved to a fresh vat. In a large dyeing operation, the dyeing yard was a forest of vats.

Fig. 74. American resist print in two blues on white cloth in a design of sinuous branches and flowers with a complicated picotage pattern. Courtesy, Metropolitan Museum of Art, Gift of Mrs. Robert W. de Forest, 1924

The color was not what we would call today a bright or intense blue, but was a rather soft color — although it could be very dark — but it was very resistant to sun and washing, or "fast," and this alone made it a treasure among dyes.

In the early days of indigo dyeing, or when it was done on a small scale entirely by hand, cloth simply was folded and dipped by hand into the vats. Later, in a more complicated operation, the problem of handling a length of cloth, particularly if it was coated with a stiff paste and had to be dyed to produce a pattern, became a formidable one. However, an ingenious device was used called a "star-frame" which could be wound with as many as 80 yards of cloth for dyeing the piece. The frame was like an octagonal reel with a slender center pole the length of the width of the cloth, and a star-shaped wheel with eight wooden spokes, but no rim, at each end. Each spoke of the two wheels had tenterhooks at equal and matching intervals that clipped the cloth in place at each hem, The reel was temporarily placed on a horizontal, turning rack and the cloth was wound on the reel starting at the center, turning the rack, and matching the two sets of hooks for stretching the cloth until the whole, gradually-growing-larger spiral was wound. From the end, when wound, the edge of the cloth looked like the pattern of a giant spider web. The spaces between layers allowed free circulation of the dye. The frame was then upended and attached to chains with ceiling pulleys, and hung directly over the dye vat. It was lowered into the vat, then pulled up and reversed for another dipping to dye the other half of the width of the cloth. Thus, the dye vats did not have to be very large or very deep to take a long length of cloth, and the fabric never had to be moved, folded or disturbed during dyeing. The tenterhooks (origin of an expressive phrase) left slight marks on the edge of the print if the background was dyed a solid color. After dyeing, the frame was hung in the air so that the color could oxidize and the cloth could dry; then the reel was put back on the horizontal axis and the cloth was unwound onto another roller for final washing and finishing.

Now, to return to the original Cooper Union Museum study which gives us page after page of descriptions of this long, redolent dyeing process; one

Fig. 75. Resist printed cotton in one shade of blue on white, 18th century, source uncertain — France or England possibly. Overall pattern of foliage, flowers, and pomegranates with delicate picotage parts. Courtesy, Cooper-Hewitt Museum of Design, Smithsonian Institution

book will be enough to quote. A Frenchman, Dorette Berthoud, tells us how the vats for dyeing were set up, and it is enough to discourage anyone from the trade just to read about it!

> "FIRST VAT. In a vat containing about 2500 pots of cold water, one puts 100 to 120 pounds of quicklime. One stirs it well ... if one were to dip more than 50 pieces in the same lime, one would have poor work. Better to empty the vat after 40 or 50 pieces.
> "SECOND VAT. This vat serves for rinsing .. in water, a little lime and a few pounds of vitriol.
> "THIRD VAT. One prepares it with a sufficient quantity of iron sulphate ... and it should be perfectly refreshed the following day, which is indispensable.
> "FOURTH VAT. Water acidulated with sulfuric acid
> "FIFTH VAT. Processing or dipping. One arranges the piece in a rack and places it in the first vat of agitated lime for 10 minutes .. etc.
> "THIRD VITRIOL VAT. . . .
> "FIRST LIME VAT. . . .
> "THE CHALK VAT. . . .
> ". . . it is now rinsed and passed to the washing wheel . . . one clears it up in boiling water . . ."

"One" hopes that this is the end, but it is not. Other processes had to follow: drying, stretching, sometimes steaming, sometimes waxing and polishing (glazing) with a smooth stone; bolt-lengths (usually about 30 yards) had to be measured off, cut, wound, wrapped, and labeled. The process sounds endless, but in a 20th century fabric-printing operation the whole procedure is about as complicated, only mechanized.

Although it is true that for many years it was impossible to *print* with indigo (and now we understand why) — or to achieve a blue and white print of any kind except by resist dyeing — there were two other ways later worked out to use indigo blue, before the discovery of synthetic mauve and aniline.

English printers, about 1730, were the first to work out a way of applying indigo by painting it on by hand with a brush. The stuff they used was called "pencil blue" and was made by mixing ground indigo, potash, *orpiment* (arsenic trisulphide), and lime, boiling these in water, then adding gum Senegal to thicken the mixture. This combination kept the indigo from oxidizing just long enough to allow time for putting it on the cloth with a brush, or by drawing it on with what is referred to as "an iron pencil." By 1760 a similar but improved mixture could be used for block printing, but was never completely satisfactory. This orpiment recipe was called "bleu d'Angleterre" in France and "Englischblau" in Germany, and its discovery was considered a "very important advance in European textile printing."[98]

Fig. 76. Typical European resist print with white figure on blue background, 18th century French or English. Courtesy, Cooper-Hewitt Museum of Design, Smithsonian Institution

Printers and chemists sought to improve the method and another way was found called "China blue." This was a radically different principle of printing indigo in an undissolved state (without lime), and then arranging its simultaneous *reduction* and *solution* on the cloth *after* printing. "Indigo was mixed with ferrous sulphate and thickened as a finely-ground printing paste, printed on, and then the cloth was alternately immersed in lime [to dissolve the indigo] and in ferrous sulphate [to reduce it] as many times as necessary to achieve the desired strength of blue."[98] The method could not be combined with madder and mordants, but was a satisfactory way to print in one color — particularly from copper plates, and later from copper rollers.

The first method, "Pencil blue," was used until about 1850 wherever small touches of blue and green (with yellow) were needed to add to a madder-printed design to produce what was called a "full-chintz." The later "China blue" was used for monochrome prints in England and France in blues or purples. There are American colonial references to "pencilers" who were paid so much per stroke to paint on indigo; one reference says that "Pencil colors are laid on by young boys and girls with a pencil after the piece is printed."[16] The "China blue" method may not be what is sometimes referred to as a China-blue print, meaning simply printed in blue like the popular imported blue ceramic wares from England and the Orient — but it could, of course, mean both.

What about the people who carried on this dyer's trade — a handcraft from early Biblical times? In India, where the skill may have begun and was developed, the dyer was not especially highly-regarded — his trade was classified as part of the tailor's, and he belonged to a fairly low caste in that country's complicated social system. In Malaya and Sumatra, all dyeing was an art strictly reserved for women and it was considered an unlucky omen to have a man anywhere near the operation. In many countries there was an aura of magic about the dyer's trade — nobody really understood how it worked. In Japan, printing and dyeing were considered high arts and the craftsmen were honored as artists. In Europe, the dyer's skill came to be highly regarded and was respected; the first American colonial dyers and printers to come to the New World from European print works came as respected tradesmen and they were among the first to set themselves up as independent artisans in the colonies.

THE BLOCK-PRINTING METHOD AS ILLUSTRATED: *time for a few questions*

Several factors in the block-printed resist method as illustrated in the progress drawings (Figs. 61-64) are puzzling. We must keep in mind that most of the American blue resists have a *white* background with a blue figure; almost all other resist designs are a *white* figure on a dyed background, with some exceptions as shown, and Java batiks. There are five parts to the puzzle.

1. Why the reserved ground?

We know that indigo was at first impossible to use for direct printing because it oxidized and sometimes thickened on contact with air, so we wonder how it happened that these prints flew in the face of that fact and came to be designed so that the large background areas had to be printed with a resist, and the smaller, or "positive," areas of the design were the parts that had to be dyed to produce the pattern. This is doing an already somewhat complicated feat an even harder way! Most of the technical explanations given in the books consulted and quoted make no specific mention of a reserved background area, but seem to be describing a dyed background with reserved figures like those shown in the Slovak folk art prints, Figs. 70 and 72. This is a puzzling, illogical aspect of the American prints.

2. Why the style?

How does it happen that the blue resist prints seem to be not even first cousins to other designs of the same date — assuming we have the approximate date? Is it logical that English printers or Eastern printers working on order from England would devise a style of design that differed noticeably from the proven-to-be-popular Indian chintzes at a time when trade with the colonies was being built up in every possible way by the British? The fabrics are regarded as "different" in several ways — and anything regarded as different was *new* at its inception. A new printer in a new situation might be expected to devise it. It is hard to imagine skilled English printers or experienced Indian dyers turning out these bold, slapdash, one-color prints that have a kind of primitive bravado of feeling previously unknown, and not especially "in style" at the time. Would it not be logical to imagine that an American-colonist printer with more enterprise and daring than skill may have devised this new kind of print in an attempt to copy what he had seen in England or France, where he had learned the whole technique of indigo dyeing? The style of the blue and whites suggests that the designers either did not own a library of pattern-books or were not very good at following them; or possibly they simply did not feel at all constrained to use them. Since there are so few fragments left, nobody knows for sure how many there were originally — and the records may be lacking because there *were* so few. Could two or three colonial printers have turned out the entire amount?

3. Why the block assumption?

Technically it is difficult to understand how a block covered solidly with paste could be placed with any accuracy in a pattern without the use of pitchpins. If the blocks were rectangular, pitch-pins could have been used, but would have left reserved dots at regular intervals on the cloth. No such marks can be discovered. In a design like the one with the bird (Fig. 57) the block might have been free-form, following the contours of the unit, and if that were so, each resist-paste area would have had to meet (or slightly overlap) the edge of the adjoining print in order to reserve the whole background. This would have been an extremely difficult block to place accurately, and since most printing blocks are generally rectangular or square, such a form would be most unusual; not impossible, but unlikely.

4. How was the light blue reserved?

In a design with two blues there had to be two dye baths, as we have read — the first for the light blue, then the light blue parts had to be completely covered or printed over with resist paste so that they would not take on the final, double-dyed darker blue. If we assume that blocks were used for the whole job, then two blocks were necessary for a two-blue print, and the second one would present some register problems, too. It would be easier, however, to place this one by eye, following the previously printed parts.

5. If the designs were block printed, why the variations?

When measurements are taken from several blue and white designs we discover that there is irregularity in the size of the units; for instance, no two birds measure quite the same from beak to tail, though this is not readily evident to the eye. Since a carved wooden block never shrinks or stretches, and prints exactly the same every time, with only minor variations in the outline, one must question the idea that the reserved parts of the design (the outlines of all the blue forms and the background) were printed from a *block*. One large-scale print at the Cooper-Hewitt Museum has a bird with a tail of sometimes seven feathers, sometimes eight feathers. What kind of a block could have printed that bird? The picotage dots *do*, without doubt, resemble any metal-pin block print, and the number of dots in each unit remains constantly the same.

Fig. 77. Resist print in one blue on white cotton, France or England, 18th century; one of the prints that is a forerunner of American blue resists, but this one has very complicated picotage detail and a sense of refinement. Courtesy, Cooper-Hewitt Museum of Design, Smithsonian Institution

SPECULATIONS ON AN ALTERNATIVE METHOD

We now have read enough technical descriptions of the use of resists to give us a background knowledge of several methods by which resists could be applied — painted, stenciled, or printed — so we may be in a position to explore the possibility of other methods, or at least a combination of methods not usually ascribed to these prints.

1. The most obvious and simple way to coat a large area with paste or wax in the early stages of any resist print is just to draw the design on the cloth somehow, then paint on the resist with a brush.

2. Painting would have been easy to do in either of two ways. One, by using a paper or metal cut-out pattern of the outline of one complete design unit, and to paint while holding it in place, so that it shielded the parts of the cloth that were to be dyed blue. Or, second, a pricked stencil could have been used to pounce on the design. In either case, the shield or stencil could have been put in place and moved each time *by eye* by an experienced printer, with only small variations or "movements" of a quarter of an inch or so. It is much easier to place a positive pattern (representing the blue parts of the design) than it is to work with a negative pattern that must, by its edges, form only the background areas of a design. If the craftsman worked in this rather free way, it is easy to understand how a bird could have seven tail feathers one time and eight the next. It also seems consistent with the freedom of the whole design.

3. *If* the blue and whites *were* done by the use of pricked stencils or cut-out patterns and painted with a brush, then a coppered block with metal pins could have been dipped into the paste subsequently and printed within the parts that were left to be dyed blue — the only places where the dots appear. The few heavier white details, such as those dashes seen on the back of the bird (Fig. 57), could have been cut in wood on the same block. It is almost certain that the painted-on paste would have had a slightly grayish (or other) tone so that it could be seen on the cloth. If this was done, and if the first painting were regarded as a sort of preliminary operation, then the prints *would* have been called block prints.

4. It might even be that the dots were painted on also, through another punched stencil, though this would not be easy with a thick paste. The Japanese used a spatula to force the paste through very intricate stencils, but the patience and care of Oriental printers is in no way shown by the character of these prints. Nevertheless, it is possible, though not probable, that the prints were done entirely without blocks.

5. The dashed-on outlines of the light blues lead us to think that the second resist could be painted on easily by following the dots outlining the

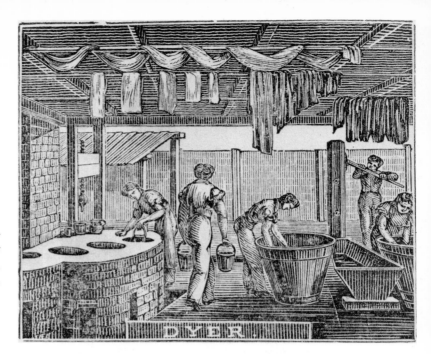

Fig. 78. "Dyer" wood engraving from *Panorama of Professions and Trades*, by Edward Hazen, Philadelphia, 1836. Courtesy, Smithsonian Institution

details. The dots are followed very freely and inaccurately, and the light blue areas have a painted-on look that conjures up the picture of a man with a brush in his hand putting on the final touch.

SOME SPECULATIVE CONCLUSIONS

The idea that paper shields or stencils were used as guides for painting on the resist would explain the fact that no blocks seem to exist that appear to be "reverse" or background-printing blocks. They are generally uncommon, if not nonexistent, elsewhere in the world, too. A close look at the photos of any of our fabrics, concentrating only on the white background, will show you what a puzzling sort of block it would be, and therefore it would be easily indentifiable. A second block for printing reserve for only the light blue would look even more unreasonable and puzzling.

There is another factor that seems very important to a technician, but may not seem so important (or so obvious) to a scholar: *all* the outlines have the *look* of a painted-in background. There is no other way to describe them.

Any kind of pattern stencil would have been rather perishable and might be discarded after use. If this is what happened, then along with those pricked or cut-out patterns went the only evidence of how the fabrics were made. What happened to the coppered blocks — and it seems probable that there were some — is hard to explain, too, unless we imagine the ashes of many bonfires with a bunch of wire nails scattered through them. Such a bonfire is not wholly imaginary — there is an historical record of large bonfires fed by the hand-carved wood blocks of Jouy, as they were discarded for "more modern" methods. Coppered blocks of many kinds do exist, but most of those called American appear to be printing blocks for patterns of braid-work or embroidery of the 19th century rather than for the picotage of the supposedly earlier blue and whites.

If the stencil-shield theory is correct, then the blue and whites were done in essentially the same way as the India resist and mordant-dyed chintzes or calicoes, the Japanese stencil fabrics, and Java batiks. If a block was used for only a part of the design, then our fabrics are like the tjap batiks of Java. The primary differences are that (1) a resist *paste* must almost certainly have been used instead of wax, as there is no trace of crackling, and (2) there is always the characteristic white background with a blue figure that is distinctive and unusual, but not absolutely unique.

AN EVEN MORE SPECULATIVE CONCLUSION

And now for the benefit of knowledgeable readers who cannot agree with any of the foregoing ideas and speculations and who do not accept any of the facts, we quote from *Antiques* magazine, Vol. XX, November, 1931, from the column called the "Editor's Attic," written by Homer Eaton Keyes. He described the identical design we have used in our diagrams of technique (Figs. 61-64), made from the example now owned by the Metropolitan Museum of Art (Fig. 57):

"The blue and white textile reproduced on this month's cover has, by various authorities in and out of sundry museums been admired, condemned, and viewed with complete indifference . . . [the editor] has learned that the piece was made in New Jersey, in Java, on the continent of Europe, and in Japan. Its date has been set at from 1650 to 1900. It is a thin cotton cloth loosely woven of handspun thread. On this foundation the pattern appears to have been printed from wood blocks in a uniform dark blue from which lighter passages were produced by brushing parts of the design with some bleaching compound before the dye had fully set.

"The piece was acquired in Northampton from a descendant of a mariner who was fond of bringing home souvenirs of his voyages. On one occasion his trophies were: this specimen, a few bits of decorated porcelain, and a print quilt. [It] . . may have typified the inexpensive commercial flotsam about the international ports of the early 1800's."

Mr. Keyes held an important editorial post and was respected for his knowledge of many things, so we would *wish* him to be entirely right. Most experts date these prints somewhat before 1800, and even if Mr. Keyes' date is right, it was a good many years later before blue could be printed with any kind of perfection from wood blocks. And the complications of carving *out* all those little white dots in the design would be of concern to some people, but seem to have escaped the editor's attention entirely. "Brushing some parts of the design with some bleaching compound" is a description of a casual way of making a discharge print — ordinarily a rather complicated process and not done in this way. It is our impression that indigo is "set" within a few minutes after hitting the air, and bleaching it in a pattern would be a neat trick.

The caption can probably be taken as an authoritative but almost impossible explanation of the technique. The fact remains that the "commercial flotsam" made an exceedingly handsome cover for a fine magazine!

TWO SCHOLARLY CONCLUSIONS

There are two internationally-known museum curators who have seen and studied (either the pieces or photographs and slides of them) almost all of the blue resists in existence, as well as hundreds upon hundreds of other world textiles. We should listen to their conclusions.

Alice B. Beer, for years curator of textiles of the Cooper Union Museum in New York City (now the Cooper-Hewitt Museum of Design, Smithsonian Institution) says, "For years in this country such blue-on-white resists have been attributed to American dyers of the 18th century. This museum, despite thorough search, has found no clear evidence up to the present, for the printing of such textiles in this country before the 19th century. Moreover, as a piece exists in the Albany Institute of History and Art bearing on its end an English Crown tax-frame and the word *calicoe*, we believe, until other evidence may develop, that such pieces may be attributed to England, second half of the 18th century."[79]

Peter Floud, late curator of the Victoria and Albert Museum in London, says, "It would be satisfactory to think that the whole group were English — but in that case it seems extraordinary that they *never* turn up in England — or indeed in Europe generally. Until some further, positive evidence is assembled, they will remain a mystery."[100]

THE LAST WORD — A YANKEE CONCLUSION

The idea that blue resists were printed "elsewhere" is given wide credence in spite of the fact that only one bit of concrete evidence exists to support it (the Albany Institute piece). The feeling is strong among museum curators and others that the prints simply *could not be* American-made, but this seems to have grown out of the insights of professional knowledge, not out of facts. One wonders if some day there may be the discovery of well-preserved examples of prints made in a remote East Indian village, dated

Fig. 79. American blue resist in dark indigo on white cotton — design of branches and foliage with a very decorative, if precariously-perched, bird eating. Courtesy, Cooper-Hewitt Museum of Design, Smithsonian Institution

1760, that prove to be exactly like the "American" examples. This would be a comforting affirmation of scholarly feelings and it could actually happen, but it does appear rather improbable.

How does it happen that only *one* piece has been found bearing the British tax stamp out of perhaps more than a hundred in existence? The

English had every reason to put identifying marks on their colonial imports — if we assume that the one known piece indicates that such a marking was customary or required. An American printer had absolutely no reason to put identifying marks on his printed cottons, and might even have been adjudged to be stupid if he did.

If we have dated the prints in the right century it is important to remember that Britain was actively suppressing all American enterprises at the time. A smart American printer who worked between the early 1700's and 1800 would logically and purposely leave all identifying marks *off* his fabrics. Historians tell us of many occasions when Americans took illegal ways of gettings things when the British left so few ways for them to gain money in business. Ship captains made it possible for American tobacco to travel to France and Holland where it was bartered for cheese, brandy, and printed cottons. Molasses for rum was smuggled out, and rum was smuggled in, so that "rum-running" became a common term. When John Hancock signed the Declaration of Independence he had a price on his head in London as a smuggler.

The rough British tactics employed to monopolize American trade continued long past the Revolution and led one skilled Irish-American calico printer to write in his diary, in 1797, that because of English harassment, "being wearied and disgusted I determined to break up the Works" — after one year in business in Delaware. (See Section IV, 8)

Is it too much to suspect that a more determined printer who was not too "wearied" to fight intimidation might *forge* a British excise tax stamp in order to make his cottons saleable? If this idea seems at all probable, then we must give the wily and enterprising colonial printer credit for a successful deception that has lasted for 200 years!

No flat conclusion about the nationality of the blue and white resists can carry any weight as long as so much of the evidence is circumstantial. However, it *should* be said flatly: it is unfortunate that parenthetical question marks or quotation marks have stuck like glue to the word *American* in any description of the blue and white fabrics. It is unfortunate because it has had the effect of keeping them in semi-obscurity in textile history. Since they now exist, and have existed always *only* in America — no matter where they were made — they deserve to be widely known as the most independently original and distinctive American printed fabrics of the New World's first 300 years.

It would be reassuring to be able to think of these boldly handsome prints as American members of the family of historic textiles rather than having to regard them as fabrics without a country — or as relics of uncertain age that are colonial mavericks, unrelated to anything and dyed in limbo.

8. A MID-VOLUME GUIDEPOST

To make a story out of the scattered factual information about colonial American printers and print works some writers fill up their pages with a procession of names, dates, and places, hitched together with conjunctions. The parade is not very long, but it is 300 years old and not much more interesting than an old telephone book. Therefore, *herein*, at the end of Sections III and IV, you will find the procession in the form of two lists of facts about printers, as complete and accurate as it seems possible to make them. And following each of these lists are charts of all the dates that have anything to do with fabric printing, and some other dates to remind you of what was happening in the world at the time.

The facts thus dismissed, our text can be confined to the people about whom, and the events about which, enough is known to bring them more nearly to life. The pictures are part of the story.

9. PAINTED FLOOR CLOTHS AND OILCLOTH

The first cabins built in the colonies were put together of wood as simply and quickly as possible to provide necessary shelter. They had no other floors than the dirt neatly leveled and packed, then spread with sand for cleanliness. Even after board floors were commonly installed the custom of sanding was continued up to as late as 1750. "The first patterned floors were made by swishing a faggot broom in the fresh sand"[63] — and this was the origin of some of the painted floors to follow. Many later ones were done in place of expensive carpets but did not necessarily imitate their designs. Plain floors began to be painted about 1725, and the colors that looked most like sand were used: pumpkin yellow, brown, and gray, and later Indian red. The plain floors did not seem fancy enough, so the next step was to "spatter," paint freehand designs, or paint imitations of marble with black and white on gray; then there were carefully stenciled designs of the same period as the stenciled walls, and possibly sometimes done by the same itinerant artists.

These steps did not necessarily lead to painted floor cloths, because the two seem to have existed at the same time. According to Carl Drepperd, the first date that "Painted Floor Cloths" were mentioned was about 1720, and they were heavy canvas "thickly painted in diapered and chequered patterns."[19]

One of the first specific bits of information about painted floor cloths is found in a book at Williamsburg published in London in 1739. It is illustrated with engravings by John Carwitham of designs that were recommended for use either as "pavements of marble or for painted floor cloths."[15] The book must have been used by an American artisan as a reference book.

Fig. 80. Portion of very early painted floor cloth; almost the only remaining example in museums in condition to be photographed. Courtesy, Henry Francis duPont Winterthur Museum, Delaware

In 1728, Governor William Burnett of New York and Massachusetts died and left a will bequeathing various things to his heirs, among which were "two old checkered canvas to lay under a table."[15] These must have been small, painted forerunners of linoleum, and in all probability served exactly the same practical purpose. In 1761, an advertisement in the *Boston Gazette* offered for sale "Wilton or Marble Cloths,"[7] and ten years later the painted floor cloths were described as a type of homemade linoleum of hand-sewn canvas and painted according to directions given in one of the instruction books of the period. "In the first half of the 18th century they were decorated with a design in imitation of marble-tiled floors, but later designs kept pace with the times"[7] In 1769, an upholsterer in Williamsburg advertised that he "paints floor cloths according to directions."[15] Other newspaper ads called the stuff "Oyl Cloth for Floors and Tables" and "False Carpets."[21] If the floor cloth shown in the portrait in Fig. 81 is any indication, these cloths were used in elegant homes as well as for utilitarian purposes.

These floor coverings, both decorative and practical, were used up to 1850, but almost none have been saved. One more description tells how they were made. "A manufactory of a new article of patent Floor Cloth or summer carpet was in operation in Philadelphia in 1807. It is described as strongly woven, for the purpose of the best floor, on a 7-yard loom without seam and

Fig. 81. Portrait of John Phillips by Joseph Steward, 1793. It shows painted floor cloths in two rooms, and in the rear room, bands of stenciling decorate the wall. Owned by Dartmouth College

of any peculiar size or shape. The carpets were furnished plain or in colors with borders to match from $1.25 to $2.00 per square yard, according to the number of colors; and when partly worn could be recoated, painted, or ornamented with appropriate borders. By the same process, old woolen or worsted carpets could be coated on one side at half price, and baize or coverings for trunks and baggage made water-proof."[9]

In 1828, the *Boston Daily Advertiser* described "Painted Floor Cloths without seams — some in imitation of Brussels carpeting." Evidently there were home-crafted floor cloths without the enameled surface of the coated canvas ones so much advertised. The detail shown in Fig. 82 is described by the owner, Nina Fletcher Little, author of *American Decorative Wall Painting*, as being "made of soft, woven cotton and must have been used with padding under it. The pattern is hand-stenciled with a coral background, dividing squares of dark brown and black with petalled motifs in yellow and green on white."

There are few fragments of the painted cloth left, or even examples of early painted floors. It is due to the change of styles that we have some "saved" examples. Some old painted floors were preserved by having "modern" straw matting tacked down over them, and at least one painted floor cloth on cotton was used as padding under a wool carpet and was thus preserved.

Fig. 82. Hand stenciled floor carpet from New Hampshire, c. 1850. Courtesy, Nina Fletcher Little

BOSTON NEWS-LETTER, May 5, 1774:

"PAPER HANGER. George Killcup jun. advertises that he paints carpets and other articles, and Papers Rooms in the neatest manner. He will take English or West Indies Goods as pay."[17]

Closely related to the painted floor cloths are some large squares of *block-printed* oilcloth, probably used as tablecloths mostly for decoration. They are printed in four or five bright colors in what looks like enamel on black oilcloth (canvas coated with black, glossy paint) by incredibly detailed picotage blocks with hundreds of tiny pins. They are very expertly printed — certainly not done by home craftsmen, and are probably of the period around 1825 or earlier. If they were professionally produced there must have been many of them, but almost no museums own them or are even familiar with them. One example is owned by the Lyman Allyn Museum in New London, Connecticut, but it is in too poor condition to photograph well. *Antiques* magazine (August, 1945, p. 108) describes the piece: "Oilcloth panel 46″ x 52″ with an elaborate design rendered by a multitude of dots, from pin-prick to pin-head size and a few solid lines. The design shows George Washington on horseback in the center. Surrounding scrolled motifs suggest stenciled and painted decorations of about 1830 to 1840 with many repeats of separate small motifs. Colors are orange, red, yellow, gray, white, dark blue, and dark green on a black background. Probably painted from blocks set with nails or pins of various sizes, and metal strips. In order to make a smooth printing surface of all the metal parts, they are set in, then covered with a metal plate which is hammered until the printing surface of the block is level. Probable use of the cloth is uncertain — it could have been a table cover or wall hanging." We seriously doubt that it ever hung on a wall. The piece shown in Figs. 83 and 84 could be described in almost identical terms, except the central figure is an eagle; it has been preserved folded, and the folds made photographing very difficult.

Fig. 83.   Painted oilcloth table cover, block printed in six colors on black, size 54″ x 59″. Collection of Wm. E. Montague, Norristown, Pa. Courtesy, Bucks County Historical Society, Doylestown, Pennsylvania

Fig. 84.   *Right:* Corner detail. Cover shown in Fig. 83. Same source

"HOUSE FURNISHINGS — Handsome oyl cloths for Tables."[17]

In our days of many kinds of plastic sheeting for everything from rain-coats and place-mats to painters' drop-cloths, we forget that there were days when similar articles were quite different and often handmade. Oilcloth was used for other articles beside floor coverings and tablecloths. Sturdy canvas with many coats of paint made a protective cape for a soldier and the one shown in Fig. 85 is decorated with an eagle and regimental identification. The little girl's sewing kit in Fig. 86 was probably her mother's way of providing a durable and inexpensive but neat little case that simply was not to be bought at the time.

Fig. 85. Militiaman's marching cape, found in Foxboro, Massachusetts. Many layers of paint on heavy canvas with painted and stenciled design, c. 1850. Courtesy, Old Sturbridge Village, Sturbridge, Mass.

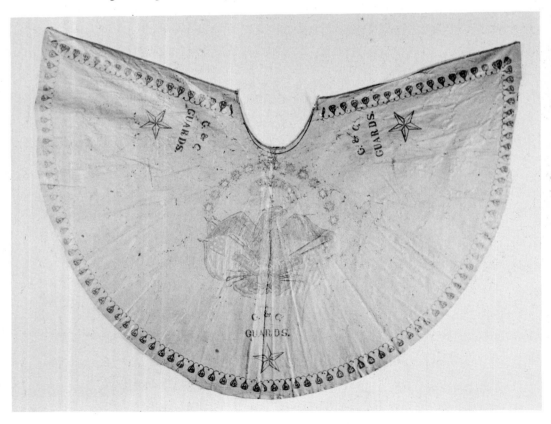

Fig. 87. Oilcloth (painted canvas or tow) dispatch bag or saddle bag, painted in blue on tan ground. Courtesy, Dedham Historical Society, Dedham, Mass.

Fig. 86. Sewing Kit, painted oilcloth, size 5″ x 7″, made of homespun linen coated with layers of paint until stiff, then decorated with fine brush-work pattern in a geometric design — buff on brown. Kit contains thread and a receipt for sewing lessons for Theresa, Julia, and Frances Gilmore, c. 1800. Courtesy, Dedham Historical Society, Dedham, Mass.

Fighting men who had to be in the field in all kinds of weather must have been grateful to have some of their gear made of weatherproof oil-cloth. Another piece from Massachusetts is the oilcloth dispatch bag shown in Fig. 87 and painted with the owner's initials, "D. I.," and marked "Ist Reg. M. M." (Massachusetts Militia?)

10. WALLPAPER — FIRST COUSIN TO EARLY CALICO

The history of wallpaper-making in England, France, and America is closely related to fabric-printing because often the same designers made drawings for both wallpapers and printed calicoes — and some early print works turned out both. Two famous designers worked in both trades: Jean Baptiste Huet, chief designer of the toiles de Jouy in France, was employed also by the Reveillon wallpaper factory, and William Morris, the noted 19th century English textile printer, is almost as well known for his wallpaper designs. It is probable that many anonymous craftsmen served both crafts as designers and block cutters.

Wallpaper was first made as early as 1509 in England, and only a few years later in France. It was made originally to take the place of more costly tapestries and hangings that had been used from mediaeval times to decorate and insulate walls. The designs, therefore, were made to look like patterned fabrics such as damasks and brocades.

How were these papers made? The process was like — and seems to have developed in much the same way as — fabric printing and on a similar schedule. In England, in 1738, it was reported that paper was printed from wooden blocks of the same size as the sheets of paper — about 14″ x 18″. Blocks were fastened to the table with the carved face up, inked with leather pads, and the damp paper was pressed into the block with a cloth-covered roller used like a rolling pin. After the paper was dried and pressed, other colors of the design were mixed with glue and painted on freehand or through stencils. A decade later some papers were printed by hand from carved wooden rollers, and in another ten years engraved copper plates were tried out in a flatbed press, but never came to be used much. Block printing continued to be the usual method and was also finally done in a press with a long lever being used to apply the necessary pressure. In 1778, there was a British decree that paper should be 20″ wide and nine yards long — this became standard until about 1840 and is not very different from today's best papers.[80] Eventually roller-printing machines were used, and today the more expensive papers are done by silk-screen stencils by hand.

In 1739, the first wallpaper factory was founded in the colonies by Plunket and Fleeson in Philadelphia. Other "Paper Stainers" advertised their work in 1765, in New York and in 1788, in Boston. Their papers were not highly regarded by the French who reported, in 1788, that "Americans are unable to produce and hence must import from France: wines, cloths, linens, silk stockings, stained papers, etc."[41]

BOSTON NEWS-LETTER, December 12, 1765:

"MADE IN NEW YORK — At a numerous Meeting of the Society for promoting Arts &c. in this Province . . . John Rugar produced several Patterns of Paper Hangings made in this Province . . . and said Rugar has now a considerable Quantity on Hand, and lives in Bayard Street next door to Mr. Heyman Levi."[17]

In 1797, in Philadelphia, two Frenchmen, Chardon and LaCollay, started a wallpaper "staining" factory and also printed calicoes. They advertised: "WANTED. Two good Calico Printers who will find suitable encouragement and constant employ at the Calico Manufactory of said Chardon and LaColloy; if they are workmen."[41] In 1800, Ebenezer Clough of Boston printed a memorial paper upon the death of the first President called "Sacred to Washington," with an assortment of allegorical and patriotic figures and symbols and is said to have presented enough to the Governors of the 16 States for each to paper a room.[41] Apparently none of these cheerful salons survives, but some of the paper is on exhibition in the Cooper-Hewitt Museum in New York.

Fig. 88. Wallpaper panel, block printed in white and black on gray, "Sacred to Washington," 1800. Courtesy, Cooper-Hewitt Museum of Design, Smithsonian Institution

French papers continued to be imported to the mid-1800's and they included many elegant scenic patterns and others imitating (again) sumptuous fabrics with velvety flocking and fake satins and damasks. They were very expensive and their popularity gave impetus to the vogue for stenciled walls in colonial homes where the high-priced imports were too costly. French scenic papers probably provided the idea for some of the rare painted murals done in a chamingly primitive style in some early American homes.

Wallpaper factories also turned out some special papers about 10″ wide, printed from blocks and used to cover that colonial carryall and boudoir shelf ornament, the bandbox. The first ones were small and were intended to be used as collar boxes — a collar was called a "band." They were made in many sizes and used also as hatboxes and as light, decorative hand luggage by lady travelers and were the first carry-on bags for fashionable stagecoach passengers. The boxes were made of thin wood or cardboard in round or oval shapes with a decorated lid and a carrying cord. The pictorial papers used to cover them included a variety of subjects from historic scenes to advertisements for the box-makers. Some were made as "nested" sets and the smallest were called ribbon boxes. Many of them have been preserved by historical societies and museums and are a charming souvenir of about 1800.

By 1800, American paper mills had begun to flourish and printers could obtain more and cheaper paper. In 1844, the first color-printing machine for wallpapers was imported from England by John Howell of Albany, New York, and this started the industry rolling. Our plain word *wallpaper*, by standardization, has lost some of its early romantic connotations when it was called "painted papers," "Stayned papers," and "room hangings."

Fig. 89. Oval bandbox with hand-blocked paper cover, c. 1800, with scenes of wide variety on one box. Courtesy, Cooper-Hewitt Museum of Design, Smithsonian Institution

The NEW-ENGLAND
Weekly JOURNAL,

Containing the moſt Remarkable Occurrences Foreign & Domeſtick.

Monday May 29. 1 7 2 7.

THE NEW ENGLAND WEEKLY JOURNAL, October 26, 1730:

"STAMPT PAPER — John Phillips, bookseller, sells Stampt Paper in Rolls for to Paper Rooms."[17]

Fig. 90

11. FIRE SACKS

Many fine, large homes and increasing numbers of smaller one were established in all the larger eastern cities and many outlying areas in the years just before and after the Revolution. The large homes were sometimes of brick or stone, but the typical colonial houses of the period — large or small — were built entirely of wood.

With wood-burning stoves and fireplaces, candles for lighting, and, later, open gas flames, the wooden houses gave rise to concern about the dangers of fire, since few communities had water systems and these were small and inadequate. Homeowners had an outdoor well, and sometimes a hand-pump in the kitchen sink; sometimes the family carried water from some distance. Volunteer fire companies were formed and their early hand-operated pumpers, hose carts, and hook and ladder carts were pulled to the fire by red-helmeted, red-shirted firemen shouting through their brass fire trumpets to clear the streets. Later, the fire wagons were pulled by teams of horses with fancy harness riggings. Some of the houses had cast iron insignia called "firemarks" over the doors to show that they were insured, and in a combination of neighborly aid and reward payments by fire insurance companies, the firemen *did* save some houses. If there was no pond or river near enough to be reached by the hose, or if the bucket brigade was too slow, the whole abode just went up in smoke.

All this left the householder pretty much on his own to save his belongings and his own neck when fire broke out. In Providence, the earliest mention of fire buckets was in 1754. These, at that period, and up to the mid-1800's, were leather or canvas water buckets kept hanging in several rooms of the house. Because they had to be so much in evidence they came to be decorated with initials, patriotic insignia, and brass ornaments. Inside of the bucket — which was to be filled with water in an emergency — was kept rolled up a canvas bag to be grabbed out and filled with the valuables that had to be saved from the fire. Sometimes there were two — the large one, called a fire-sack, was for silverware, hollow ware and miscellaneous heirlooms; a smaller one, about 18″ long, was called a fire-pocket. The housewife or a maid was responsible for seizing the latter and filling it with smaller treasures, money, jewelry, and personal trinkets; it was fitted with long cords so that it could be tied around a woman's waist under her skirts to conceal it from thieves and looters. The image of a colonial fire becomes a rather dramatic scene!

The large canvas fire-sacks were also sometimes hung separately on a hook near the entrance door, and they were painted with the owner's name, the date, and sometimes with fancy medallions and borders. We know these fire-sacks were common in Providence from 1790 or earlier until about 1835, and they must have been used in many communities. One Providence home-owner whose fire-sack is preserved in the Rhode Island Historical Society was Zachariah Allen, one of the several self-styled "first" calico printers in New England. Thrifty Mr. Allen had painted his name over that of a Mr. Freeman, who might have been a former owner of the house; the earlier name shows clearly through the red medallion of later date.

The members of the volunteer fire campanies grabbed their own fire buckets and canvas fire-sacks to take to fires, too, and others were hung on the "enjines." Many buckets were needed to form the bucket brigade — two

Fig. 91. Painted canvas fire-sack, owned by the Rhode Island Historical Society, Courtesy of *Antiques* magazine

lines of volunteers, one handing along full water buckets from the pond or tank to douse the fire and the other returning empties to be refilled. Thus it was imperative to have names on buckets and sacks in order that everything could be sorted out when the action was over.

The fire-sack in the photograph in Fig. 91 is about 2' x 4' in size, made of sturdy canvas, and is decorated with a red medallion, with the name of "A. Throop" painted in white. Probably "No. 2" sack was reserved for certain treasures and possibly assigned to the care of one individual in the family. Dr. Amos Throop was a distinguished doctor, born in Woodstock, Connecticut, in 1738, and he practiced medicine in Providence; he served in the State General Assembly and was also president of the Exchange Bank.[57] The fire-sacks are a little-known example of decorative painting on a most vital utilitarian cloth object that was used through a comparatively short history in American homes.

12. POCKETS, KITS AND CASES

Public-spirited citizens in colonial days took an interest in their young people and in the year 1685, a Quaker gentleman wrote a tract called "Good Order established in Pennsylvania and New Jersey" in which he urged that schools be started where girls could learn "the spinning of flax, sewing, and making all sorts of useful needlework, knitting of gloves and stockings, making of straw-works as hats, baskets, &c. or any other useful art or mystery." In the same year, Cotton Mather said in a sermon that "New England Youth in this country are very sharp and early Ripe in their Capacities."[20]

Colonial boys and girls were sent at an early age to "dame schools" — schools with female teachers — where the boys learned numbers, Latin, history, and religion and the girls learned to cook, sew, embroider, spin, weave, and knit. They all learned how to read from hornbooks — the first primers. These were printed alphabets and prayers or religious verses fastened between two polished and transparent sheets of horn, shaped like a small, rectangular paddle with a hole in the handle. The children wore these durable books hanging at their waists and the sheets were changed as the lessons progressed. In 1716, a Boston schoolmaster advertised that he taught "Young Gentle Women and Children all sorts of Fine Works, as Leather Works, Filigree, Painting on Glass, Embroidering in a new way, Turkey-work for handkerchiefs in two new ways, fine fashion purses and flourishing and plain Work."[20]

Miss Polly Darling of Plymouth, Massachusetts, a descendant of Richard Warren of the *Mayflower*, might have been a product of one of these schools. In 1775, she herself was teaching in a "dame school." Her pupils would have learned a great deal from her about the hand arts, for she was skilled in them.

This lady is said to have made herself a dress that was *entirely* of her own making. She spun the thread for it on her own spinning wheel, wove the cloth on her loom, probably brewed the red and brown dyes over her own kitchen fire, and colored the cloth by block printing. The wooden blocks for her pattern may have been carved for her — or bought from — an itinerant calico printer, but possibly she even made them herself. The homespun she made and printed was sturdy enough to last more than 200 years, and her design is a neat little pattern we can admire today. The Plymouth Antiquarian Society in Massachusetts owns these bits of Aunt Polly Darling's work, carefully saved and labeled by her descendants.

A piece of her dress was made into a "huswif" — a small case for needles and trinkets (Fig. 92), which is carefully preserved, though the dress disappeared long ago. The colors are red and brown figures in small white ovals against a dark brown background. The case is monogrammed in cross-stitch, "P. D.", and is patched with a bit of madras where a thimble may have rubbed a hole. Grandma Howard's needle case (Fig. 93) was made by Aunt Polly about 1760, of two kinds of printed cotton and with a red flannel heart to be stabbed with the needles.

A "huswif" was rolled up and sometimes carried in a pocket like the one shown in Fig. 94, which also belonged to Miss Darling; the word *pocket* comes from the French "pouche," meaning a carrying pouch, and that is exactly what these pockets were. It is made of a plain homespun back and a printed patchwork front; it is a capacious 15 inches long and has a slit opening in the front. Two long handwoven cords were used to tie the pocket around the housewife's waist, or to attach it to her belt, and in it she carried her personal treasures and necessities. These tie-on pockets were worn as early as 1650 and continued to be used to 1850.[23] Fabrics were hard to come by, expensive if imported, and mostly handwoven, so every scrap was saved to make quilts, petticoats, and pockets such as these.

The pocket at lower right is made of a few hand-printed squares arranged in a pattern with other squares of calico and chintz. Pockets such as these were worn on the outside of the skirt while women went about their daily tasks. Fine embroidered linen ones were worn under the skirt for special occasions and were a favorite gift for the bride. They were sometimes made in pairs on one cord, to hang at each hip and tie in back. Now we see how it happened that "Lucy Locket lost her pocket" in the verse — it just came untied.

Lucy Locket lost her pocket
Lydia Fisher found it
Not a bit of money in it
Only 'broidery 'round it
(To the tune of *Yankee Doodle*, after a fashion.)

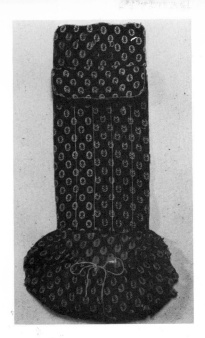

Fig. 92. "Huswif" made of hand-blocked cotton in red and brown, 4½″ wide x 14″ long, trimmed with long rows of tiny chain-stitch. Courtesy, Plymouth Antiquarian Society, Plymouth, Massachusetts

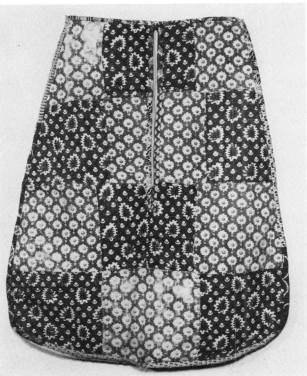

Fig. 94. Patchwork pocket made from squares of hand-blocked homespun printed in brown and red; 12″ wide near bottom, 14″ long, with slit opening 7½″ long; cords missing. Plymouth Antiquarian Society

Fig. 93. Grandma Howard's needle case made by Aunt Polly Darling c. 1760; hand-blocked cotton lined with glazed chintz, with red flannel hearts. Plymouth Antiquarian Society

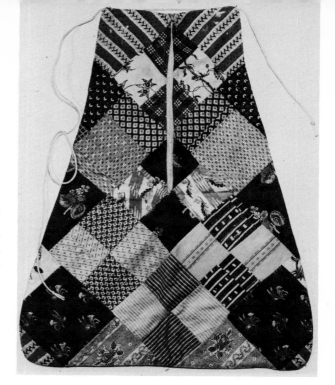

Fig. 95. Patchwork pocket 2″ longer than the one at left with cords intact. Very neatly sewn and symetrically arranged. Plymouth Antiquarian Society

Fancy embroidered pockets were sometimes left to the daughter of the family in wills. One New England woman left her daughter a dimity pocket in 1795 — complete with its "pocket-glass, comforter, and strong-waters bottle." These were: a small mirror, a hand-warmer, and a Bristol glass flask for rum. It was more than a hundred years after Polly Darling's time that pockets were commonly made into women's skirts. The small draw-string purse called a "reticule" was derived from the tie-on pockets, and our word "pocket-book"

Fig. 96. Heddle-type tape loom that could weave fabric up to 12″ in width, using two foot pedals. On this type of loom colonial women wove linen threads to make all kinds of tapes and cords, belting, ties for corsets, shoe laces, cords for bandboxes, loops for buttons, collars, etc. Courtesy, Smithsonian Institution

comes from them, too. Today we have purses, shoulder-bags, clutches, and totes for a lady's personal property, which might include a little leather case stamped "Likker Lugger" for her strong waters.

13. COUNTERPANES AND COVERLETS

From earliest times bed coverings have been an important decorative accessory, whether on the throne-like beds of European kings or on the simplest pine bed of an American colonist. Bedspreads, counterpanes, coverlets, and quilts have always been decorated in some way — a plain one without color, texture, or design of some sort is almost unthinkable.

Fig. 97. Coverlet stenciled boldly in green, yellow, and orange on unbleached cotton. The four sides are bound in pink cotton, with bottom corners cut out to fit the bedposts. Signed on the back: "Hannah Corbin, Woodstock, Connecticut"; a rural home craft work, 1780-1800. Courtesy, Old Sturbridge Village, Sturbridge, Massachusetts

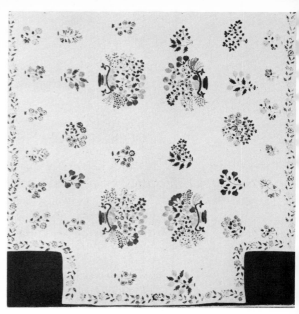

Fig. 98. Stenciled bolster cover with bold floral border and central sprigs in red, blue and green opaque paints; c. 1800. Courtesy, Cooper-Hewitt Museum of Design, Smithsonian Institution

Fig. 99. Stenciled coverlet with hearts and flowers; from Lisle, Broome County, N. Y., c. 1831; from the collection of Mrs. Mary L. Wright. Courtesy, *Antiques* magazine

Sometimes the large colonial four-poster beds were used as a daytime storage place for feather mattresses from trundle beds and "settles" where children slept, and an enormous counterpane was required to cover the pile. India cottons were used as bed hangings and coverlets in more elegant homes, and since they were much admired as well as expensive, it is probable that some early home-art counterpanes were made as a homespun substitute for early costly imports. Some were embroidered and some were hand-stenciled or block-printed. Quilts were primarily for warmth, but were made of all kinds of treasured bits of fabrics in hundreds of patterns.

The famous printed coverlet now in the Philadelphia Museum of Art, printed by the professional calico printer, John Hewson (Fig.109), very clearly shows the style of an imported one he also owned and bequeathed to his daughter, and it is truly elegant. The primitively stenciled flowers and branches done by hand on the cotton coverlet of a housewife for her own bed represented the simplest kind of decorative style, but it was an attempt at the same elegance. Sometimes only a pillow-cover was decorated and the coverlet had only a border. There are not many examples of hand-printed coverlets left to us and those few are in museums, historic houses, or in private collections. Many are not dated or signed and their origins are difficult to establish.

Fig. 100. Patchwork coverlet from New Hampshire. Alternate squares of figured chintz and hand-stenciled and painted squares, all different, c. 1850. Courtesy, Old Sturbridge Village, Sturbridge, Massachusetts

One rare "wool-on-wool" coverlet was preserved in Chelsea, Vermont, by the simple circumstance of its being used as a padding for a carpet; it was dated 1774.[46] Professional printers advertised their services at a very early date, as this one from Boston:

BOSTON EVENING POST, November 16, 1747:

"COUNTERPANE STAMPER. Whereas a certain Person, who followed the business of stamping counterpanes is going out of the Country, and has intirely dropt the Business here: These are to inform all Shopkeepers and others, that they may have Counterpanes and Curtains, &c. stampt after the same Manner and at the same Rates that the Said Person stampt them at the House of John Williams in King Street."[17]

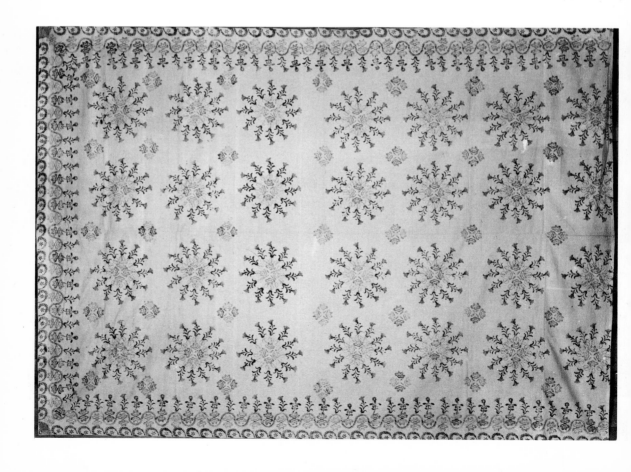

Fig. 103. Quilt made of alternating squares of (1) Resist-dyed blue and white print, and (2) hand-stenciled squares of red roses with green leaves. Courtesy, Shelburne Museum, Shelburne, Vermont

OPPOSITE PAGE:

Fig. 102. Hand-blocked coverlet in red and green. The Shelburne Museum says: "Most supposedly home decorated coverlets of this type were stenciled; this one is blocked and therefore rare." The coverlet might have been professionally "stampt," as the corner-turnings are very well planned and neatly done; home craftsmen could never figure out how to get around corners with a border. Courtesy, Shelburne Museum, Shelburne, Vermont

The big colonial beds were, of course, the birthplace of American children, and apparently in winter the beds were hung with heavy curtains, which made a warm and discreet delivery room. Describing the circumstances of the birth of a Puritan baby in 1770, one writer says. "The first scene of gayety upon which the chilled baby opened his sad eyes was when his mother was taken from her great bed and laid on a pallat and the heavy curtains and valances of harrateen or serge were hung within and freshened with curteyns and vallants of cheney or calico."[21]

BOSTON NEWS-LETTER, May 13, 1773:

"HOUSEHOLD FURNISHINGS — furniture of the late Joseph Apthorp, Esq. to be sold at auction — A neat blue and white Copper-plate bed with Window Curtains and Chairs for ditto. Four very handsome Window Curtains of red-and-white Copper-Plate almost new."[17]

14. FASHION DOLLS AND OTHER FANCY FURBELOWS

It is hard for us to imagine a time when no television, no radio, no telegraph, no newspaper, no magazine, and not even any real mail service existed to carry news. The information — important or unimportant — arrived long after the happening. Colonial men eagerly waited for shipping and political news, but colonial women were as curious in 1725 about the newest French styles as women are today.

As early as 1391, fashion-conscious French designers and dressmakers hit upon a way of spreading the fashion news — and the method was used in Europe, then continued to America until as late as 1800. This was to dress dolls, completely outfitted from corsets to gloves, carefully designed and made in appropriate style, with the figurines coifed and hatted in the latest fashion. They were called "Doll Babies," "Fashion Babies," or, more often, "Fashion Dolls." Hairdressers, milliners, and dressmakers in America imported the dressed dolls from France and England, then took orders and copied the styles down to the finest detail for colonial ladies. One dressmaker charged each customer five shillings to look at the doll, undress it, and examine every tiny article of clothing.[21] The arrival of a ship with a new set of dolls and bundles of silks, calicoes, and trimmings created as great a stir as a French fashion preview of today. Most of the dolls were about 18″ tall with cloth bodies and china heads and hands. Many of them eventually were purchased and found their way into nurseries and little girls' doll houses. Their "not-to-be-touched" elegance may account for the fact that some of them have been preserved by collectors and museums. Colonial calico printers had an important stake in the new styles on the dolls, because if a new doll came dressed in a printed calico, he would have a rush of requests for printed cotton.

Fashion magazines did not appear until about 1800 — the *Ladies Monthly Museum* was published in England about 1799. In America, the most famous one started as *Lady's Magazine* in 1828, and, in 1837, it merged with another to become *Godey's Lady's Book*, named for its owner, Louis Antoine Godey. Its editor and moving spirit was Sarah Hale, an ardent feminist who advocated women's education and emancipation; her magazine contained fiction, editorials, and recipes as well as the fashion illustrations that made it "The Victorian Bible of the Parlor." Each issue contained two double-page steel engravings of fashion plates, colored by hand, as well as many black and white woodcuts. This parade of lovely ladies and angelic children, ruffled and ribboned in the latest style, meant an end to the need for the Fashion Dolls which had served well their graceful if trivial purpose for an unbelievable 400 years — almost 200 in America.

1786:

Mrs. John Adams described a dress as "*A sacque of blue and white copper-plate calico, over a blue gauze petticoat, an apron of fur-belowed gauze, straw ribbons and green morocco slippers.*"[23]

A Roster of the First American Calico Printers

1712	George Leason	Boston
1713	James Franklin & Wife	Boston
1715	Francis Dewing	Boston
1735	Francis Gray	Roxbury
1747	John Williams	Boston
1747	Sarah Hunt	Boston
1759	John Hickey	Boston
1760	Hunt and Torrey	Boston
1761	Mrs. John Haugen	Boston
1774	Joseph Barth	Philadelphia
1774	John Hewson	Philadelphia
1775	William Lang	Philadelphia
1775	John Walters	Philadelphia
1775	Thomas Bedwell	Philadelphia

Things That Went On from 1607 to 1776

Note: American dates are shown against left margin;
foreign dates are indented five spaces

1607 The London Company established in Virginia the first permanent English settlement in America at Jamestown (first "right to colonize")

1619 First American Legislative Assembly — the Virginia House of Burgesses

     1619 First English patents granted for the "staining of fabrics"

1620 Pilgrims landed at Plymouth, Massachusetts; Mayflower Compact signed

1621 New Amsterdam (New York) founded by the Dutch

1625 Jamestown colony was so much in debt that England annulled its charter and made it a Royal Province

1626 Peter Minuit purchased all of Manhattan Island for the Dutch and paid the Indians in trinkets worth $24

1629 Massachusetts Bay Colony chartered to the Puritans

     1631 English East India Company granted permission to import India calico into England (painted cottons) — these became very fashionable with all Europeans and were soon known in America

1632 Maryland colonial charter granted to Lord Baltimore

1638 New Hampshire colony established at Exeter

1638 West Indian cotton shipped into Salem, Massachusetts

1640 Massachusetts General Court ordered manufacture of wool and linen cloth. By this date colonists were arriving less often. Population of New England: 20,000

1643 First professional textile industry established in America at Rowley, near Ipswich, Massachusetts; spun wool and cotton

1644 Rhode Island settlements became chartered as part of the Bay colony

1645 Massachusetts Bay colony published an appeal exhorting people to care for and increase their sheep and to write their friends in England to bring more sheep for wool

1652 Maine became part of the Bay Colony

1656 Anne Hibbins executed as a witch in Salem, Massachusetts; an inventory of her belongings listed "Five painted Callicoe curtains & vallients"

1662 Connecticut colony chartered

1663 Rhode Island chartered as a separate colony

1664 New York colony was established by the English; they took it from the Dutch without a battle

1664 New Jersey established by the English who took it from the Dutch

1664 Delaware established by the English; it was originally held by the Swedes and Dutch

1665 Taxes were paid in *wool* in Rhode Island

1665 North Carolina was granted a Proprietorship

1665 Bills were paid in *tobacco* in Virginia

    1676 "First" print works were established in England by William Sherwin at West Ham. Print works were said to exist in Germany and France

    1678 Holland claimed establishment of the "first" European print works for printing and dyeing

1679 New Hampshire given separate status as a colony (from Massachusetts)

    1680 Print works were established in Germany, Switzerland, and Austria

1681 Pennsylvania chartered with William Penn as Proprietor

1683 Swedish and Finnish colonists in Delaware were raising sheep, spinning and weaving wool; they exported some to Sweden; some linens were woven

1683 Germantown, Pennsylvania, settled

1684 German workers were well established in Pennsylvania and became celebrated weavers and later printers of cotton and linen

1685 William Penn wrote that the quality of linens woven at Germantown was unusually good; by this date American textile manufacturing had become important enough to begin to worry English merchants

    1689 Manufacture of "indiennes" started at Neuchâtel, Switzerland

    1690 A French refugee named Cabannes set up the "first" print works in Richmond, England. A French edict in 1687 prohibited printers from copying India prints; many printers fled to England

1697 A cloth manufactory was in operation in New Jersey

1699 The Wool Act forbade exportation of wool of any kind from the American colonies. This only stiffened opposition and many governors continued to encourage textile manufacturers and offered bounties for linens and woolens

1700 By now England was in real apprehension that colonial manufactures might lessen the demand for English goods

    1700 Print works were started at Crayford, England — later called the mecca of English printing

    1700 The British Parliament enacted a law saying "all calicoes of China, Persia or the East Indies that are painted, dyed or printed or stained there, which are, or shall be imported into this kingdom, shall not be worn or otherwise used in Great Britain."

1700 Household inventories in Rhode Island included many looms and spinning wheels — proof that home industries were flourishing (even in cities). Connecticut, Maine, New Hampshire, and Massachusetts all recorded spinning and weaving

1712 George Leason set up a print works in Boston and advertised that he printed "all sorts of Linnens"; this is the earliest dated reference to a domestic cotton-printing establishment in America

1713 James Franklin, founder of the *New England Courant* in Boston, printed, in addition to his newspaper, linens, calicoes, and silks

1715 It was reported that the colonies from Carolina to New England produced "much of the same thing" as did England, and that they were capable of subsisting independently

1715 Francis Dewing of Boston advertised that he "Engraveth and Printeth Copper Plates — likewise cuts neatly in wood and printeth callicoes"

1720 *The Boston Gazette* advertised that it was also a "linen printer"

    1720 Printed cotton of England, Switzerland, and Holland were said to rival the prints of India

1729 North and South Carolina became independent provinces

1732 Georgia became a chartered trusteeship

    1733 John Kay of Bury, England, patented the flying shuttle; this freed one hand of the weaver, as he could operate the loom by pulling a cord, and the invention soon found its way into the American colonies

    1738 Lewis Paul and John Wyatt took out the first patents on cotton-spinning machinery in England

    1746 Cloth printing was started at Mulhouse, France, by Kocchlin

1750 A linen manufactory in Boston advertised that "persons may have their yarn wove"; it was a cooperative manufactory that failed and was abandoned

    1752 The first copper-plate printing was done by Francis Nixon near Dublin, Ireland, at the Drumconda Printworks

    1754 Copper-plate printing began in London — transmitted from Ireland

1756 Seven Years War with France

1760 John Hickey of Boston advertised that he "prints linnens with true Blues and Whites"

    1760 No *all* cotton fabrics were made in England before this date

    1760 Oberkampf began printing at Jouy, France, using mostly cottons woven in India

1760 Many efforts were made to foster American manufactures to lessen colonial dependence on England

    1761 The earliest *dated* English printed cloth recorded by "R. Jones at Old Ford"

1761 Mrs. John Haugen of Boston advertised that she "stamps linens china blue or deep blue or any colour that gentlemen and Ladies fancies"

1766 The Society for the Promotion of Arts and Economy gave many awards for excellence in the linen industry

    1766 Some English prints were done from copper plates in chinoiserie style, signed by Collin Woolmers

    1766 Printing and dyeing establishments existed in Switzerland

1767 On George Washington's estate at Mount Vernon, linens, cottons, and woolens were woven for more than 25 families in the neighborhood

    1769 Richard Arkwright patented machinery for spinning cotton in England

1768 The senior class at Harvard wore suits made of homespun wool for its graduation

    1770 James Hargreaves invented the spinning jenny in England — a device that spun several threads at one time

    1770 Thomas Bell invented copper-plate printing on cloth in England

    1770 Frédéric Oberkampf took knowledge of copper-plate printing to Jouy, France, from Morat, Switzerland

    1770 Print works were founded by Robert Peel (1750-1830) in Bury, Lancashire, England; he became the outstanding printer of 18th century England. Peel and Yates exported many bolts of fabric to America and their designs were copied for many years

    1771 First cotton-printing works at Glasgow, Scotland

1774 First Continental Congress met at Philadelphia

1774 John Hewson, a protégé of Benjamin Franklin, came from England and set up a print works in Philadelphia. His progress has been well recorded and some of his fabrics still exist. Other linen printers advertised their services in Philadelphia at this time

    1774 The use of chlorine as a bleach was discovered in England by Scheele — a significant discovery for the fabric industry

1775 The first spinning jenny was used in America in Philadelphia at the plant of Samuel Wetherell; this plant survived the Revolution and operated until about 1790

1775 The American Revolution; April 19, the battles of Lexington and Concord

160 • English documentary copper-plate (possibly roller) print in sepia and red. "Death and Burial of Lord Nelson, January 8, 1806." Subject taken from a series of aqua tints by Ackerman. Panel 26½" wide, vertical repeat 21". A prototype of the story-telling historical toiles with scenes and events in profusion. Most copper plates were printed in one color — the red may have been over-printed by block but appears to be a second copper plate. Courtesy, Cooper-Hewitt Museum of Design, Smithsonian Institution

IV

From the Revolution to 1900

1. JOHN HEWSON, ESQR. OF PHILADELPHIA
c. 1745-1821

THERE appears to be only one 18th century American calico printer whose life story is known and, more importantly, whose prints still exist in good condition in at least two American museums. It is probable that few of the European artisans who came to America to set up "manufactories" had as active and romantic a life as John Hewson of Philadelphia, but other printing enterprises undoubtedly progressed in much the same way as his. The Hewson story is therefore of historical interest to our fabric narrative.

> THE PENNSYLVANIA GAZETTE, January 30, 1772, quoted a letter from Baltimore which said:
> *"We learn that a person who has for many years been a master in several large manufactories for linen, cotton and Calico printing, likewise cutting and stamping of copper plates for same, intends sometime this month to leave England for America with six journeymen and all machinery for carrying on the same business, which unknown to the English manufacturers, has been shipped."*

It is generally thought that the "person" was John Hewson. The journeymen are unknown, but could well be some of the several early printers who advertised their services and worked in Philadelphia. A careful second reading of that brief notice tells us some interesting things. First, that since the printer "likewise" did cutting and stamping of copper plates, his principal craft

Detail of the center of hand printed coverlet made by John Hewson in Philadelphia, late 18th century. (See Fig. 109) Pink, red, light green, dark green, gold and sepia on natural cotton or linen. Vase is 10″ high. Courtesy, Philadelphia Museum of Art

was probably wood-block printing of cotton, linen, and calico. Secondly, the "machinery" could only have been a press for copper-plate printing and was most certainly smuggled out of England, who was doing all she could to keep British inventions and machines at home to discourage colonial enterprises.

Benjamin Franklin was in London in 1758, and wrote to his wife, Deborah, that he had bought "fifty six yards of cotton, printed curiously from copper plates, a new invention, to make bed and window curtains, and seven yards of chair bottoms, printed in the same way, very neat."[103] It is possible that at that time, or on a later trip, Franklin visited one of the largest manufactories and bleach-yards near London — Bromley Hall — where John Hewson was employed as a calico printer and bleacher. The two men struck up a friendship and Franklin encouraged Hewson's wish to go to America and gave him letters of introduction to acquaintances in New York and Philadelphia. The Hewson family — husband, wife, son, and three small daughters — sailed for the New World and reached Philadelphia in the Fall of 1773.

Nine months later Hewson had set up his business and his first advertisement appeared in the *Pennsylvania Gazette* of July 20, 1774:

A CALICOE PRINTING MANUFACTORY, and BLEACH-YARD, is juſt opened, near the Glaſs-Houſe, at the upper end of Kenſington, about one mile from the city of Philadelphia;

JOHN HEWSON,

The Proprietor thereof, begs leave to inform the public, that he has, at a conſiderable expence, imported prints from London, and compleated works ſufficient for carrying on the above buſineſs to perfection; ſhould the public encourage him in his preſent undertaking, he hopes to merit their favour, as well in the execution as price, being brought up regularly to the buſineſs, at Bromley-Hall, near London, one of the moſt conſiderable Manufactories and Bleach-yards in England. He engages his work ſhall be equal in colour, and will ſtand waſhing, as well as any imported from London or elſewhere, otherwiſe will require no pay. Linen ſent for bleaching, from one yard to a thouſand, ſhall be punctually returned in three weeks, compleatly finiſhed, at 4d. per yard. The different colours that may be ordered, renders his publiſhing the prices of printing impoſſible, or he would inſert them here; ſuch as he has done, he has the pleaſure to find have given general ſatisfaction; his preſent ſett of prints conſiſts of patterns for printing calicoes and lineps for gowns, &c. coverlids, handkerchiefs, nankeens, janes and velverets, for waiſtcoats and breeches, &c. Orders from town or country are taken in at the Manufactory, or by the following gentlemen, in Philadelphia, who have been pleaſed to encourage the work,---Mr. Jonathan Zane, Mr. Sharp Delany, Dr. William Drewet Smith, in Second-ſtreet; Joel Zane, between Race and Vine-ſtreets, in Second-ſtreet; Jonathan Zane, jun. in Vine-ſtreet, between Third and Fourth-ſtreets, and at the New-Ferry. Patterns of the different prints may be ſeen at the Manufactory, or on notice he will do himſelf the pleaſure to wait on any perſon with them. §

Fig. 104

By this time there was increasing prosperity in the colonies, particularly in the larger cities, and there was money to be spent on fine clothing materials and prints for bed hangings and coverlets in "neat and elegant" patterns as described in the advertisements. Hewson lost no time in acquiring property where the Aramingo Canal emptied into the Delaware River, providing an ideal supply of the fresh, running water necessary to his manufacturing operations. If he carried on printing as it was done at Bromley Hall, he did both block and copper-plate prints and had enough meadow-land to do bleaching in the sun out of doors. It might be noted here that since there are no known American examples of copper-plate printing it is said by most experts that *none* was done in the colonies. There is clear evidence here that Hewson probably did print from copper plates. By 1774, the enterprising young Britisher had acquired five agents — or at least five friends — "who have been pleased to encourage the work." There can be little doubt that Franklin's interest in printing and his wide circle of acquaintances in the Quaker City helped to give Hewson a good start. The only known printers in Philadelphia who might have offered competition to Hewson's business were John Walters and Thomas Bedwell. The latter had come from England in 1722, and joined Walters to start their printing establishment in 1775 — just when Hewson was well started. In two years — after the start of the Revolution — they "entirely quitted the linen-stamping business."[76]

> PENNSYLVANIA PACKET, March 13, 1775:
> *"LINEN PRINTING — In all its Branches, performed by the subscribers, John Walters and Thomas Bedwell, at their Manufactory near the Three-Mile Stone on Germantown Road. They show their goods every Wednesday and Saturday from eleven o'clock till two at Mrs. Krider's at the Golden Swan, in Third Street . . . they print linens and muslins for curtains, chair bottoms and bed furniture, handkerchiefs and for men's waistcoats. As the subscribers have been at great expense in bringing this Manufactory to America, they hope they shall meet with encouragement, as the prices they print for will make what they do considerably cheaper than what comes from Europe."*[103]

John Hewson's British wife died in 1774, and, following the typical colonial custom of quickly finding a new wife and mother for small children, he remarried in 1775. His American wife, Zibiah Smallwood, had a brother who was a lieutenant in the "patriot" army and this family connection may have helped speed the very rapid Americanization of John Hewson. He enlisted in the army and, in 1776, was commissioned a captain in the Philadelphia County Militia. He left his new wife, young family, and a barely-established business to fight in the Revolution, where he made a fine military record. In 1778, he was captured by the British and imprisoned, but he managed to escape from a Long Island jail and make his way safely back to Philadelphia in spite of the fact that the British offered a reward of five guineas "for his body, dead or alive."[14]

Hewson returned to find that his printing manufactory had been destroyed by the British upon order of General Howe, who sought to revenge the fact that a London "gentleman" had joined the American army after only four years in the country. Hewson took on a partner, Englishman William Lang, possibly one of the original "journeymen," and as soon as the British evacuated the city, set about re-establishing his business. In his first postwar advertisement, he said that "the savage foe of Britain have made such destruction of their works and materials that renders them unable to carry on the business in all branches." The bleachery — which was probably the largest volume activity of his former factory — seems to have been abandoned.

The *Pennsylvania Packet* of November 9, 1779, carried this notice:

LINEN PRINTING.

THE subscribers beg leave to inform the public, that they have removed to Kensington, on purpose to carry on the business at the original factory, joining the glass-house. The savage foe of Britain have made such destruction of their works and materials, that renders them unable to carry on the business in all its branches. The branch of business they mean to carry on, is the printing of blue handkerchiefs, with deep blue grounds and white spots; also very neat gown-patterns of the same colour, which they will warrant to be as durable in their washing and colour, as any imported from Europe or elsewhere, or they will have nothing for doing them. Little need be said as to the abilities of the subscribers, as there are numbers of yards now in wear, done by them, equal to any done by the boasted Britons. The works will be ready this week, and work received at the factory, by   HEWSON and LANG.
   N.B. A quantity of Pot-ash is wanted.

Fig. 105

Renewing of any businesses following the war was not easy and Hewson had a hard time of it for awhile. He finally applied for — and was granted — an interest-free loan of 200 pounds by the General Assembly of the State.

In the *Pennsylvania Packet* of March 24, 1790, his advertisement says modestly that he had been awarded a "Plate of Gold" by the Pennsylvania Society for the Encouragement of Manufactures of the Useful Arts; this "plate" was the gold medal mentioned in Hewson's will and bequeathed to his son, John Jr.

Calico Printing.

THE Bufinefs of Calico Printing is carried on by the fubfcribers at their Factory in Kenfington, in the Northern-Liberties of the city of Philadelphia, where Merchants and others may have Work done in that art elegantly and with expedition—They alfo, upon moderate terms, preferve Sailcloth, without injuring its texture, from the deftructive effects of mildew, though ufed upon the longeft voyages.

The fubfcribers were always averfe to mentioning performances which exifted but in a newfpaper: they however think it proper to mention, that fuch proof of their abilities have been exhibited to the Legiflature of this ftate, as met the approbation of, and induced that Honorable Body to grant a fmall encouragement to the performers; and as a further proof of having excelled in their line of bufinefs, the Board of managers of the Manufacturing Society of the city of Philadelphia, adjudged to John Hewfon the Plate of Gold propofed as a premium for the beft Specimen of Calico Printing done within this ftate.

A favourable opportunity now prefents itfelf for carrying on the Bufinefs of Calico Printing in this country extenfively, and with great advantage, particularly to thofe concerned in the Eaft-India trade, who have it in their power to reap many and great benefits that are peculiar to thofe only

Any perfon or perfons, willing to enter into the abovementioned branch of bufinefs in an extenfive manner, may have further information on the fubject by applying to

March 23. 3t1aw   JOHN HEWSON & CO.

Fig. 106

Hewson's prints were of good quality in the best English tradition, as far as we know, and his business prospered. In 1810, at the age of about 65, he retired and turned over the print works to his son, John. Hewson died in 1821, and his son continued in the business until about 1825. The Hewson estate included fine furniture and silver — the acquisitions of a man of some wealth — and these were left to his eight children. Chintz curtains and bed covers were left to Ann Hodgson, his daughter, whose grandchildren carefully labelled and preserved the early Hewson prints that eventually were acquired (principally) by the Philadelphia Museum of Art.

One of the highlights of Hewson's professional life occurred on July 4, 1788, when the city of Philadelphia celebrated the adoption of the United States Constitution. His high standing in civic affairs is attested to by the fact that he was selected to represent the "Manufactory Society" in the Great Federal Procession, the biggest event of the celebration. The *Gazette* of July 9, 1788, describes the parade and provides us with a bit of Americana that is as animated and charming as a scene from an historical novel.

The float, or "carriage," was 29th in the long procession and consisted of a low, flat bed 13 feet wide by 30 feet long, covered with white cotton cloth woven and bleached in Philadephia. The whole display was so heavy that

PENNSYLVANIA GAZETTE.

WEDNESDAY, JULY 9, 1788.

Grand Federal Proceſſion.

PHILADELPHIA, July 9.

ON FRIDAY, the 4th inſtant, the citizens of Philadelphia celebrated the DECLARATION OF INDEPENDENCE, made by the Thirteen United States of America on the 4th of July, 1776, and the ESTABLISHMENT of THE CONSTITUTION, or Frame of Government propoſed by the late General Convention, and now ſolemnly adopted and ratified by Ten of thoſe States.

flag of white ſilk, having three fleurs de lys and thirteen ſtars in union, over the words " 6th of " February, 1778," in gold letters. The horſe he rode belonged formerly to Count Rochambeau.

VI.
Corps of Light-Infantry, commanded by Capt. A. G. Claypoole, with the ſtandard of the 1ſt regiment.

VII.
DEFINITIVE TREATY OF PEACE.
George Clymer, Eſq; on horſeback, carrying a ſtaff,

XVIII.
The Conſuls and Repreſentatives of foreign States in alliance with America, in an ornamented Car, drawn by four horſes.—Captain Thomas Bril, with the flag of The United States of America,—Barbé de Marbois, Eſq; Vice Conful of France, that of France,—J. H C. Heinecken, Eſquire, Conful of The United Netherlands, that of The United Netherlands,—Charles Hellſtedt, Conful General of Sweden, that of Sweden, —Charles William Lecke, Eſq; that of Pruſſia,—Thomas Barclay, Eſq; that of Morocco.

XIX.

Fig. 107

ten large bay horses were required to draw it. The entire panoply of cotton manufacturing was in action on the platform. First, there was a cotton-carding machine operated by two men, then there was a spinning jenny with a woman operator, then a large lace-loom on which scarlet and white lace was being woven, and then a large fly-shuttle loom (just introduced in America) on which cotton was being hand woven. These represented all the steps in the making of cotton fabric — with a little lace added for decoration.

Then John Hewson and his associate, William Lang, and Mrs. Hewson and the four Hewson daughters were at work in all phases of the printing operation. Lang was cutting a wood block for printing shawls and Hewson was hand-block printing a length of chintz. The Hewson ladies (the youngest was then about 12) — all dressed in Hewson-printed cottons — were seated around a table "pencilling" a chintz of Hewson manufacture (painting in color, perhaps indigo, by hand). On a high flagpole at the rear of the float waved the flag of the calico printers. In the center there were 13 white stars on a blue field and 13 blue and white stripes. Around the edges were 37 different patterns printed in many colors. The flag also carried the motto of the Society: "May the Union Government protect the manufacturers of America."[14] What a pity that the flag, the lace, the cotton, and everything has disappeared! The whole celebration sounds like a resplendent 4th of July send-off for the new nation.

One further distinction of Hewson's career is that Martha Washington visited his first manufactory in 1775, and "expressed a desire to have handkerchiefs printed with a representation of Washington on horseback. Hewson took for his model a miniature showing Washington on horseback in full military dress and sent the first examples of these prints, which achieved great popularity to Mrs. Washington in Virginia."[37] The Washington kerchief shown in Fig. 108 cannot be identified positively as the Hewson design, but it is of the same date and is undoubtedly very much like it; the size is 30"

Fig. 108. Washington Historical Kerchief — the figure is taken from a print published in 1775 by C. Shepherd in London. It has not been substantiated that this is the kerchief printed by Hewson. Sepia print, probably from a copper plate. Courtesy of the New York Historical Society, New York City

square. Washington and his wife were known to have ordered both clothing and cloth often from England and both had a taste for elegant dress. But Martha Washington was much taken with Hewson's prints and must have ordered dress fabrics later, as Washington "pointed with pride to the Hewson calicoes worn by Mrs. Washington."[37]

Fig. 109. Hand-printed cotton coverlet made by John Hewson in Philadelphia, late 18th century. Courtesy, the Philadelphia Museum of Art

OPPOSITE PAGE
Fig. 110. Printed cotton bedspread (patchwork) with fabrics printed by John Hewson in Philadelphia and probably some others. Courtesy, the Philadelphia Museum of Art

The printed coverlet shown in Fig. 109 has a paper attached to it written by a Hewson grandson stating its origin and that it was printed by John Hewson. This is possibly the finest and most famous piece of printing done in America during its first 300 years. The fabric is a soft, loosely-woven cotton or cotton and linen, now an ivory color, but it probably was originally white. The coverlet is just a few inches less than three yards square, and is made of two pieces sewn together down the center (each the width of a loom), as were most colonial coverlets. The colors have probably softened somewhat in the nearly 200 years since they were printed, but the whole effect is still remarkably lively in pink, red, light green, dark green, light brown, or gold and sepia. In the center is an ornate vase about 10″ high with delicate handles, holding a bouquet of red flowers topped by a butterfly and guarded by two birds on the wing. Surrounding the bouquet inside an inner border of red, green, and brown are bunches of pink flowers with more butterflies and birds; one small bird on the branch is repeated eight times throughout the design between flower units. Outside the square, standing in a row along the 10-inch wide ornate border in browns and reds, are repeated one of the center sprigs (or bushes), alternating with two other bird units. The whole design is edged with a printed simulated fringe — an elegant finishing touch. As with most professionally-printed coverlets, separate blocks are used for the corners of the borders.

Fig. 111. Hewson Quilt #2, discovered in 1953 by Florence Peto, author of *American Quilts and Coverlets*, and verified to contain Hewson prints by the Philadelphia Museum of Art. The darkish spots on the alternate white squares in the center section are feathers, printed from copper plates. Courtesy of the Henry Ford Museum, Dearborn, Michigan

OPPOSITE PAGE

Fig. 112. Detail of Quilt shown abov

The coverlet is the personification of that description used so often in the 18th century — neat and elegant; to 20th century eyes it also has an air of charming naiveté. It also represents clearly what is meant when we say the design shows the Indian influence. The coverlet is in remarkably good condition and is a real treasure among American prints. The piece is usually described as a block print, but examination of the finely detailed parts of the design suggests that it could be partly copper-plate printed.

Another coverlet (Fig. 110) is sometimes described as the Hewson Quilt. It is of patchwork and was originally owned by a Hewson descendant, Miss Ella Hodgson, a great-granddaughter. It supposedly was made by Zibiah Smallwood Hewson of bits of fabrics printed by her husband and the center design is the identical vase with butterfly and some of the same birds as those in the center of the other coverlet. Some of the surrounding squares appear to be hand prints of a similar style, but others show similarity to prints typical of a later period, c. 1805, after roller printing was invented. It is possible that the coverlet was sewn together at a later date, and made use of fabrics of that year along with the early ones.

A second quilt (Fig. 111) was found in the 1950's and was discovered to have some squares printed with the same three Hewson birds on the branches that are used on the first coverlet. The history of this piece is a mystery — it was found in Massachusetts and is now owned by the Henry Ford Museum in Michigan. The birds are combined with a patchwork of squares and a heavy border of pieces that appear to be early 19th century roller prints, but are possibly block prints. Because of the unmistakable birds (also shown in detail) this quilt, too, is called a Hewson Quilt. No other swatches or printed cloth or clothing are known to remain of Hewson's work — but one may hope that those birds may still turn up again.

The Philadelphia Museum also owns an Italian mezzaro (Fig. 113) that was given to them by Hewson's descendants who inherited it, too, from his daughter, Ann Hodgson. In his will, this was described as "my largest India chintz Bedquilt." It is made of two widths of cotton sewn together down the center. The mezzari were generally printed from wood blocks and another piece almost identical to this is owned by the Boston Museum of Fine Arts and is marked with the printers' names: "Fratelli Speich, Cornigliano," a suburb of Genoa. One of the Speich brothers was undoubtedly that Michele who left Switzerland to start printing near Genoa about 1787, as mentioned in Section II. The mezzaro was obviously prized by Hewson and by comparing its border with that of his coverlet (Fig. 109) we see that he may have been influenced by its style.

2. THE ROAD TO INDEPENDENCE — STRAIGHT BUT ROCKY
1776-1800

From about 1760 to 1765, before the Revolution, British ships were arriving regularly in New York, Philadelphia, and Boston laden with most of the commodities, including dress goods and interior furnishing fabrics, required by the colonists. The home industries that had been essential in the early days to supply household linens and woolens for clothing had declined with the increase in imports. The few artisan-printers could not make a dent in the demands so amply filled by British goods.

As friction between the British and colonial citizens increased, and when Americans began to chafe under excessive taxation, trade began to dwindle. Beginning with the Stamp Act of 1765, the Revolution started to brew. The Boston Tea Party in 1773, and the firm stand taken by the Daughters of Liberty who burned their dresses rather than wear British calicoes, were a few of many acts of open defiance that preceded the beginning of the war.

The Revolution put a temporary end to trade with England, but only so long as ships were needed for transporting men and equipment for the conflict. The war ended in 1781, but a final treaty was not signed until 1783, and it took another year before all British troops were on their way home. But trading ships soon came again.

"Through all the turmoil of war and the activities connected with it, the work of civil government, local and general, was carried on in the United States. While British governors were being driven from power, or fleeing for their lives, eleven of the thirteen States set about drawing up plans for full self-government and at the end of the war had constitutions of their own. Absorbing as the war was, it would be a conservative estimate to say that at least three-fourths of the men as well as all the women and young people devoted themselves mainly to civilian affairs, though often engaged in war production."[7] Business had to go on as usual.

Fig. 113. Italian mezzaro owned by John Hewson; block-printed in blue, red, pink, brown, purple, and black on white cotton. The design is a copy of an East Indian palampore with "Tree of Life" design. Mezzari were supposedly not used as coverlets but were a sort of shawl-robe worn over the head. Courtesy, the Philadelphia Museum of Art

PENNSYLVANIA EVENING POST, March 1, 1777:

"NATHANIEL NORGROVE, from Kensington, begs leave to inform the public that he has opened a manufactory for printing linen, cotton, calico and velverets . . . at the house of Widow Myers, four doors above Poolsbridge in Front Street, Northern Liberties."[103]

England was slow to see anything radically new in America and although encouragement for all sorts of business began to come from State governments and professional organizations, Britain held on to her manufacturing secrets, and competed with all business enterprises.

PENNSYLVANIA PACKET, September 18, 1785:

"Henry Royl & Co. began a Calico Printing Manufactory on the Germantown Road, two miles from Philadelphia, at the place commonly known by the name of Bakeovens Place. The undertakers of this work have been regularly brought up to the business, they flatter themselves capable of giving entire satisfaction."[103]

"In 1786, one Abell Buell, an ingenious mechanic of Killingsworth, Connecticut, who had been engaged in engraving, type-founding and the manufacture of copper coins for the State, visited England ostensibly to purchase copper, but in reality, it is said, to obtain a knowledge of machinery used in cloth manufacture."[9] Subterfuge continued to be necessary!

PENNSYLVANIA PACKET, 1786:

"Robert Taylor is fitting up the Bleachfield in Lower Merion Township, ten miles from Philadelphia, laid out and lately possessed by Daniel Bunce, where he intends carrying on the bleaching and printing business on the same principles they are conducted in Britain. Pattern books will be lodged in different places for the convenience of the public."[103]

In 1787, a gold medal was offered by the Society of the University of Pennsylvania for — among other things — "the best specimens or patterns of printed linens or cotton goods stained within the State."[9] Societies for the encouragement of domestic industry "were formed before 1792 in Philadelphia, New York City, Baltimore, Wilmington, Boston, Morristown, Newark, and Burlington, N.J. The legislatures of New York, Massachusetts, and New Hampshire exempted manufacturing establishments from taxation and New York released men engaged in them from militia and jury duty.

"In 1789, everything seemed to indicate that the economic future of America for at least two generations lay in agriculture and in commerce. Shipping had revived after the Revolution until trade with England was becoming as thriving as it had been during colonial times. Just thirteen years after the beginning of the war the United States was the largest single purchaser of English goods. And it was returning to Great Britain or its colonies nearly one half of its exports — chiefly rice, tobacco and timber.

"The storekeepers of the commercial towns carried a stock made up almost wholly of imports from abroad. American manufacturing had not really begun and its meagre showing was not enough to divert attention from the flourishing state of agriculture and commerce. There was no surplus population yet to furnish a ready labor supply, and the scarcity of labor was an obstacle to industry so long as western lands were open on easy terms to discontented easterners. There was a lasting prejudice against industrial labor, lest American factories should degrade the worker, as had been done in England."[54] Nevertheless, this was the time when American enterprise began to assert itself.

NEW YORK JOURNAL & PATRIOTIC REGISTER, September 4, 1791:

"Moses Phillip and Son Walkie will engage to die the following colours viz. Deep and pale blue, Bottle, grass, amoke and sage green, lead, plumb, garnet, dark olive, damson, slate, buff, claret, crow and ash colours, London and Hartford smoke; London snuff, olive, slate and federal drab, Hartford mud and crow black."[28]

Hartford must have been a distinctly dingy city at the time!

The map shown in Fig. 114 was printed in sepia on white cotton or linen from a copper plate. At the upper left it says, "The United States of America with the British and Spanish Dominions adjoining. From the best Authorities and latest Observations." The date 1791 was written in. In the lower right corner it says, "Evan's Polymetric Table of America, Corrected and Improved, Showing the Distances between the Principal Towns." Marked by symbols are Towns, Forts, and Indian Towns. Careful examination with a magnifying glass discloses the four letters "ndon" near a torn section at the lower left, which means it was probably printed in London. It lists the counties in New York, Long Island, and Massachusetts, and just east of the Mississippi is the "Louisiana Spanish Dom."; to the north is the "New British Dominion," and "West Florida" is bounded on the west by the Mississippi. It is surprising to find a mileage chart just like the ones on our maps at every gas station.

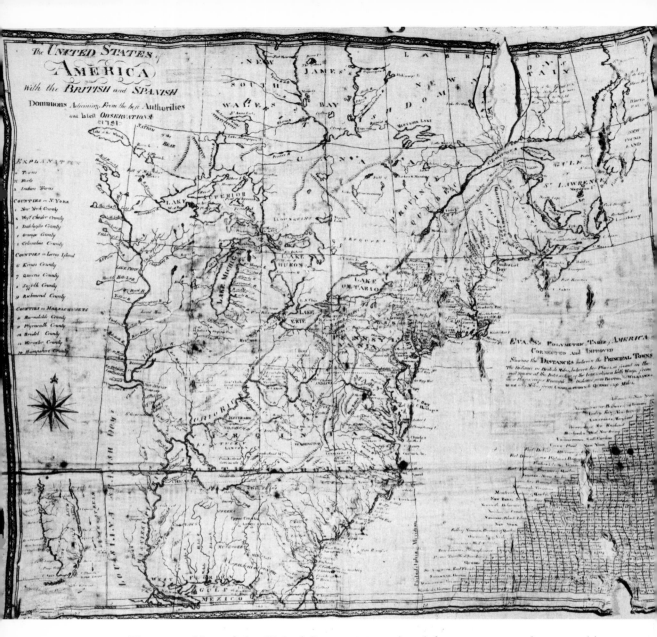

Fig. 114. Map of the United States, 1791, printed from a copper plate on white cotton (?) or linen in sepia, size 23″ x 26″. Courtesy of the Rare Book Division, N. Y. Public Library, Astor, Lenox and Tilden Foundations

American artisans continued to depend on English pattern books, swatch books, and French and Italian design books. A treatise on calico printing published in London, in 1789, said, "By a good Pattern Drawer should be understood one who possess a fertility of invention, with judgment to adapt that

Fig. 115. "Calico Printer," engraving from *The Book of Trades*, published in 1807 by Jacob Johnson's Publishing Co., Whitehall, N. Y., Vol. III. Courtesy the Smithsonian Institution

fertility to the best purpose, as it regards taste, effect, execution and experience; or at least one who can improve on what is being done by others, or readily catch the reigning style, and by adapting it, form his designs accordingly . . . [one who] can produce that variety which gives *a spring to business* ever dependent on the capriciousness of taste."[69] It can be said that the colonial citizens of about 1800 who were by then *United States* citizens were about to "give a spring to business" the likes of which had never been seen before!

THE DIARY OR LOUDEN'S REGISTER, September 20, 1792:

"CALICO PRINTING AND DYEING. Stephen Addington, Respectfully informs the public he has established a Manufactory at Springfield, Essex County, New Jersey for Printing Muslins, Muslinettes, Dimities, Calicoes and Linen &c. Dyeing of Brown cloth."[28]

AMERICAN MINERVA AND EVENING ADVERTISER (N. Y.), September 20, 1795:

"PRINT CUTTER — Wanted a Print Cutter, at the new Callicoe Manufactory in Boston, Any one being Master of the branch of business, may find encouragement by applying to Wm. Codman, No. 18, Pearl Street, New York."[28]

Fig. 116. Three wood blocks, cut in hardwood on the end-grain in typical floral motifs — the largest is about 3¼″ across. Believed to have been used by Herman Vandausen. Courtesy, Rhode Island Historical Society, Providence

3. SOME RHODE ISLAND PRINTERS

The Rhode Island Historical Society in Providence owns the three wood blocks shown in Fig. 116. These are supposed to have come from a calico-printing business started in 1780, in East Greenwich, R.I., and the blocks may have been cut and used by one Herman Vandausen. If so, they are possibly the oldest *dated* calico printing blocks in America. Vandausen was a German who had learned his trade at Mulhouse, a great printing center in France. He came to Philadelphia hoping to set up his own business and tried to interest a Providence importer, John Brown, in establishing a cotton-printing enterprise that would make use of the calicoes Brown was already importing from India. The trader considered that there was too much financial risk in the printing business, so Vandausen began working on his own. In 1790, he had the typical small and modest establishment where he cut blocks and printed on the homespun brought in by women of his district near Providence. The competition with the plentiful imported goods and his lack of funds finally forced him to seek another arrangement. He then joined the printing business of Zachariah Allen. Both Vandausen and Allen are members of the group of self-styled "first calico printers in America."

A slightly different version of the Vandausen story was found in a manuscript written 50 years later by one Anthony Arnold, to record some Providence history. Since it was written after the fact, it is hard to say whether it is completely accurate.

"Some Account of the First Beginning of the Calico Printing in Providence.

"In the year 1780 Alverson a painter and Jeremiah Eddy agreed to go into the printing of cloth with oil colors, Jeremiah Eddy cut the tipes on the end of small pieces of hard wood and put on the paint on the tipes with a brush, stamping the cloth by hand in small flowers to please the eye, and the work was done in a shop belonging to Charles Lei, near Stone Pond. The health of Alverson becoming poor in the fall he gave up the business and Col. Benjamin Hopper took his place as partner. They carried on the business until the Spring of 1781. They then dissolved the Partnership and about that time there came a German into Providence from the British servis who had worked in the printing business and he gave the said Eddy knowledge of printing with water colors, he then cut larger tipes in blocks and pieces of boards of hard wood and printed running vines and large flowers and he printed hundreds of various figures, the women brought in their sheets made of Tow and lining taken from their beads, and had them printed and made into grounds, and in the fall of 1781 or the Spring of 1782, the rumor of Peace, and the arrival of calicoes through various channells reduced the price so much that he gave up the business. Herewith is presented some of the tipes that was used in 1780.

ANTHONY ARNOLD"[15]

D. Graeme Keith, museum curator and writer of the calico-printing section in the Comstock *Concise Encyclopedia of American Antiques*, says that the wood blocks shown were more probably cut by Jeremiah Eddy, but there is nothing in the story to determine that. If the "German who came into Providence" *was* Vandausen, it seems as if his European experience and training would have given him the greater skill and knowledge of the business. This brief quotation from an obscure writing gives us a definite picture of the fact that women *did* bring in their sheets — "lining taken from their beads" — to be printed. The "water colors" were undoubtedly dyes, and the ink first used by Eddy was probably plain printer's ink.

Fig. 117. Wax rubbings on cloth made by the author from the three printing blocks; the designs are not reversed, as they would be in printing. Same source as Fig. 116

Fig. 118. Printing block cut on the long grain of the wood; date and use unknown. Owned by the Museum of Art, Rhode Island School of Design, Providence

Fig. 119. Resist print made by Mrs. Anna C. Mautner from the 18th century wood block shown above. Size of block 6″ x 10¾″

In 1794, another French-trained group of three printers set up a print works in Providence. Little is known of their work, except that Vandausen, Allen, and the new firm of Schaub (or possibly Schwab), Tissot and Du-Bosque all printed from wood blocks on imported India cottons and on homespun linens, and that if glazing was done, it was by the use of flint stones set into handles. Peter Shaub left his first firm and joined with Robert Newell to set up another business in 1797. By the middle of the 19th century there were said to be 17 dyers and calico printers in Rhode Island.

Another Rhode Island block that is probably from about the same date is shown in Fig. 118. It is very primitively executed and the motif of a hunter with a gun, animals, and birds is of very old folk-art origin. It is doubtful if this block was intended for use on fabric, but a contemporary resist print in blue and white was made from the block, and is shown in Fig. 119. The block may have been used by a printer as a heading for a broadside, a primitive and often charming give-away advertising handbill decorated with woodcuts; or the block may have been used as the line block for a bandbox paper.

Figure 120 shows another print from about the same date, c. 1790; it is possibly block printed. The color is rose on a natural linen; the eagle and serpent are carefully drawn, probably taken from an engraving; the willow tree (a popular American symbol at this date) seems to be incongruously stuck into the design, and very amateurishly drawn. The eagle, serpent, and tree appear to have been added to an English floral chintz to make it "American." This odd print is difficult to explain; the above is mostly speculation.

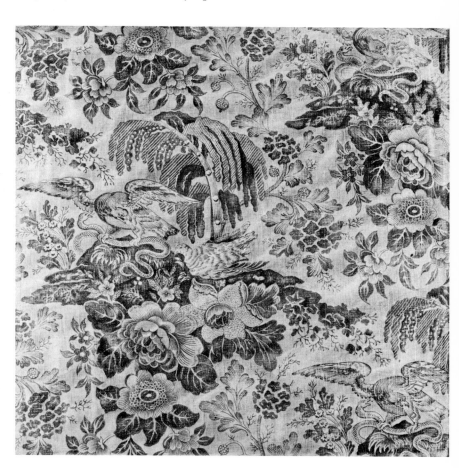

. 120. Linen drapery fabric, e monochrome on cream ound. Courtesy, Index of Amer- n Design, National Gallery of t

4. COTTON — AMERICA'S FIRST INDUSTRY
and Samuel Slater, "The Father of American Manufactures"

Samuel Slater was a bright young Englishman who had gone to work in 1783 as an apprentice cotton spinner in a mill a Derby, England, where Sir Richard Arkwright, the inventor of the cotton-spinning machine, was a partner. Slater learned his trade well and left England in 1789, in answer to an advertisement for a reward offered by a Philadelphia factory for the design of a machine to make "cotton rollers." The records do not say whether or not he got the reward, but in 1790, he went to Providence to join the firm of Almy and Brown, who were also seeking an engineer-inventor. Arkwright's mill guarded all the plans of their machinery, and Samuel Slater came with no designs or drawings, but he began building wooden machinery entirely from his memory of the English machines. He designed and supervised the building of carding, drawing, roving, and spinning machines and planned the whole factory to run by water power at the mill in Pawtucket. When completed, this was the first cotton mill in America in which all the processes were done by "Arkwright" machinery under one roof. Spinning, bleaching, dyeing, and finishing of cotton yarns were done in the building, but the weaving was still done in private homes on hand looms in 1793.

The project represented an enormous achievement and Slater's biographer says "this was a circumstance worthy of the atention of the whole nation, and worthy also of a fair page of her history — the art and mystery of making cloth with machinery by water power."[55] (Power looms were finally added to the mill.) The engineer's adopted nation agreed with the opinion, and today two of Samuel Slater's original wooden machines, with a beautiful, smooth patina that came from use, are on exhibition in the Smithsonian Institution in Washington, D.C.; they are a carding engine and a spinning frame of 48 spindles. There is also now a museum at "The Old Slater Mill" in Pawtucket which is entirely devoted to Slater's achievements. He later became a partner in three other mills, one of which was the Amoskeag Manufacturing Co. in Manchester, N.H. It is interesting to note that "The Father of American Manufactures" was paid a salary of $3 per day in 1801 for supervising two mills, one at Pawtucket and the other in Massachusetts.

In the same year that the water wheel started the machinery at Pawtucket (1793), Eli Whitney invented the cotton gin, and also in that year the southern States sold 138,000 pounds of cotton to English mills. This combination of circumstances in that year — efficient machinery for cleaning harvested cotton, machines to prepare thread and weave the cotton, and adequate manpower in the fields to harvest the crops — was the essential beginning of the industrialization of America. The Slater mill was the first of hundreds to swing into operation, and the cotton industry was the first factory system in the country.

American textile printers were soon no longer dependent on imported India cottons, or on small bits of hand-woven homespun for the material of their trade.

There were good reasons for the industry's development in New England rather than in the South, where cotton was grown. In New England there were many streams and small swift-running rivers where the pure water provided both power and washing facility, the steady "medium" humidity of New England made the spinning machines work well, coastal ports were better for receiving raw materials and for shipping goods, and the labor supply, mercantile capital, and land transportations systems were all superior in "the North."[54]

As mills were established, the first mill workers came mainly from farms, but did not intend to give up their land, and regarded mill work as a temporary change from agriculture. It was some time before there was a permanent "factory class." The cotton mills gave employment to the first body of women workers and provided them with new economic independence; it also used the first paid child labor. Factories at first had to overcome a new atmosphere of social stigma attached to factory work; women in the mills were regarded as immoral and were socially ostracized; men were criticized for shirking their duty as farmers.

Many Americans — even some in the government — found it hard to think of America as anything but an agricultural nation and believed that its other needs should be met by England and Europe. Thomas Jefferson wrote in 1785, "Cultivators of the earth are the most valuable citizens . . .as long as they can find employment in this line, I would not convert them into mariners, artisans or anything else. I consider the class of artificers as the panders of vice and the instruments by which the liberties of a country are generally overturned."[54] The War of 1812 finally made it evident that industry was a necessity for complete independence, and even Jefferson changed his mind and spoke equally vehemently when he finally said, "To be independent for the comforts of life, we must fabricate them ourselves. He who is now against domestic manufactures must be for reducing us either to a dependence on England or to be clothed in skins and live like wild beasts in dens and caverns."[54] And so cloth and clothing became an example of *necessary* manufacturing.

An English power loom was secretly shipped to Massachusetts in 1827, and was soon copied, but it took time to manufacture enough of these complicated, mostly handmade machines to make any great change in cloth production. It was not until after the Civil War that anything but ordinary sheetings, called "domestics," were woven on power looms.

Many mills eventually added printing to their manufacturing operation. Calico printing completely changed the character and uses of plain cotton goods, but did not materially alter the basic process of making cloth. In 1829, after a general depression, calico printing came to the rescue of New England manufacturers; it opened up a new market for dress goods, interior furnishing fabrics, and "fancy goods," provided employment for a whole new class of artisans (mostly from Europe), and brought new sales to the companies.

The Merrimack Company in Lowell, Massachusetts, and the Cocheco Company of Dover, N.H., were among the first to add print works to their manufactories. Others were started — many for doing printing *only* — around Boston, Providence, and Philadelphia, and, by 1833, calico printing was publicly credited with bringing a return to prosperity in the manufacturing states.[54]

The War between the States had very little immediate adverse effect on the cotton industry and, in 1862, "Providence traded four million pieces" — about 120 million yards. Mills continud to expand to include printing, and in 1864, three years after the Civil War, "the Manchester Print Works were going, as usual, full blast,"[13] as were dozens of others. It took the southern cotton-producing states much longer, however, to recover financially from the war.

The records and swatch-books of the early mills have disappeared so completely that it is now rare to find more than one or two from the same factory. For the few surviving mill books in attics or archives there must have been hundreds that were destroyed. The Cranston Print Works in Rhode Island lost all its books by their being burned to "clear out old papers." The books of the Arnold Print Works of North Adams, Mass., represent a rare, almost intact collection in the Museum of Art of the Rhode Island School of Design in Providence.

Most histories of early manufacturing are written in a colorless style, as dry as dust, and are full of statistics about yards, acres, dollars, gallons, tons, and numbers of people employed. They are dynamically illustrated with steel-engraved portraits of owners and founders who appear to be already dead. To be true to history, the story should be colored bright red and green — for the brick buildings and the meadows around them. The large, neat, well-kept factories were often in a pleasant country setting of fields, trees, and rivers, with busy, lively people coming and going, or working at clattering machines making American history.

5. THE NINETEENTH CENTURY BEGINS

By 1800, America had been — officially — an independent nation for about twenty years. But England did much to make those years difficult for American business — and continued to provide not only obstacles, but competition for 50 years more.

PENNSYLVANIA PACKET, June 27, 1797:

*"OAKFORD AND LA COLLAY will carry on the calico print-
ing in its various branches, having a variety of new patterns, both
for calico and for shawls."*[103]

PENNSYLVANIA PACKET, 1798:

*"DAVY, ROBERTS CO. — Calicoes printed at Germantown
equal to any London work. Calicoes printed and completely finished by skilfull workmen with punctuality and expedition at the
lowest prices, to patterns suitable for the West Indies or this country."*[103]

Machinery was at first smuggled in and when we read that in 1802, the
first power loom was used in Rhode Island, it meant that quite a few more
years had to elapse before there was any considerable number of looms made
and distributed for use in American mills. In 1803, England herself was still
trying to perfect power looms. The real American manufacturing progress
did not begin until after the War of 1812, and it was 1850, before the nation
was industrialized. From 1812 to 1900, the story becomes a series of vignettes
of the progress of inventions and the building of machines, and the books do
not always agree as to dates and facts.

MERCANTILE ADVERTISER, February 2, 1801:

*"John M. Gibbon respectfully informs the public in and about
New York, that he has begun printing of Shawls and Calico on
the most reasonable terms, at Paterson; and considering the excellence of the place for business, the long practice of the colour-
maker and dyer in England, the public may expect work well
done. Enquire of Moses Gomez & Co. 75 Wall St. N. Y."*[28]

1806 Discharge printing was first used in the United States,[15] although it was
supposedly patented in 1813.

1810 "Several attempts had been made to print calicoes, but the manufacturers
did not seem able, without additional duties [tariffs] to withstand foreign
competition. Their difficulties were stated in a petition of the calico
printers of Philadelphia to Congress. Considerable capital was invested
in an establishment near Baltimore which could print 12,000 yards per
week — and might considerably extend it if the profits and demand afforded sufficient encouragement.

"The first lot of cotton goods printed in the United States by engraved rollers and machinery driven by water power reached Philadelphia on October 6, 1810, from the Bleach and Print Works of Thorp,
Siddall and Co., about six miles from Philadelphia. The cylinder ma-

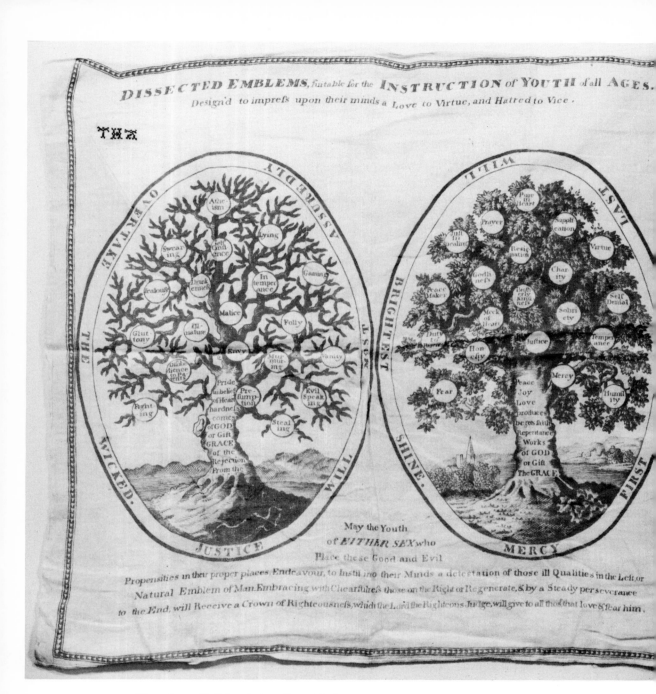

Fig. 121. Children's handkerchief, 15½" square. Red on white cotton. "Dissected emblems suitable for the Instruction of Youth of all Ages. Designed to impress upon their minds a love to Virtue and Hatred to Vice. Justice will most assuredly overtake the wicked. Mercy first and last will brightest shine." Courtesy, Dedham Historical Society, Dedham, Massachusetts

chine was brought from England by Mr. Siddall and was the first to supersede the tedious process of block printing previously in use. One man and two boys were able to print 10,000 yards of cloth or 50,000 children's handkerchiefs in one day. Cotton and linen goods were stained and dyed one color for various uses by similar means within the next two years."[9]

1822 "Messrs. David H. Mason and Matthew W. Baldwin, manufacturers of bookbinder's tools in Philadelphia, commenced the first engraving of cylinders for calico printing in the United States."[9]

1822 By this year there were established "print works on a large scale at Taunton, Fall River, and Lowell, Massachusetts, Dover, New Hampshire, Baltimore, and Columbiaville, N.Y., and elswhere. Within a few years they were prosperous businesses. The invention and manufacture of tools and machinery adapted to their use [some of which were patented in this year] led to the construction of calico-printing machines and drying chambers."[9]

1823 Print works were started at Paterson, N.J., North Adams, Mass., and Sanford, Maine."[13]

1824 "The New Jersey Bleaching, Printing and Dyeing Company was incorporated at Belleville, N.J."[9]

1826 "Joseph and Benjamin Marshall established the Hudson Calico Print works at Columbiaville or Stockport — five miles above Hudson, N.Y. They started with one roller-printing machine and in two years they imported three more. By this year New England was printing 60,000 yards of cotton per week."[9]

1836 "The United States printed one hundred and twenty million yards of calicoes. The Hudson Calico Print Works of Marshall, Carville, and Taylor was in a high state of efficiency, having 42 block hand printers and five printing machines. Two machines printed four colors at a time, and three printed three colors. The machines were all the best from England and could print over five million yards per year."[9]

1837 "The largest establishment for printing ginghams and silks was the Phillips Mills at Lynn, Massachusetts."[9]

ENGLISH · 1812

REDINGOTE · 1812

6. FASHION NOTES, 1800-1850

1800 "This year can be set as the time when what were called "women's trousers" first were worn to any extent. Their adoption — first called Pantaloons, later called Pantalets — was brought about by the transparence of the Indian stuffs employed for dresses."[23]

1801 "The extraordinary influx of Oriental fabrics into this country, caused by the sudden growth and prosperity of the East Indian Trade, was shown distinctly in men's apparel in the wear of *nankeen*. In one year over a million dollars' worth of yellow nankeen came to the U.S. It was a smooth, sturdy cotton fabric originally from Nanking, China".[23]

1820 Empire styles were made popular and were worn by all women during the time of Dolly Madison.[23]

1821 The *Lady's magazine* says that "female children" all wore, in winter, pantaloons of merino with short petticoats. In summer they wore pantaloons of white dimity or colored calico.[23]

It was the small-patterned cotton goods so favored by American women for daytime dresses that kept the roller-printing presses running.

7. MASSACHUSETTS MILLS

In the early 1800's, there were many print works that started their operations with hand-block printing. "In Massachusetts a pioneer printer was Andrew Robeson of New Bedford who entered the business in Fall River in the early 19th century with imported Scotch and English help. He printed at first in *simple blue and white*, later adding block printing in several colors."[37] We wish there were samples of the blue and whites done at Fall River, as the description fits the blue and white resists thought to have been done much earlier. The Franklin Institute in Philadelphia encouraged American manufacturers by holding annual competitive exhibits of all kinds of products. In 1832, the judges reported that "the premium went to Andrew Robeson for their printed cottons — for their fineness, coloring and elegance of execution."[15]

The American Print Works of Fall River was another that grew to be one of the largest producers of calicoes in the country by 1850, and its prints also won awards in Philadelphia, "noted for their beauty of designs, rich and agreeable effect in combination, delicacy and exactness in the execution that lead this season [1840] the first premium."[15] Other print works in the area of Fall River, Tiverton, and Taunton won awards for their work, too. All these factories began using roller-printing methods as soon as the copper rollers were perfected. Rollers were imported from England at first and were soon copied in America.

Rollers were engraved by hand for a number of years and skilled artisans trained in Europe were valued employees of the American print works. In

1822, in a continuing search for speed, Matthias Baldwin, who had invented the first locomotives, worked out a method of mechanical engraving. He drew the design on a wax plate, which was soft and easy to work on. This was then placed on a steel plate, face down, and treated with acid that bit into the steel to the proper depth in a reverse pattern to the design. The steel plate was then hardened, and the seamless copper cylinder was rolled against it under great pressure. The resulting impression became the printing cylinder and the steel master could be used to make any number of duplicates.

The history of two others of the Massachusetts group, the Waltham Manufactory and the Merrimack Mills at Lowell, is a rather typical story of how American industries made their start.

A Boston gentleman with two "first family" names, Francis Cabot Lowell, traveled widely in England and Scotland in the early 1800's and in Lanchashire saw for the first time power machinery in operation for all phases of cotton manufacturing. Lowell was ambitious to promote American industry and, about 1812, he set up a company, found investors, and enlisted his brother-in-law's aid in a venture at Waltham. The war with Britain meant that further travel or purchase of English machinery was impossible at the time, so Lowell reconstructed from memory the power loom he had seen in England. His feat was similar to that of Samuel Slater, who built all the machinery for his plant from memory *except* the loom. The Waltham Manufactory developed the new power loom so that by 1816, the 36″ cotton woven on it was said to be comparable to India cottons. After the War of 1812, England again flooded American markets with imports and tried to discourage new industries, still hoping to make the country a *customer* instead of a *competitor*, and always seeking profits. Nevertheless, the Waltham Manufactory and many others were successful and the company expanded by starting another factory, in 1823, on the Merrimack River, and named the town that grew up around the mill Lowell, after Francis Cabot, founder of the parent company. The Merrimack Company began printing calicoes immediately, and employed engravers brought from England to make their cylinders, and within 15 years Lowell had grown into a large, thriving textile center with hundreds of workers, new homes, and other buildings. Skilled technicians in all branches of the business were brought over from England, and the British superintendant of the works was at one time paid more than the Governor of the State.

Merrimack prints won many awards for excellence, and in "1839 at Boston the committee for the Second Annual Exhibition of the Massachusetts Charitable Mechanic Association reported the Merrimack prints a 'gorgeous product.' The width, durability and beauty of texture, the rich, original designs, the superior execution and the brilliance of coloring are beyond any work of the kind that has before been brought to the notice of the committee."[15]

Fig. 122. Roller-printed cotton in green, pink, and brown made at the Merrimack Mills in Lowell, Mass., about 1845. Courtesy, the Metropolitan Museum of Art, Gift of Mrs. Eli Fordham, 1927

Fig. 123. Roller-printed cotton in a combination of floral ornament and patriotic fervor. The figure on horseback among the scrolls is General Zachary Taylor at the Battle of Palo Alto. Taylor was President from 1849 to 1850. Courtesy, the Metropolitan Museum of Art, Gift of Mrs. Leonard Ralph Ballard, 1936

Fig. 124. Campaign ribbon, white silk, copper-plate printed in black; Harrison was President eight years before Zachary Taylor, and won on the Whig ticket. Courtesy, the Dedham Historical Society, Dedham, Massachusetts

Fig. 125. Printed silk kerchief showing General Zachary Taylor; lithographed by Bauer & Co., Louisville, Ky., probably for the campaign of 1848; black on tan (white originally?). Courtesy of the New York Historical Society, New York City

Many American companies had become sizeable operations by 1870, and the selling agents began to be responsible for the design of prints. Eventually the "textile converter" came into existence — the man who buys the fabric from the mills, chooses the designs, and supervises the printing and sale of the finished product.

The entire industry was soon mechanized and more and better power machinery was built — the early wooden parts had long since been replaced by steel and brass. James Watt's invention of the steam engine in 1782, was eventually adapted to all phases of cotton manufacturing and printing. The picturesque mill wheels stopped turning and became historic American relics.

8. ARCHIBALD HAMILTON ROWAN, ESQR., OF DELAWARE

In 1823, the editor of the *Baltimore Register* reported the receipt of some "American calicoes or chintzes in seven or eight colors, fast and brilliant as any imported, accompanied by specimens of jaconet muslins suitable for gents' neck cloths — spun and woven on the Brandywine. The printed cottons, being made of American cotton, were better than English prints of similar kind which were usually made of the inferior Bengal or Surat cotton. They sold for 25¢ per yard."[9]

This is the first known reference to something from England or the East being inferior to an American product. Other references to a print works "on the Brandywine," and some samples of work in museums done by Archibald Hamilton Rowan, have now been more positively identified by the Henry Francis DuPont Museum in Winterthur, Delaware. In *Antiques* for October, 1968, curator Florence Montgomery reported a new acquisition:

"Winterthur recently discovered and acquired a pattern-book containing over 140 block impressions on paper, many colored with water colors. [It bore a label that says] 'This book of paterns belonged to Archibald Hamilton Rowan, Esqr. He had it in America; it was given to me by his daughter, Miss Rowan.' Rowan was a native of Ireland who had come to America in 1795 when he was 44, and who became a calico printer on the Brandywine River near Wilmington; he died in 1834.

"The Rowan enterprise was doomed from the start. British merchants still controlled American trade. As Rowan and Aldred sought orders for their printed goods they were told that the British would not tolerate competition. 'Riders' or salesmen informed the merchants that accounts would be payable forthwith if *American* printed textiles were discovered along with British goods. Finally, Rowan wrote in his journal, 'being wearied and disgusted I determined to break up the Works.'

Fig. 126. Copper-engraved sample of the work of Archibald Hamilton Rowan. Sewn to the back of the piece is the legend, "Piece of the first Calico printed in America. In the year 1796 Archibald Hamilton Rowan commenced the printing of Calico on the Brandywine. The business was not a success, and he quit it in a little more than a year with a loss of $500.00. His stock was bought by a Wilmington merchant and sent to South America." Owned by the Museum of Art, Rhode Island School of Design, Providence

"What amounted to British monopoly hindered American printers. Despite State and Federal grants and protective tariffs enacted by the United States government for the printers' benefit, English goods continued to find a ready sale in America, and supplied the bulk of the market until about 1850."[76] Rowan is one of the six "first" American calico printers, and is assured of his rather late place on the list because of a copper-engraved sample from his "Works," shown in Fig. 126.

The pieces are obviously copper-engraved, and are evidence that this method *was* employed in America, if only for a year. The legend on the book of samples acquired by Winterthur does not say that the block impressions were *done* by Rowan, even though it is natural to assume this. The book may have been *owned* by him as a pattern-book; this is uncertain.

9. THEOREM PAINTING — ELEGANT PARLOR ART

For many years embroidery has been a favorite domestic art for ladies, and in colonial days and later — especially for young girls — it was a way of exhibiting great skill in subjects varying all the way from the tiniest sprig of flowers on a baby dress to a whole embroidered carpet or bedspread. From about 1800 to 1840, embroidery somehow temporarily went out of favor and a new art became the rage. This was *Theorem Painting*, and since it was largely a matter of using ready-cut stencils, anyone could learn how to do it and for a while almost everyone did. Instruction books, itinerant teachers, and schools that advertised the art appeared on the scene, and all proper young ladies began to paint. Even before 1800, this advertisement appeared,

Boston Gazette, October 19, 1767:

> *"EMBROIDERY SCHOOL . . . also classes in that most ingenious art of Painting on Gauze and Catgut . . ."*[17]

The new domestic art was a way of decorating velvet, linen, silk, paper, and even light-colored wood panels to make original art works to be framed for the parlor walls; it was also used for fire-screens, small handbags and other articles. White cotton velveteen and white satin were the favorite materials used. The technique was simply to paint on oil colors by dabbing with a stiff

Fig. 127. India Muslin printed at Barley Mill on Brandywine by Archibald Hamilton Rowan. Preserved by Mrs. Samuel Hilles and presented to the Historical Society of Delaware by her daughter, Mrs. Charles W. Howland, 1895. Courtesy of that Society

Fig. 128. Painting on white velvet, c. 1815, size 15½″ x 19½″; colors blues and browns (probably faded red) with fine outlines in black. The container is typical of theorem paintings, but this one is more refined and delicate than most and is mostly hand painted and not stenciled. Courtesy, Fairbanks House, Dedham Historical Society, Dedham, Mass.

brush or cloth dauber through a paper stencil which one could cut from a pattern with a small knife or scissors, or which was supplied by the teacher who also had a full-color example to be followed. After various parts of the design had been stenciled, details such as grape tendrils, seeds in cut melons or fruits, veins in leaves, and other lacy parts were painted in freehand with a very small artist's brush.

The subjects were almost always still lifes of fruits, flowers, and leaves in an assortment of fancy bowls, baskets, and vases, with birds and butterflies hovering about. Some venturesome artists painted religious scenes, but these were mostly hand-painted and could not be called true stencil paintings. At about the same time that the ladies were painting their theorems, shop-made furniture and tinware were decorated in a similar but more professional manner.

Fig. 129. Painting on white velvet, c. 1815, size 10½″ x 13½″; mostly blue and brown. Melon, pears, peaches, grapes, seemingly mostly painted, but shapes may have been stenciled first. Theorem painters were inordinately fond of melons. Courtesy, Fairbanks House, Dedham Historical Society, Dedham, Mass.

Fig. 130. Stenciled and painted Masonic apron, c. 1830; 16½″ wide x 17½″ deep, white velvet bound with blue taffeta ribbon; colors: blue, ochre, tan, brown, and black. Courtesy, Fairbanks House, Dedham Historical Society, Dedham, Mass.

Many names were given to the art, but all of them were the same thing; the names somehow convey the whole aspect of the work: Oriental Painting, Poonah Painting, Formula Painting, Velvet Painting, and India Tint-work. The stencils themselves were also called *theorems* and *poonahs*.

By 1835, there were professional stencil-cutters turning out their patterns by the hundreds for theorem painters, and also for lampshade makers, glass decorators, and shippers. Thus, the amateurs were spared the laborious job of cutting their stencils, and the art was surely the ancestor of "numbers painting," which spares the artist the work of creating. Some of the colonial women who made stenciled coverlets may have learned their art in a theorem painting class. Interest in the craft seems to have died suddenly about 1840, and was almost never seen again. Many historical societies own the framed pictures and some of them are quite charming. All of them represent the style of the time, whether they were very skillfully done, or were of the most primitive execution. The style was so much admired that a roller-printed fabric was made, using the same out-of-drawing design as the theorems.

Stenciling of a more stylized kind was practiced on other objects besides coverlets. Fig. 133 shows a stenciled cotton table cover (undoubtedly for "best") in five colors, made with unusual care, with only one corner that didn't come out right.

Fig. 131. Roller-printed glazed cotton (chintz) with a fruit basket resembling the-orem paintings, with added scrolls and leaves. The repeat is 23½″ x 14″. Courtesy, Index of American Design, National Gallery of Art

Fig 132. Velvet bag painted by Lucy Maria (Harrison) Brown, c. 1820 ("In 1968 it is 148 years old."), 8″ wide x 9″ high. Border of pink stars scattered among feathery green branches and leaves; brown basket with pink and yellow roses. White velvet bound with pleated white satin. Courtesy, Fairbanks House, Dedham Historical Society, Dedham, Mass.

Fig. 133. Stenciled cotton table cover, 27½" square, found in New Hampshire. Colors are rose, yellow, green, brown, and blue. Courtesy, Old Sturbridge Village, Sturbridge, Massachusetts

10. AMERICAN INDIANS

The arts of the American Indian are seldom shown or described as real *art*, or even as handcrafts, but are more often known as natural history or ethnic relics. In the fabric arts — or arts in which Indians used other materials such as woven grasses or skins as we use fabrics — we have no intention of discounting American Indian arts. A kinship to arts of other western Indians of Mexico and Central and South America is obvious, but somehow the North American art has come to be evaluated differently.

Central American Indians of a very early date made pottery stamps of both rectangular and cylindrical forms to be painted with dye or color and applied to the skins of their bodies, or possibly to woven clothing and mats. Such designs almost certainly designated a tribal rank or skill and were the first badges of authority and status. They represent, in the view of many, the first "printed" clothing of all times.

American Indians had a highly developed sense of design and created some very complex geometrical patterns. Their dyeing and weaving skills were considerable, and their woven fabrics, made on the simplest of two-dimensional tapestry looms, were well done. Many tribes knew how to paint on animal skins and on cloth; the Hopis and the Pueblos were highly skilled artists.[35]

The Plains Indians painted on skins using earth colors and their tool often was a thin, spongy piece of buffalo-knee bone.[18] Their paintings were "picture writing" on animal skin robes and rawhide and were often representative of battle and hunting scenes and historical records.[2] Before 1800, dye-stuffs of European origin seem to have been used for painting on skins and cinnabar (red mercuric sulphide) was a favorite object of barter of the fur trader who did business with the Indians. Other colored powders and pastes were sold to the Indians, and except for powdered earth colors and berry juices, Indian pigments were obtained from European traders. Drawing was often done by incising soft, tanned leather with a sharp bone or pointed wooden stick, then the colors were applied with roughened sticks or bones.[89]

In Quebec, the Algonkian Indians wove sturdy splint baskets of wide strips of oak and other woods and decorated them by printing with carved turnip stamps dipped in fruit juices and vegetable colors. The Mohegan tribe in Connecticut made almost the same kind of printed baskets. Indians of Oklahoma and South Dakota used painted muslin (bought from white-man traders) as a backdrop decoration for ceremonies and for tent-hangings for chiefs — mostly of hunting scenes and tribal battles. These are charmingly primitive and sometimes are reminiscent of prehistoric cave paintings in southern Europe.

Delaware Indians in Oklahoma devised a most ingenious way of making "stamps" serving as printing blocks to decorate baskets by rolling up strips of

Fig. 134. Painting on tanned buckskin; Sioux Indians stealing horses. Courtesy, the Smithsonian Institution

Fig. 135. Sioux Indians' panoramic painting on muslin of Indians stealing horses and engaged in running battle. Courtesy, the Smithsonian Institution

thick deerskin in various doubling-back patterns, tying the roll tightly with rawhide strips, and printing with the end (edges of the skin) of the roll; they also printed from inked rope knots of different kinds. Many tribes painted dance dresses for important ceremonial occasions and robes for chiefs and others with decorative patterns. The Tlingit tribes of Alaska had a unique style of decoration that was powerfully stylized and bore a relation to the arts of the South Seas. They wove capes, skirts, and hats out of pieces of finely split and twisted cedar bark that looked almost like straw, and on the finished woven garments they painted handsome, simple decorations.

Any history of American fabrics that ignores the American Indian is overlooking a very ingenious and skillful contribution to the art of fabric decoration, even though some of the work is decidedly primitive, and notwithstanding the fact that the Red Man may be best known for his handsome and colorful weaving.

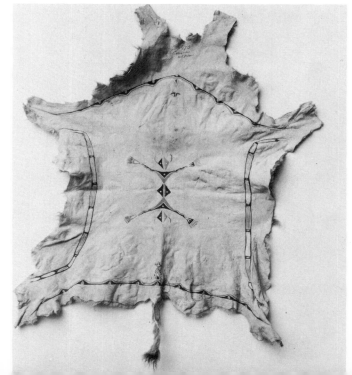

Fig. 136. Comanche Indian Ghost Dance "Shirt" of incised and painted doeskin. Courtesy, the Smithsonian Institution

11. THE CRANSTON PRINT WORKS

One of the few — possibly the only one — of the early print works that continues in business today under almost the same name is the Cranston Print Works of Rhode Island. Not one early printing block or sample book seems to remain, but the company history is recorded in the story of the Sprague family — one of the most distinguished in the State's history. The Spragues served their government well over the generations but they were also dogged by a variety of unusual experiences that have served as subjects of at least one novel and of several histories. The stages of development of the Cranston Mills tells us one complete story of a fabric manufacturing and printing enterprise from the early 17th century to today, so it is worth knowing.

The first William Sprague came to Cranston from England about 1620, settled his family there and began farming. He started a sawmill and a gristmill, as many early landowners did — at first to meet his own needs, then as a business — and called it Cranston Mills. This enterprise in a rural setting on the Pocasset River grew to be one of the wealthiest and probably the first of the American industrial empires when it was converted or expanded to cotton mills and print works. The several direct descendants and one nephew of the original Sprague continued in the business until 1873, when the fortunes of the country declined and the company failed with one of the most resounding crashes heard in the New World. Even so, the reputation of its products was such that it was said, ". . perhaps no concern in the country ever shared more the respect and confidence of the people."[31] Not long after the failure the company was reorganized, and, building on its old record, rose again to eminence so that it now has a venerable history of almost 350 years (in 1969), counting from the year the first William Sprague settled in New England.

Jonathan Sprague, of the second generation, continued in his father's enterprises and was the first to appear in public life when he served as Speaker of the Rhode Island General Assembly in 1703.

William Sprague II (1773-1836) was extremely energetic in enlarging the family business interests and continued to build more mills. In 1808, he converted a gristmill into a small factory to card and spin cotton yarns, using crude wooden machinery — and this was the beginning of the business that became an empire. At that time cotton was imported and was only beginning to come from the South by merchant vessels and barges. For a number of years the factory did only carding and spinning, and the thread was loaned out to farm wives to be woven into cloth on their home looms and returned to the mill to be finished. Loops were sewn into the selvage of the lengths of cloth and these were used to stake down the fabrics on the ground in fields where they were alternately wetted down with sprinkling cans, then left to

Fig. 137. Chintz, 1834, similar to the first prints from the Cranston Mills. This piece was part of a "wedding set-out" for a family in Bergen, N. Y., and was used as four-poster bed curtains and window curtains. Source unknown — possibly American or English. Courtesy, Index of American Design, National Gallery of Art

bleach in the sun. No other bleaching agents were available then, although chlorine had been discovered in England in 1774.

In 1821, Sprague purchased half the water power at Natick Falls, R.I., and built a 42-loom cotton mill for new power-operated machines, and for carding and spinning. Machinery for these operations had been introduced into America from England around 1800, but it was not improved much, or built in quantity for a number of years. Within 15 years, the Spragues owned five more mills in various locations — always seeking the water so necessary to their operations. In 1824, the original mill at Cranston became a bleaching, dyeing, and printing factory, making the design known as "indigo blues." This gives Sprague (along with the five others) the name "First Calico Printer in America." The early printing must have been done from wooden blocks, and, in 1837, the first power-printing machine with rollers was "tried out" by millworker James Doran. Before long there were 30 roller-printing machines in use and the plant could turn out thousands of prints of about 40 yards in one week.

William II had five children and was a prosperous farmer, cattleman, and lumberman in addition to being the administrator of his extensive mills and print works. His wealth had become considerable, but records show that not all of this rich man's offspring promised to continue as industrious as their fore-bears. One of his sons "loved his fiddle and pleasant company better than manu-facturing cotton or printing calico or anything concerned therewith."[37] In spite of his many occupations, Sprague became interested in politics and devel-oped strong anti-Masonic sentiments; he ran unsuccessfully for Governor on that ticket in 1832. At the age of 64 he died violently, by choking on a bone caught in his throat.

By the year 1836, there were many successful print works in addition to the Sprague mills. In Rhode Island there were also the works of Philip Allen in Providence and Crawford Allen in Pawtucket; in Massachusetts there were works at Lowell, Lynn, Taunton, Fall River, and North Adams. There was a factory at Dover, N.H., two at Cheshire, two or three in New Jersey, 10 or 12 in Pennsylvania, and a few in Baltimore. The total quantity of calicoes printed in that year was 120,000,000 yards.[31] It is hard to believe, but appar-ently true, that almost no records and even fewer examples remain to us of the work of all these printing establishments.

The next William Sprague's biography is less extensively recorded than the others, but the pattern of violence appears again. He is said to have in-creased the family holdings considerably, and, in 1843, was murdered while walking alone at night — supposedly because he had influenced the town coun-cil against granting a license to sell liquor near his factory. The murderer was caught, tried, convicted, and executed, but sentiment ran high because many felt that the identity of the murderer had not been proven. As a result of the trial, the State of Rhode Island was one of the first to abolish capital punish-ment.

His son, the next William, distinguished himself in several high positions in the State and also was president of two banks and a railroad company. He served in the General Assembly, in the Federal House of Representatives, was Governor, and a Federal Senator. At his death, in 1856, the company had nine mills in Rhode Island and Connecticut capable of an output of 1,400,000 yards of printed calico and 800,000 yards of plain cloth per week, and their holdings were said to be the largest in the world.[31]

A son, another William, assumed control of the Sprague properties at the age of 26. He was elected Governor of the State twice, fought at the Battle of Bull Run in the Civil War, and was later elected a Federal Senator — following his distinguished father's footsteps very closely. In 1863, his mar-riage to the beautiful Kate Chase, daughter of the Republican leader and Supreme Court Justice, Salmon P. Chase, was the social event of the year on the national scene, but it was a tempestuous and ill-fated union and ended in

Fig. 138. Roller-printed cotton, American, c. 1851, in four colors. Courtesy, the Philadelphia Museum of Art

a sensational divorce case 20 years later, after some domestic gunplay. In 1890, their son committed suicide; the pattern of family violence seemed relentless.

The Civil War (1861) marked the almost imperceptible beginning of the decline of the great Sprague fortunes. But the dimensions of its holdings were the result of many lifetimes of achievement; the manufacturing interests were scattered all over New England and represented an immense outlay of capital. There was a saying, "In Rhody, where there's smoke, there's a Sprague Mill" (*Cranston Herald*, June 11, 1953). Some reports compare the Sprague empire to a feudal state, and it did in many ways represent a completely self-sustaining community in Cranston. Railroad tracks of the family-owned company were laid throughout the buildings; stores, a meat market, an icehouse, and a vegetable farm were set up for the needs of the employees, numbering about 1200. A private fire department protected them and a private gas line provided fuel in homes built for families, and in "tenements" for single workers. The "works" were said to be the most extensive in New England.[31] At first the war seemed to have little effect on operations; French-Canadians were imported to take the place of men going to war. The Spragues seemed to be firmly in command, with controlling interests in five banks, their own steamboats to transport cotton, and their agents in all the principal cities in the East.

Fig. 139. Children's kerchief, copper-plate printed on cotton in Boston — prayers and poems titled "Sunday Lesson No. 1." These were printed in black or one color on job-printing presses in another style typical of the same period as the later fabrics of Cranston by the yard from roller presses. Courtesy of the Philadelphia Museum of Art

Fig. 140. Cotton kerchief or broadside, c. 1860, size 17″ x 23½″, probably partly engraved with red, dark blue, light blue, and yellow added by block. It was a form of advertisement or Christmas souvenir of the "Oriental Print Works" as per the label on the sled under Santa Claus' arm. From the collection of Mrs. Sherman P. Haight, N. Y. C.

Their interests proved, in the end, to be too extensive. There was a financial panic in 1837, and litigation involving $20,000,000 wiped out the company. The failure was considered to be the greatest financial disaster ever to hit the State. The last William Sprague remarried in 1883, and retired to Canonchet — his estate at Narragansett Pier — by then a symbol of his former status. Misfortune pursued him and the huge house burned completely; he finally moved to Paris where he died in 1915.

In 1888, the Cranston Print Works — most of whose properties were still in good condition — were acquired and refinanced by B. B. and R. Knight, well-known cotton manufacturers in Rhode Island. The company continued to expand and finally came to specialize in color printing of fine fabrics, and they are still known for their dependable quality as the Cranston Print Works Company.

Up until 1920, the Cranston Company had preserved all its order-books, swatch-books, and records and these had been stored in an attic during several changes of management. Fire insurance inspectors finally ordered the "papers" cleared out, and everything was burned. The present company has not been able to locate any blocks, swatch-books, samples, or even any old photographs of the mills.

The Cranston story has more color and scope than most, and is tied by personal connections to American history, but it followed the pattern of calico printing in early days. First, hand-printing operations were carried on by artisans who had pursued the trade, mostly in England. As cotton became more plentiful, carding, spinning, and weaving increased and almost all cotton mills eventually added bleaching, dyeing, and printing operations. Few of the early works were able to survive the fortunes of a developing nation through its economic ups and downs. Few produced anything that is now thought to be of great aesthetic or stylistic importance; but their usefulness was great in their times, and they are now simply a part of our history.

As historians point out, the early American settlers had a "quality of energy, enterprise, daring, and aspiration"[7] that was inherited or acquired by generation after generation. Both men and women had an opportunity never before known in the world to freely shape their own lives, and they seized it eagerly. The story is not likely to have happened anywhere else.

12. ENGLISH INFLUENCE ON EARLY AMERICAN ROLLER-PRINTED DESIGNS

The Peel Works

Robert Peel of Bury, Lancashire, one of Britain's most successful printers (already mentioned in Section II), turned out hundreds of the small-patterned, copper-roller printed fabrics that served as examples for the American factories which began to operate around 1805. During the period of transition from hand-blocked prints to copper-roller printing, two Englishmen, Charles Taylor and Thomas Walker, invented a method of printing cotton and linen by means of wooden rollers about 1770, but the method never became practical and almost none of these rollers can be found now.[92]

The prints from Bury, including the simple block prints, were not only copied in America but colonial women bought yards and yards of them to make into cotton dresses. Since the source of the prints was well known, about 1775, "...with the disfavor into which English manufactures fell at the time of the Revolution, these Peel prints were eschewed also. Boston citizens forbade their wives to use them and they were probably among the English-printed gowns that were burned by patriotic women who refused to wear any article on which a tax was paid to Britain."[37] So tea was not the only thing that disappeared in Boston!

 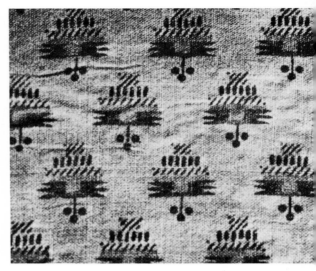

Fig. 142. Right: Geometric, two-color block print from the Peel Works, Lancashire. Same source as Fig. 141

The Peel and Yates works at Bury and Peel's of Church (a son) are credited with several inventions, some very short-lived and some important ones that formed a part of textile-printing history — the same as some inventions from Jouy in France. James Burton, one of Peel's engineers, invented a "mule" machine, in 1805, which combined engraved copper rollers with carved wooden rollers, thus printing by intaglio and relief methods on the same fabric. This process never came to be used universally. Peel is supposed to have been the first to use (in 1802) the process of resist printing called "neutral work," which consisted of printing various mordants on the parts of the cloth to be dyed, and a paste or resist wax on the parts that were to remain white. This became a common process in the fabric-printing industry. To the hardworking 19th century dye-master who worked out the process it may have seemed very original, unless he, too, had studied fabric history and knew that the Egyptians and East Indians used a very similar procedure.

There is a picturesque story of how the first Robert Peel acquired his nickname from one of his designs. His daughter Nancy was working in the kitchen and was struck by the beauty of a freshly-picked parsley sprig and asked her father if it might be imitated as a print on cloth. Then and there, father drew the sprig's outline on a wooden block and cut the design.

"Nancy's Pattern" caught on immediately and was done in many variations and was a favorite for so long that the printer became known as "Parsley Peel."[92] (See Fig. 143) One version of the parsley pattern shown here is from the swatch in the Peel and Yates sample book owned by the Metropolitan Museum of Art in New York. In 1850, someone wrote a descriptive note next to this small swatch which says, "This Pattern of a Leaf is from the same disien of a plain Leaf — like this in outline said to be the first Pattern tried by Sir Robert Peel's father. Patterns or styles did not then [70 years earlier] change so quickly as now: and this Leaf plain or combined was in use for a long time." Inside the front cover of the swatch-book, written in a fine hand is this inscription:

> "His High Mightiness, King Cotton — Potentate of Printing — Prince of Patchwork — Duke de Laine — Marquis of Muslin — Lord of Lawn — Baron Barege Balzaine — and Count of Calico and Cambric."

The poetic humor might have come from the pen of Edward Lear, but it also shows a subtle respect for the cotton-printing profession.

Fig. 143. Parsley leaf pattern, block print from the Peel Works, Lancashire. From *Painted and Printed Fabrics*, by Clouzot and Morris, Metropolitan Museum of Art, 1927

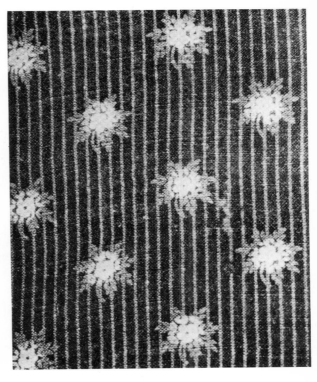

Fig. 144. Right: Small sprigged pattern block print from the Peel Works, Lancashire. From *Painted and Printed Fabrics*, by Clouzot and Morris, Metropolitan Museum of Art, 1927

There were three generations of Peels, and the grandson of the original Robert became *Sir* Robert, who also prospered in the business and became known in British government. He was much concerned over the fact that British coypright laws were ineffective as protection for original designs, and he suggested the formation of a Parliamentary committee to study the statutes. A "Bill of 1840" was introduced in the House of Commons protesting the fact that designs covered by a copyright of only three months (then in effect) could be copied, reproduced, and put on the market before the originator had even begun to recover his production costs; a 12-month copyright period was asked. During the hearing it was said that "in the U.S. no law of copyright exists";[51] American printers had reason to be interested in the British decision. Some time later copyrights were extended in England.

From 1820 to 1830, the "foreign trade" (in England) was from two to three times the volume of "home trade." The petitioners included manufacturers of Ireland and Scotland as well as of England, and the wording of part of their petition gives an idea of their view of the market for British prints: "The natural progress of civilization, refinement and intercourse, is to assimilate the wants and tastes of different and distant countries — thus in articles of dress there is at this day [1840] not much difference between London, Paris, Vienna, and New York; and the printed muslins, challis, cambrics, and other fabrics manufactured by your Petitioners for the first of these cities, are well-suited to the last."[51]

In America, designs were copied from anything and everything — and sometimes with dizzying speed and efficiency. "It seems that some patterned *Mousselaine de laine* arrived from France and was discovered in the New York market by an agent of a Rhode Island printing establishment. The imported fabric was selling at 14¢ a yard by the case. Obtaining a piece of the goods, he sent it to Rhode Island, where the pattern was immediately engraved on a copper cylinder and in sixteen days the American copy was placed on sale in New York at 10¢ a yard. This was in about 1840."[14] This record appeared originally in Edward Field's *History of the Providence Plantations* and happened in exactly the same year that Sir Robert Peel and his friends were being heard before Parliament. American copyright laws were slow in coming and even today are difficult to enforce; modern "design pirates" work in much the same way as they did in the 19th century.

The prints involved in the copyright discussions were mainly of two popular kinds — small "sprigged" patterns that had been used for years, ever since the first hand-blocked dress muslins were made at Jouy in 1760, and another new style called "Excentrics." These were small, complicated geometric designs and the story of their origin is interesting and amusing, since it involves two *accidents*, both of which occurred because of the nature of roller-engraving and printing.

Fig. 145. "Lane's Net," the original British Excentric roller-print design, which supposedly gave rise to the others; this was the most-copied of the group. From the book *A Treatise on the Copyright of Designs for Printed Fabrics*, by J. Emerson Tennent, London, 1841

Fig. 146. *Right:* "Diorama," the British Excentric designed by a printing machine that went wrong. From the same source as Fig. 145

The three most popular Excentrics were of English origin and all were copied in America; the names were the same for many variations: *Lane's Net,* Fig. 145; *Diorama,* Fig. 146, and *Hoyle's Wave,* in two versions, Figs. 147 and 148. It appears that Lane's Net was the original, carefully engraved design of the geometrics, and when a firm in Foxhillbank — Messrs. Simpson & Co. — was printing cloth from a roller bearing this design, "a series of creases occurred in the cloth under the inked roller and the accident "at no cost whatever" for the designing produced a number of yards of the mistake in which the original parallel stripe was repeated at an angle and produced a new and unexpected effect."[51] This was so well liked that it, in turn, was engraved as a new design and became known as the "Diorama" and was produced in several variations. It "was a favorite with the public — a simple figure upon a pattern for neck cloths [ties] and was supposed to have brought the manufacturer a profit of three hundred pounds."[51]

Another famous design was called "Hoyle's Wave" — probably because it may have originated at Thomas Hoyle and Sons, well-known British printers. It was supposed to have been a variation produced by means of something called "Perkins' eccentric lathe," which engraved facsimiles of bas reliefs on copper rollers, and was thought to have been another "mistake" meant to come out as Lane's Net. "It is even possible it may have been as accidentally fallen upon as the chance which threw out the 'Diorama.'"[51]

In 1840, when the Excentrics were popular, one English company produced as many as 12,000,000 yards of geometric prints on cotton in various designs (mostly in one color) in one year, and these were sold in 28-yard "pieces," or bolts.

It is sometimes impossible to substantiate the fact that a fabric made by an American printer is of specific European design origin. In the case of Lane's Net our Fig. 145 is taken from the British book published in 1841, and the three center swatches in Fig. 174 are taken from an 1887 sample-book of the Arnold Print Works in North Adams, Massachusetts.

Almost all of the dress fabrics used by American women from the early 1800's to 1880 were these one-color (sometimes two), small-patterned cotton prints; they were used for children's clothes and for women's everyday dresses. They were the patterns that gave most of us our mental picture of the word "calico" today. Party dresses, mourning clothes, ball gowns, and wedding dresses were made of much more elegant fabrics, such as French silks, taffetas, moires, brocades, and velvets. Of all these, only velvet was ever printed; the others, if patterned, were woven designs.

American printers began producing the small-patterned dress cottons as soon as roller printing was introduced. Cottons with larger patterns used for draperies and furniture continued to be imported from England for some time, and American printers could not compete with English chintzes.

In 1860, the magazine *American Woman's Home* had an article by Catherine Beecher and Harriet Beecher Stowe wherein the ladies suggested a practical budget for decorating a living room:

"Wallpaper and border	$5.50
Thirty yards of matting	15.00
Center table and cloth	15.00
Muslin for three windows	6.75
30 yds. green English chintz	7.50
6 chairs @ $2	12.00

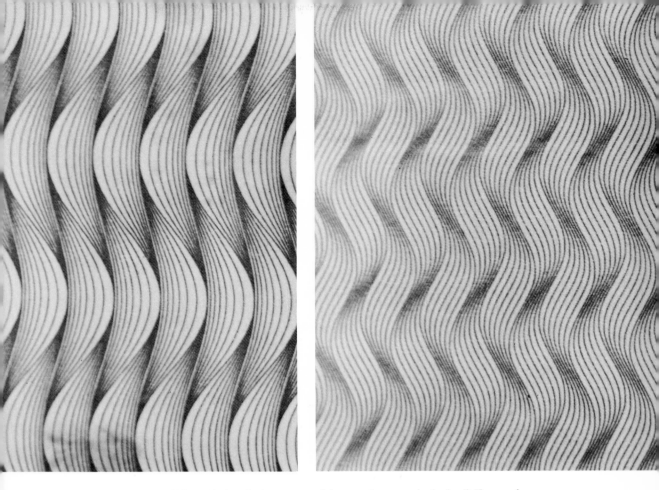

Fig. 147. "Hoyle's Wave," the design created by an "eccentric lathe." From the same source as Fig. 145

Fig. 148. *Right:* Another version of the pattern "Hoyle's Wave." From the same source as Fig. 145

"List of 4 selected 'chromos'
   for the walls entitled:
'The Little Scrap-book Maker'   7.50
'Barefoot Boy'   5.00
'Blue Fringed Gentians'   6.00
'Sunset in Yosemite Valley'   12.00."[39]

So, for $92.25 the whole room was furnished, including imported chintz at 25¢ a yard — for about the cost of one chair today!

Fig. 149. Two silk kerchiefs, 32½″ x 35″, c. 1825, block printed (possibly later machine printed) in red and yellow. Courtesy, Bucks County Historical Society, Doylestown, Pennsylvania

SPORTS COSTUME · 1868

Fig. 150. Kit found in Pennsylvania, c. 1860, with all the necessary supplies and instructions for stamping embroidery or braid patterns; probably distributed for home use. Courtesy, *Antiques* magazine. Below: *left*, Blocks in all sizes and shapes, and *right*, Pad, brush, bottle for gum and box of powdered color from kit shown in Fig. 150

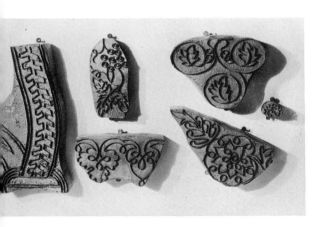

From the Revolution to 1900 • 215

13. PAINTED WINDOW SHADES

The word "Victorian," when used to describe a decorative style, probably conjures up a surprisingly consistent picture in the mind of almost everyone. But one of the *most* Victorian interior accessories of all is perhaps the least familiar: American painted and printed window shades. No home with any claim to elegance would have been without them from 1830 to 1860, and they fulfilled a different purpose — or more purposes — than our room-darkening shades. They were often the sole "window treatment" of parlors and dining rooms and although they did serve to keep out sun and provide privacy, they were primarily decorative — sometimes dramatically so — and were made to be admired from outside, inside, or both. These shades were hung at the top of the window and operated on rollers, but not by the springs that flip up a window shade today. The 3″ wooden rollers had a grooved wheel at one end and a cord went over the wheel and ran through a small pulley fastened to the window frame; the shade was raised or lowered by the cord hanging down at one side, rather like Venetian blinds.

Window shade factories were started about 1830 in the East and within 10 years the successful industry spread to the Middle West where new homes were being built at a great rate in growing industrial towns. A major concern of the manufacturers was the source of cotton cloth suitably made and economically priced. Imported English shade cloth cost 15¢ a yard in 1848; some factories started their own bleach-works and were able to bring the cost down to about 10¢ a yard by buying "gray goods" as it came from the mills. Various processes of sizing or oiling were necessary before colors could be block printed, stenciled or painted on; the latter process was called *slap-dashing*. The earliest shades were printed from blocks, then painted by hand in colors over a glue sizing. Stenciled colors were also used, but the most popular ones were scenic shades hand-painted in a size of about 2′ x 5′. Some of the subjects were: "Battle of Bunker Hill," "Grecian Fount," "Washington and Mount Vernon," "Jefferson and Monticello," and a whole series called "Shepherds and Moonlight." About 1850, the Sawyer, Ashton & Company's Great Western Oil Cloth and Window Shade Manufactory of Cincinnati advertised:

> *"We now have a complete assortment of these tasteful and neat shades for parlors, chambers, etc. both in plain borders and with center pieces. In these goods we keep none but the best, made on the finest cambric, and of pure gold leaf. Painted shades are particularly recommended — of every description, comprising Fancy Borders, Landscapes, Gothics and IMITATION Venetians suitable for halls, dining-rooms, chambers, etc."*[66]

Fig. 151. A typical hand-painted Venetian transparent shade to be hung facing the street. It was made by the Sawyer, Ashton & Co.'s Great Western Oil Cloth & Window Shade Manufactory of Cincinnati, Ohio, which was in business from 1849 to 1856. It was painted on fine muslin, double-sized, and smoothed with pumice. The outlines were copied, traced, stenciled or pounced on, then painted. Skies were sometimes put in with a sponge and paints were mixed with Japan gold size so they would dry fast and not run.[66] This was called "slap-dashing" and probably describes quite well the scene where many identical shades could be turned out in one day to sell for less than $2.00. Courtesy, *Antiques* magazine

Fig. 152. This is a border "transparency" painted in an obviously sketchy and primitive technique and must have been the 75¢ variety sold by the same Cincinnati factory where the Venetian scene was also done, about 1850. Courtesy, *Antiques* magazine

Fig. 153. Stenciled cotton cloth used as window shade; found in New Hampshire, c. 1780. The urns and vases are yellow, the flowers are red and rose, and the foliage green. Courtesy, Old Sturbridge Village, Sturbridge, Massachusetts

The style called "Gothic" was extremely popular for many years and was simply the shape of a Gothic Window painted on the panel, and could be ordered with or without landscape. These and the scenic paintings were transparent and were hung with the painted side toward the street to be admired by passers-by. The light came through the colors in changing intensity, so the scene could be admired from inside, too. On a rainy day, the painted landscape must have been as dreary as the outdoors! These masterpieces of interior decoration could be enjoyed by anyone who could afford the cost of from 75¢ to $2.00 each.

Other shades were painted with opaque colors and gold leaf in all sorts of borders, and sometimes in imitation drapery treatments with swags, fringe, and tie-backs; these were to be seen only from inside the room.

Godey's Lady's Book finally found the flamboyant shades a bit too much and advised readers that "sprawling bouquets or flower baskets in gaudy colors are not considered *in taste*."[66]

The commercially-made window shades were for urban homes, and in rural areas the women who decorated their own coverlets and table covers with hand-stenciling, also did window shades. One is shown in Fig. 153.

By the 1860's, the vogue was out of favor, and although the shades spanned 30 years of Queen Victoria's style-setting reign, and were used by Americans during the administrations of eight presidents from Andrew Jackson to Abraham Lincoln, even the remnants have almost disappeared.

14. A TURBULENT FIFTY YEARS, 1850-1900

Historians Charles and Mary Beard describe the period from 1850 to 1900: "The last half of the nineteenth century was crowded with events that shook from center to circumference the economic system handed down by Andrew Jackson. The chief events were a civil war, and the abolition of slavery, an upheaval in the race and class relations of the South, occupation of the great West, disappearance of free land, growth of private corporations, expansion of industry and transportation, creation of a money aristocracy and the growth of labor unions.

"This age was also characterized by panics and depressions, strikes, unemployment, poverty, violence and property destruction."[7]

In this period of economic upheaval, industrial growth continued with its own ups and downs. Cotton mills and printing establishments grew, prospered, and failed, and there were so many in operation that few of the historians of manufacturing carry their reports beyond 1850. The field had become too vast for a chronicle like the earlier ones. The picture had grown widely varied — the East and New England were no longer the only scene in the picture. The South and Midwest became the new centers of some manufactures, though the East remained the site of most fabric industries, as it still is in the 20th century. A brief listing of some of the events of this period will remind us of the turbulence we may have forgotten.

1849   The gold rush to the West took 80,000 new citizens to California
1850   Nearly a million immigrants came to America from Ireland alone
1851   Cotton sold for 9¢ a pound (in 1820 it was 16¢) and the price of a slave field hand in Charleston was $1000

OPPOSITE PAGE

ig. 154. Machine print, c. 1875; political caricature surrounded by floral wreath. The subject is the Federal Navy pursuing the corsair Alabama on the Union Merry-go-round, while the European countries look on. The Alabama, a confederate blockade-runner, fitted out by the British, was sunk in the English channel by the Union vessel Kearsage, in 1864. Courtesy, the Index of American Design, National Gallery of Art

219

Fig. 155. An unusual 19th century print that combines roller printing with wood blocks. The entire background is printed with mill work of tiny, sprigged flowers. The main design was probably printed with an engraved cylinder over the mill-work background. The colors: blue, pink, rose, and yellow were added over the roller printing by wood blocks. Other similar pieces have been found over-printed with only two colors; others with a different mill-work background and the same over-design. One repeat is 13″ long x 25″ wide. It is possible that the engraved copper rollers were sold to several printers to over-print as they wished. Courtesy, Index of American Design, National Gallery of Art

1852   Harriet Beecher Stowe's book, *Uncle Tom's Cabin,* was published

1860-1   Eleven southern States seceded from the Union and created the Confederacy

1861   Civil War (to 1865)

1873   Financial panic and depression — the South was bankrupt

1893   Another financial crisis

1898   The Spanish-American War

In the face of a recital of these facts, we can wonder at the fact that business went on at all, but it did, and made almost complete the industrialization of America. Mechanical marvels were the only wonders of the period, and America has never outgrown the effects of the cult of that worship.

In the area of fabric printing, the times were undistinguished as to design, aesthetics, and even technical innovation. Prints rolled off the presses faster, in more colors, and with greater perfection than ever before. The technical improvement of roller printing and the repetition of small-patterned designs seemed almost entirely controlled by the method of manufacture.

The only prints that may be of interest are the few chintzes or commemorative prints that celebrated political events, which give us the tenor of the times. But the story has by now lost interest, and the fabrics have lost their one intrinsic quality — the decorative character of a printed textile.

About 1860, the English fabric printer, William Morris (1834-1896), began to exert an influence on British design and also on American fabrics and wallpapers. He created a new vogue for fine hand printing and created fabrics and wallpapers that became world famous.[36] Morris was trained as an architect but he was also a painter, designer, essayist, illustrator, typographer, woodengraver, dyer, weaver, printer, and paper-maker. His decorative designs were influenced by the Gothic revival, his love of medievalism, and his protest against commercialism. He is credited with changing the tastes of his countrymen; his stamp was put on the best of Victorian ornamental design and his influence was felt everywhere in America. There can be little question that Morris' disciples were many and that he provided the ideas that were the forerunners of "functional modern" design. It was high time for a good influence.

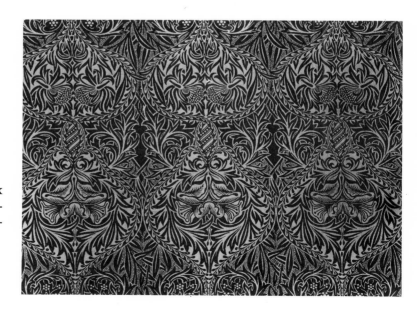

Fig. 156. Two-color wood block print by William Morris. Courtesy, Victoria and Albert Museum, London

Fig. 157. A page of prints from wood blocks, c. 1800, owned by Rolland L. Boutwell used for home printing. May have been used to print on wallpaper or "box" papers; they are too bold and crude to be supposed to have been calico printing blocks. A true folk art collection. Courtesy, *Antiques* magazine

Fig. 158. *Right:* A print in two colors "put together" with some of the blocks in the Boutwell collection. Courtesy, *Antiques* magazine

Fig. 159. Calico printing bloc[k] possibly 18th century, used b[y] Jabez Grover of Foxboro, Mass[a] chusetts, and wax rubbing fro[m] it by the author. Courtesy, De[d] ham Historical Society, Dedha[m] Massachusetts

15. FOLK ART — ITS LIFE AND DEATH

From early colonial days up the time of the Civil War practically all American art, both the so-called "professional" and the "provincial" home arts and handcrafts, had a logical place in the life of the country. The "primitive" portraits and the wood carvings, toys, block-printed and stenciled coverlets, stenciled walls and floors, hand-forged iron pieces, and weaving were what we now call folk art, because it was the expression of the common people, made by them, and intended for their use and enjoyment. It was not the expression of professional artists made for a small, cultured class and had little to do with fashionable English or French art of the period. American folk art came out of a craft tradition, but sometimes had the personal quality of the rare craftsman who was also an artist.[11] From about the middle of the 19th century a change began to come about that marked the beginning of the end of folk art. The War between the States was caused by, and also brought about, economic and social changes that marked the start of industrialism. Factories sprang up all over the East, and began to move westward. Cotton factories were among the first to draw men and women away from the farms and home industries. Machinery, for which Americans seem to have a peculiar genius, was replacing the hand craftsman. No block printer could continue to make a living at his craft once copper-printing rollers were whirling out prints by the bolt. People soon *preferred* the more precise machine prints.

"By 1865 the United States had turned the corner from a rural to an urban civilization. Machine industry was enthroned. By the last quarter of the century, the craft tradition was dying, not only in America, but everywhere in the Western World. A few of the old craftsmen remained here and there, but their production was negligible and their creative efforts met with little response from the public whose taste by then had been trained to accept only the machine-made."[11]

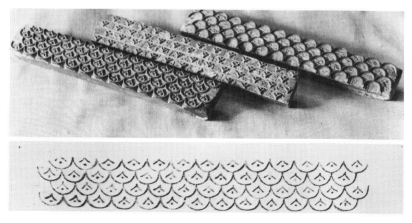

Fig. 160. Three calico printing blocks used by Jabez Grover of Foxboro, Massachusetts. Two of the blocks produce the identical pattern, when combined, as the third. Below: wax rubbing by the author from the lower "combination" block. Courtesy, Dedham Historical Society, Dedham, Massachusetts

16. INDUSTRIALISM —
Nourishment for a New Set of Tastes

In 1872, Charles L. Eastlake wrote a small book called *Hints on Household Tastes* and it became the brides' and housewives' handbook. He called his decorating style "sincere," and it was in fact a bouquet of fancy wallpaper, flowered chintz, Brussels carpets, factory-made furniture, Currier and Ives prints, John Rogers' plaster sculpture, and wax flowers under glass. Architecture at the time was in the process of changing from A. J. Downing's Gothic cottages to a sort of squared-off Queen Anne style.

Perfectly duplicated machine-made items quickly became desirable and ideal, and the conviction soon became ingrained in Americans that if you could make it more quickly and better by machinery, then there was no other reasonable way to do it. The impact of "industrial art" objects was felt in every American home. The Centennial Exposition of 1876 at Philadelphia was the grand show of the triumph of industrial production. Taking a broad point of view, there was also an Art Building where paintings and sculpture were shown and this aroused new interest in the fine arts — such as they were at the time. Possibly this even marked the start of a schism between art and industry that has proved to be very long-lived. The U.S. Government Building covered seven acres and its display of machinery was "the finest ever made, and occupied 480,000 square feet," according to the *Encyclopaedia Britannica* of 1911.

Fig. 161. Kerchief printed in black and blue on cotton, Philadelphia, 1876. Center illustration copper plate printed in black, border added by block (?) in blue. Courtesy, Philadelphia Museum of Art

The Fair attracted over 9,000,000 visitors and they found much to wonder at and admire. Critics and reviewers of 1876 would have been outraged by a contemporary opinion by Russell Lynes, who says in his book, *The Tastemakers*: "Critics today look back upon the Centennial as an architectural and artistic calamity that produced not a single new idea, but was rather, the epitome of the accumulated bad taste of the era that..[we now call] the Gilded Age, the Tragic Era and the Dreadful Decade. It was all a show of techniques, of rich materials, of virtuosity...with no intellectual substance."[39] To each era, its critics!

Fig. 162. American roller-printed glazed chintz, c. 1850; late Western variation of Indian chintz, printed in madder style; repeat of the design is 13½″ long by 23″ wide — colors yellow, red, brown, lavender, and russet. Courtesy, Index of American Design, National Gallery of Art

Fig. 163. Bolt label from the Arnold Print Works, North Adams, Massachusetts. From the collection of The Museum of Art, Rhode Island School of Design, Providence

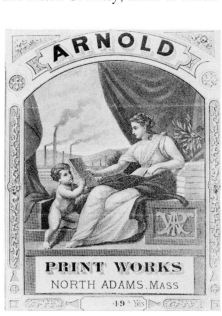

17. THE ARNOLD PRINT WORKS

One of the largest 19th century New England printing establishments was the Arnold Print Works of North Adams, Massachusetts. It is one of the few that has left many well-preserved sample books so that we can see exactly the sort of things an extensive cotton-printing business produced at the time. The company was begun about 1860 by three brothers — Harvey, Oliver and John F. Arnold — who had come to Massachusetts from Natick, Rhode Island. This was about the time of the Civil War, when the mills of the huge Cranston Print Works in Rhode Island were at their height.

The business was at first a cotton manufactory, and, in 1870, the company had about 100 employees and four cotton mills — two in North Adams on the Hoosic River and one each at North Pownal and Williamstown. The main buildings were destroyed by fire in 1872, but were reconstructed with "the latest, improved machinery" in 1874. The first calico was printed in 1883, at which time the Arnolds announced that they had a new industry called the "Blue Dip" — a pronouncement that appears in one form or another at most printing establishments. Their printing machines soon turned out 20,000 "pieces" of about 28 yards each of printed cloth per week, and employed 500 hands in the printing and dyeing establishment alone.

By 1891, the company had 2,970 employees and an annual payroll of $864,000; the total cloth output per year was 100,000,000 yards. The machinery was operated largely by steam and the consumption of coal was 20,000 tons a year. By 1900, a total of 20,000 yards of cloth was bleached and printed every day. This represents an astonishing amount of dress goods being shipped out and made into clothing by women all over the United States. There were 50 employees who did nothing but prepare swatches of fabrics and put together the sample books sent out to jobbers.

The equipment of the Arnold Print Works, in 1898, gives an idea of the magnitude of the larger American factories of the time. They owned 16 "wide" printing machines, each with a cylinder drier, 10 padding machines, a Mather and Platt continuous steaming machine with drying machines of copper capable of drying its entire product of bleached and printed fabrics. There were 300 iron indigo vats (for the Blue Dip) and 16 iron "dye becks" and a large number of "jiggers" for fancy dyeing. There was also full equipment for washing, soaping, preparing, tentering, and calendaring. The floor surface of the plant was 10 acres, and they also operated an iron repair and a woodworking shop for maintenance and had their own gas plant on the premises. The Arnold Print Works was in operation until 1937.

In the collections of the Museum of Art of the Rhode Island School of Design in Providence are many sample books of Arnold cottons, as well as their order books, labels, and other records, and — of great interest to designers — their French "copy-books." The author is indebted to the Museum for allowing photographs to be taken of much of the collection.

Anyone who has seen swatch-books of various American print works that operated between 1840 and 1900 cannot help noticing the similarities in patterns put out by half a dozen or more printers in different parts of the East. The French, and possibly some English, pattern-books must certainly account for this, as well as an exchange of employees and swiping of designs. It was about this period that there was the debate in the British Parliament about the copyright of fabric designs, and it was said then that American print works had no way of copyrighting their designs. They obviously paid no attention to British copyrights either! Most of the patterns were small geometrics, eccentric geometrics, or sprigged flower designs that were used for dress goods, so the French styles were of first importance. Probably most of the print works subscribed to the so-called "art-design" services of Europe.

The Arnold brothers subscribed to "Claude Frères" of Paris, who supplied them with books of hundreds of fine color renderings of all kinds of designs by French artists. Also, books of fabric swatches of fancy French weaves such as plissés and matelessés which the Arnold frères skillfully reproduced in *prints*, so they looked like the real thing. The idea seems entirely outlandish, but the prints seem to have just the right style for the time!

Arnold had representatives in New York whose business it was to "obtain the newest and most tasteful designs" from Paris, the leader of world fashions. Staff artists in North Adams made the drawings and skilled engravers transferred them to copper rollers for printing. A souvenir book from the North Adams Old Home Week of September 5, 1909, calls the Arnold Print Works engraving department "the equal of any establishment of its kind in the country, the Government Bureau of Engraving at Washington not being excepted." In that year there were Arnold offices in New York, Boston, Chicago, St. Louis, Philadelphia, and Baltimore and the company produced more than $5,000,000 worth of goods annually.

Until about 1900 or later, the way of life of American women had a lot to do with the success and the volume of production of the early printing factories. Ready-made clothing was almost unknown — especially outside of three or four large cities. The men went to a tailor for their suits and the women made all the family clothing themselves or hired a seamstress. The "sewing woman" who took care of the needs of three or four large families was an artist-in-residence in the homes all year around. Thus, the prints used for dresses were sold from bolts filling the shelves in the town dry-goods emporium directly to the women who were to make and wear the clothing. The garment-making industry — today's big buyer of fabrics — was yet to be born.

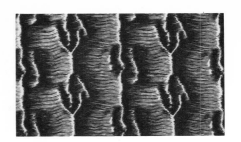

Fig. 164. Two swatches of French plissés — woven "crinkled" cottons, from one of Arnold's foreign sample books

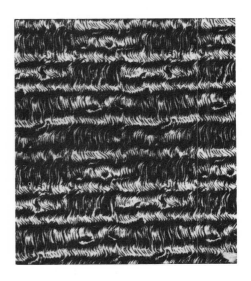

Fig. 165. *Right:* Three swatches from the Arnold Print Works sample books showing prints on buff cotton, in blue — in imitation of the French plissés

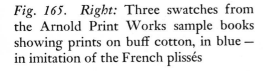

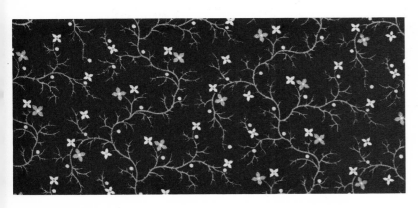

Fig. 166. Design in two colors and white on black background printed on medium-weight cotton. Sample books showed as many as six color combinations for the designs. This is a typical "sprigged" design so popular for dresses — Arnold Print Works

Fig. 167. Three-color print on heavy cotton, dated 1891, from the Arnold Print Works. Printed colored backgrounds came in a choice of gray, mauve, blue, rose, or rust. Flowers were white with stems and leaves in two darker tones of the background color. A slightly larger-scale, graceful, and summery-looking light cotton dress fabric

Fig. 168. Four swatches printed on heavy cotton, c. 1840; possibly from an English pattern book owned by the Arnold Print Works. Printed backgrounds in dark green or purple — finely engraved lines in brown and other colors, with some "shaded" colors. The effect is decidedly drab

Fig. 169. Seven prints on heavy cotton in two or three colors of drab and earth tones. The book is dated 1835, but it is uncertain if these are English swatches, or Arnold copies of English designs. At any rate, they are all the popular "Excentrics" and geometrics, and the three in the center of the page are assorted versions of the first and most famous English Excentric, "Lane's Net" (See also Fig. 145)

Fig. 170. Roller prints in black on white medium weight cotton, c. 1891. These and others similar are called "Shaker Grays"—small patterns that were named after the neutral costumes of the Shakers, a conservative religious group. It is doubtful if the Shakers ever wore them. Arnold Print Works

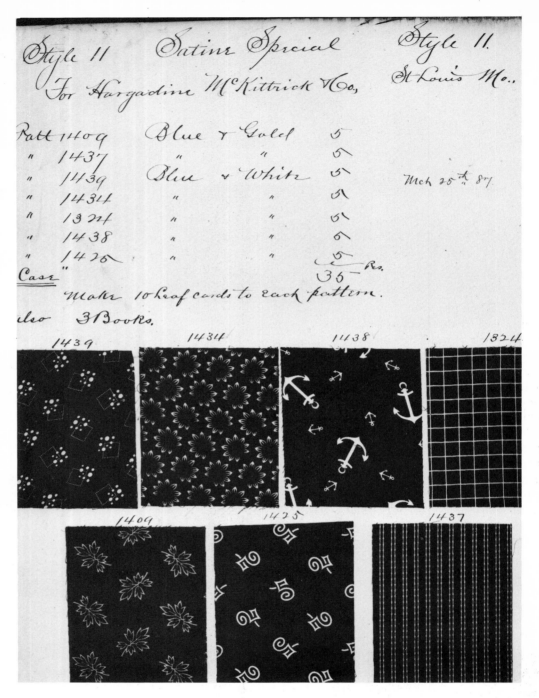

Fig. 171. A page from the Arnold Print Works' order books, dated March 25, 1887, and a record of an order of "Satine Specials" sent to Hargadine, McKittrick Co. of St. Louis, Mo. Small patterned navy blue and white cottons printed by the Arnold Print Works

Fig. 172. Print made to represent a patchwork of calicoes, from New York, c. 1850. Machine-printed in "madder style" in red, dark brown, orange, and blue. All the colors except the blue could be produced by being printed first in varying strengths of acetate of alumina (the mordant), and then dipped only once into the madder dye. The blue was then printed separately. Courtesy, Index of American Design, National Gallery of Art

Fig. 173. Printed cotton velveteen — green and black on light green background, designed by Candace Wheeler and produced by Cheney Brothers, c. 1885. Courtesy, Metropolitan Museum of Art, Gift of Mrs. Boudinot Keith, 1928

18. THE GLOUCESTER PRINT WORKS

From Bishop's *History of American Manufactures*, Vol. III, comes a quaintly vivid song of praise for a 19th century printing establishment that ends with a theme of faith in early American industries. Writing about the Gloucester Print Works and Washington Mills in 1868, the report says:

"There is at Gloucester on the Delaware River [Gloucester City, New Jersey] a large Print-Works combining facilities for calico-printing, fancy dyeing, bleaching and finishing. Their production is mainly madder prints which are attaining an enviable reputation in the market for choice styles and fast colors." Coal-fired steam engines were used for power and "one engine and boiler is used exclusively for pumping water from the Delaware River, which was found to be superior for both dyeing and bleaching, and of which a large quantity is used. Among the interesting machinery employed in the printing of calicoes is that which produces the figure with the copper rollers with matchless accuracy and delicacy. The pantograph machine is extensively used and such is the facility it affords that females are employed and found in many respects to be the best adapted in skill for executing some of the processes.

"President of the Company is David S. Brown; his establishments have capability of far greater development if the policy of the government is established in favor of its skill and industry. They constitute one of the great art schools of the country for the education of designers and chemists whose genius we may reasonably anticipate will, ere long, elevate the art products of America to a level with those of France and Great Britain."

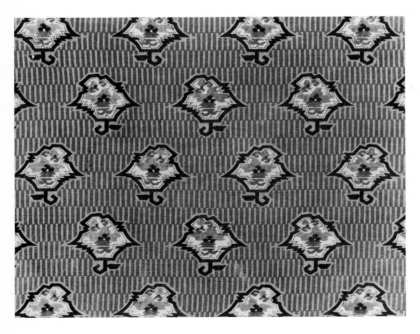

Fig. 174. Fragment of cotton material from a dress worn by Clara Barton, c. 1860. Courtesy, Metropolitan Museum of Art, Gift of Julia Brenner, 1936

CONCLUSION

If we try to imagine a Pope without a robe, a circus without a tent, a parade without banners, a home without curtains, a bride without a veil, a baby without a blanket, or a bath without a towel, we must agree that *cloth* is indispensable and that colored or printed cloth is beautiful and adds grace to living. And yet, one cannot help being aware that fabrics are, in an archeological, historical, and perhaps even in an aesthetic, sense doomed to obscurity. They are simply used up during the life of man. However resplendent his robes have made him look, they are slated to be buried on him, and however beautiful they may have made his abode, they will disappear long before the walls go down.

Significant and lasting contributions to the history of printed and painted textiles have been made by comparatively few peoples and lands. They are not too numerous to mention: the prints of the Copts and Egyptians, the painted cottons of India and the East, the batiks of Java, the stencils of Japan, the Jouy prints of France, and the block prints of England.

America came into the picture as a pioneer nation and as a British subject; both factors worked against her, making an early significant contribution to fabric history. American blue resist prints are few in number and are almost unknown outside museums and historic collections. Despite their murky ancestry, they are unique and many people find them very handsome. If they ever earn a clear title to American origin, they will probably prove to be the only truly significant fabrics of America's first three hundred years.

Beyond them, only two secondary awards for excellence can be made: one for the unself-conscious charm of some of the early folk fabrics, and one for the wonderful textile machinery that was evolving at about the time our story ends. However, it does not take an especially-tuned ear to hear the harmonious music still coming from America's fabric vocabulary:

> Banyans, drugget, dimothy and tow,
> Padusoy, kersey and braid.
>   Bombazeen and fustian of philmot and puce,
>   And
>   The Sawyer, Ashton & Company's Great Western
>   Oil Cloth and Window Shade Manufactory
>   of Cincinnati, Ohio —
>   1850.

Flo Pettit living at the Sighn of
y̆ Callico Printer in Glenbrooke
Prints Callicoes & all sorts of
Silkes and Fine Stuffs by Hand

Fig. 175.   A Textile Printer's Trade Card, American, 20th century

A Roster of
American Calico Printers and Print Works, 1776-1900

1777	Nathaniel Norgrove	Philadelphia (?)
1780	Herman Vandausen	East Greenwich, R. I.
1780	Zachariah Allen	East Greenwich, R. I.
1780	Jeremiah Eddy	East Greenwich, R. I.
1780	? Alverson	Providence, R. I.
1782	Jabez Grover	Foxboro, Mass.
1784	Henry Royl & Co.	Philadelphia
1786	Robert Taylor	Philadelphia
1791	Nicholas Mayer	Philadelphia
1791	Moses Phillip & Son Walkie	New York City (dyers?)
1792	Stephen Addington	Springfield, N. J.
1794	Schaub (Schwab?), Tissot & DuBosque	Providence, R. I.
1795	William Codman	New York City
1795	Archibald Hamilton Rowan	Delaware
1796	G. Mountcastle	Philadelphia
1796	Name unknown	Pompton, N. J.
1797	Wm. Combs & Co.	New York City
1797	Robert Newell (& Peter Schaub)	East Greenwich, R. I.
1797	Oakford & LaCollay	Philadelphia
1798	Davy, Roberts & Co.	Germantown, Pa.
1800	N. Y. Calico Printing Manufactory	New York City
1801	John M. Gibbon	Paterson, N. J.
1801	Wayne & Williamson	New York City
1803	? Stewart	Germantown, Pa.
1803	Thorp, Siddel & Co.	Philadelphia
1803	? Thorburn	Darby, Pa.
1805	Benjamin and Barney Merry	Pawtucket, R. I.
1809	Name unknown	Baltimore, Md.
1811	Francis Labbe	Philadelphia
1812	Waltham Manufactory	Waltham, Mass.
1822	Name unknown	Baltimore, Md.
1822	Name unknown	Columbiaville, N. Y.
1823	John Hewson, Jr.	Philadelphia
1823	Merrimack Manufacturing Co.	Lowell, Mass.
1823	Name unknown	Sanford, Maine
1823	Name unknown	Bronxdale, ?
1823	Taunton Manufacturing Co.	Taunton, Mass.
1824	Crocker Bros. & Co. or Crocker, Richmond & Otis	Taunton, Mass.
1825	Apponaug Print Works	Apponaug, R. I.
1825	Andrew Robeson	Fall River, Mass.
1825	William Sprague Cranston Print Works	Cranston, R. I.

1826	Hudson Calico Print Works	Stockport, Mass.
1826	Joseph & Benjamin Marshall	Stockport, Mass.
1827	The Warren Manufactory	Baltimore, Md.
1829	Cocheco Co. or Dover Mfg. Co.	Dover, N. H.
1829	Eagle Print Works	Belleview, N. J.
1829	Thomas Hunter	Philadelphia
1830	Philip Allen	Providence, R. I.
1830	Crawford Allen	Cranston, R. I.
1830	Perkins & Wendell	LaGrange, Pa.
1830	American Print Works	Fall River, Mass.
1830	Globe Print Works	Tiverton, Mass.
1830	Bay State Print Works	Tiverton, Mass.
1836	Jacob Dunnell Mfg. Co.	Pawtucket, R. I.
1836	Marshall, Carville & Taylor	Hudson, N. Y.
1837	Phillips Mills	Lynn, Mass.
1843	Benjamin Cozzens	Providence, R. I.
1844	Hamilton Mfg. Co.	Lowell, Mass.
1844	Joseph Ripka	Manayunk, Pa.
1847	Briggs & Co.	Frankfort, ?
1848	Manchester Print Works	Manchester, N. H.
	Joseph Bates & John Goodier	
1849	Lodi Print Works	Lodi, N. J.
1850	Woonsockett Co.	Woonsocket, R. I.
1850	Garner & Co.	Haverstraw, N. Y.
1853	Pacific Mills	Lawrence, Mass.
1856	William Jarvie (Merrimack Mills)	Lowell, Mass.
1861	Arnold Print Works	North Adams, Mass.
1868	Gloucester Print Works	Gloucester City, N. J.

Note: Dates given are all uncertain by a few years; the approximate starting date of factories is given, and the earliest recorded date of individual calico printers.

Things That Went on from 1776 to 1900

Note: American dates are shown against left margin;
foreign dates are indented five spaces

1776 Handwoven patterned coverlets became part of the American tradition and many survive

1777 Many printing establishments were set up in Pennsylvania between this date and 1800

    1779 The mule jenny was invented in England by Samuel Crompton — a machine for simultaneously drawing and spinning threads and winding them into cops (conical spools); this was a combination of Arkwright's spinning machine and Hargreave's spinning jenny

1780 A cotton manufactory was set up in Worcester, Mass.; horse power was used where water power was not available

1780 Herman Vandausen began printing from wood blocks in East Greenwich, R. I.; his blocks are the oldest *dated* American blocks known

1781 End of the Revolution. The last of the colonies ratified the American Articles of Confederation

1782 James Watt took out his final patent on a steam engine

1783 The Watt steam engine was applied to carding and spinning cotton

    1783 The earliest Jouy *copper-plate* prints dated for sure

1783 Last British forces left America; final treaty signed

    1785 Thomas Bell patented cylinder-printing in England, using copper rollers engraved with patterns; this was destined to change the whole printing industry from hand to machine

    1785 The power loom invented in England by Edmund Cartwright; the English would not allow the invention out of the country

1785 Cotton was first imported into Providence from Spain

1786 America was still unable to get manufacturing secrets from England

    1786 The use of acid bleach was introduced in Glasgow

1786 Models of Arkwright's spinning machines were smuggled into the United States from England

1787 The Society of the University of Pennsylvania offered a prize for "the best specimens or patterns of printed linens or cotton goods stained within the United States"

    1787 Print works were established near Genoa, Italy, by a Swiss artisan, Michele Speich

1788 Cotton was first woven by machinery in Beverly, Massachusetts, and in Philadelphia

1788 The Hartford, Connecticut, Woolen Manufactory was the first to use water power to weave woolens; George Washington ordered a dark brown wool cloth for his inaugural suit from this factory

1788 The fly shuttle was introduced into Providence by Joseph Alexander

1789 Sea-island cotton from Jamaica was first planted in America

1789 The "first" cotton mill in New England was established at Beverly, Massachusetts

1790 A cotton manufactory in Rhode Island was the first to apply water power to the mule jenny (cotton spinning machine)

1790 Samuel Slater, called "The Father of American Manufactures," came to Providence from England and set up a cotton manufactory for Almy & Brown

1790 The so-called oldest firm of block printers in England was founded as Messrs. Stead, McAlpin & Co.; the firm is still in business in 1969
1792 The first cotton thread for sewing was spun on a home wheel in Pawtucket, Rhode Island
1792 Under the sponsorship of Alexander Hamilton a complete fabric manufactory was started in Paterson, New Jersey; it had machinery for spinning, weaving, bleaching, and printing. It failed in 1795
1793 Eli Whitney invented the cotton gin — a machine that cleared seeds from cotton
1794 The firm of Schaub, Tissot & DuBosque printed calico in Rhode Island
1794 The first wool-carding machine was made at Newburyport, Massachusetts
1794 The first machine-made cotton thread for sewing was made by Samuel Slater in Rhode Island
1797 Two Frenchmen, Chardon and LaCollay, established a wallpaper "staining" factory and also printed calico in Philadelphia
1798 The Samuel Slater mill started to operate by water power at Providence
1800 By this date America had some machinery imported or smuggled in from England, and some was made in the United States. The colonies were now completely independent from England politically, but had to compete with her in trade and manufacturing
1800 India chintzes were "quite out of style" in England
1800 Copper-plate kerchiefs commemorating Washington and other government and military figures were popular
1801 Jacquard loom invented in France to weave patterns mechanically
1802 The Peel Works at Bury, Lancashire, England, began using the process of "neutral work" — a combination of resist and mordant printing which later became a common method
1802 First power looms used in America in Rhode Island
1803 First cotton factory established in New Hampshire
1803 Power looms first widely used in England after many trials and failures
1803 Engraved copper rollers used on a cylinder-printing press operated by Thorp, Siddel and Co. in Pennsylvania
1805 In England the "union" or "mule machine" was invented by James Burton and Adam Parkinson; it printed fabrics with engraved metal rollers in combination with wooden rollers on the same machine
1809 There were 87 cotton mills in operation in Rhode Island, New Hampshire, New York, Massachusetts, and Connecticut
1810 The first permanent green dye for printing fabrics was developed by Oberkampf at Jouy, France. After this other chemical dyes began to be developed in France, England, and Germany
1810 Turkey red first used by M. Daniel Koechlin at Mulhouse, France
1812 War between the United States and Great Britain
1812 The first mill in which all stages of manufacturing cotton were done under one roof began at Waltham, Massachusetts. It prepared raw materials and produced bolts of finished goods
1822 Calicoes were printed in seven or eight colors in Baltimore
1822 The first American copper-cylinder engraving was done by David H. Mason and Matthew W. Baldwin at Philadelphia
1822 Calico printing and drying machines were invented
1823 The Merrimack Mills at Lowell, Massachusetts, could print 2500 yards of cotton daily

1826 The first Jacquard loom was introduced in Philadelphia. It could weave complicated patterns automatically and radically altered the style of woven fabrics which had been done by hand until then, in much simpler patterns

1826 America began exporting cottons

1827 The first complete cylinder-printing machine was imported from England (where inventions were still guarded)

1831 By this date there were 800 cotton mills in the United States

1836 The Mexican War — mainly Texas vs. Mexico

1836 One hundred and twenty million yards of calico were printed in the United States

1836 Print works still employed a number of hand-block printers

1840 By this date copper-roller printing on power presses had almost entirely replaced all other methods of fabric printing

1844 The first color-printing machine for wallpaper was imported in Philadelphia by John Howell

 1856 An Englishman, Sir Wm. H. Perkin, discovered the first synthetic dye — aniline purple, or *mauve* — by distilling coal tar; his color gave the name to *The Mauve Decade*

1856 Painted window shades were made at Cincinnati and elsewhere and were very popular

1860 Growing industrialism had an impact on taste in every field: fancy wallpapers, Brussels carpets, factory-made chairs, and yards of flowered chintz and cretonne were the vogue

1861 The Civil War (to 1865)

1864 Thomas Holliday of Brooklyn, New York, made a synthetic magenta dye

 1868 In Germany alizarine dye (red) was made synthetically and replaced madder which had been used for centuries (from the root-herb, madder)

 1873 William Morris, foremost of the 19th century English cotton printers and designers, made his influence felt in America

1876 The Centennial Exposition at Philadelphia was a monument to "industrial art" objects

1880 A synthetic blue dye made from a coal-tar product was finally perfected to replace indigo blue

1898 Spanish-American War, after which the United States emerged as a naval and world trade power

1900 Up to this date Germany held most of the patents and secrets of dye-making, but in a few years the United States made dyes of its own invention and the fabric-printing trades were off and running

Major American Textile Exhibitions

(Catalogs available in Art Libraries except for #8 below)

1. Baltimore Museum of Art. May, 1925 — *Old Textiles*
2. Metropolitan Museum of Art, N.Y.C., 1927 — *Painted & Printed Fabrics*
3. Brooklyn Museum, N. Y., 1931 — *Early American Printed Textiles*
4. New York (City) Historical Society, 1941 — *American Scenes and Events on Textiles* — Printed Cottons, Linens and Silks from 1777 to 1941
5. Brooklyn Museum, N. Y., January–March, 1946 — *5,000 Years of Fibres and Fabrics*
6. Museum of Modern Art, N. Y. C., 1955 — *Textiles and Ornaments of India*
7. Cooper Union Museum for the Arts of Decoration, N. Y. C. (now: Cooper-Hewitt Museum of Design, Smithsonian Institution), 1956 — *Design by the Yard*
8. The Scalamandré Museum of Textiles, N. Y. C., 1956 — *The Toiles of Today and Yesterday*
9. Philadelphia Museum of Art, 1961 — College of Art *Fabrics International*
10. Los Angeles County Museum, 1961 — *Painted and Printed Textiles from A. D. 800 to 1961*

CREDITS

PHOTOGRAPHERS
1. Brook, John, Boston, Mass. #82
2. Helga Photo Studio, Inc., N. Y. C. #58
3. La Reau, Maury, Staff Photographer for Old Sturbridge Village, Sturbridge, Mass., #s 85, 97, 100, 133 and 157
4. Pettit, Robert M., Glenbrook, Conn., #s 1, 5, 11, 14, 17, 23-26, 45, 50-55, 68-72, 83-86, 87, 92-95, 116, 117, 119, 121, 125, 128-130, 140-156, 161-164, 168-174; all color plates except Plate VI
5. Wyatt, A. J., Staff Photographer for the Philadelphia Museum of Art, #s 60, 66, 138, 139 and 165

OTHER SOURCES
1. Colonial newspaper mastheads, #s 48, 49, 59, 90 and 101 are from the Rare Book Room, New York Public Library, Astor, Lenox and Tilden Foundations
2. Index of American Design, National Gallery of Art, Washington, D.C., #s 120, 131, 137, 158, 159, 166 and 176 are photographs of water-color renderings done under the Works Progress Administration Art Project under President Franklin D. Roosevelt from 1932 to 1945. Its purpose was to provide an authoritative graphic survey of American decorative arts and crafts from the days of the earliest settlements to the late 19th century. Its Curator for many years was Dr. Erwin O. Christensen, and its Curator in 1969 is Dr. Grose Evans, whom we thank.
3. Masthead of the Pennsylvania *Gazette* and the Hewson advertisements #s 104, 105, 106 and 107 are from the Historical Society of Pennsylvania, Philadelphia
4. The Bibliography of Blue Resist Printing is from a report of the Cooper Union Museum of New York, now the Cooper-Hewitt Museum of Design of the Smithsonian Institution, dated May 17, 1956 and prepared by Miss Alice B. Beer and Miss Jean Mailey
5. Drawing of the Washington Press made by Ellie Simmons is used by courtesy of the artist and copyright by *Saturday Review*

BIBLIOGRAPHY

1. *Americana, Encyclopedia:* "Calico Printing."
2. Appleton, LeRoy. *Indian Art of the Americas.* Scribner's, 1950.
3. Bagnall, Wm. R. *Textile Industries of the United States.* Cambridge, Mass.: Riverside Press, 1893.
4. Baines, Edward, Jr. *History of the Cotton Manufactory in Great Britain.* London: H. Fisher, R. Fisher and P. Jackson, 1835.
5. Baker, G. P. *Calico Printing and Printing in the East Indies in the 17th and 18th Centuries.* London, 1921.
6. Baker, Walter D. and Ida S. *Batik and Other Pattern Dyeing.* Chicago: Atkinson, Mentzer & Co., 1920.
7. Beard, Charles A. and Mary R. *A Basic History of the United States.* Philadelphia: The Blakiston Company, 1944.
8. Bendure, Zelma and Pfeiffer, Gladys. *America's Fabrics.* New York: The Macmillan Company, 1947.
9. Bishop, J. Leander. *A History of American Manufactures 1608-1860.* Philadelphia: Edward Young & Co., 1864.
10. *Britannica, Encyclopaedia:* "Textiles — history, printing, dyeing."
11. Cahill, Holger. *American Folk Art* (The Art of the Common Man in America, 1750-1900) for the Museum of Modern Art: W. W. Norton & Co., 1932.
12. Cennini, Cennino. *The Craftsman's Handbook* ("Il Libro dell' Arte") 14th century reprint. New York: Dover Publications, 1954.
13. Clark, Victor S. *History of Manufactures in the United States*, Vol. I 1607-1860, Vol. II 1860-1893, Vol. III 1893-1929. New York: for the Carnegie Institution; McGraw-Hill, 1929.
14. Clouzot, Henri and Morris, Frances. *Painted and Printed Fabrics.* New York: Metropolitan Museum of Art, 1927.
15. Comstock, Helen (editor). *The Concise Encyclopedia of American Antiques*, Vol. I & Vol. II. New York: Hawthorn Books, 1958.
16. Cooper, T. *A Practical Treatise on Dyeing and Calico Printing.* Philadelphia: Bobson, 1815.
17. Dow, George Francis. *The Arts and Crafts in New England*, 1704-1775. Wayside Press, 1927.
18. Douglas and d'Harnoncourt. *Indian Art of the United States.* New York: Museum of Modern Art, 1941.
19. Drepperd, Carl W. *American Pioneer Arts and Artists.* Pond-Ekberg Company, 1942.
20. Earle, Alice Morse. *Child Life in Colonial Days.* Macmillan, 1896.
21. Earle, Alice Morse. *Customs and Fashions in Old New England.* Scribner's 1893.
22. Earle, Alice Morse. *Home Life in Colonial Days.* Macmillan, 1898.
23. Earle, Alice Morse. *Two Centuries of Costume*, Vol. I and Vol. II. Macmillan, 1898.
24. Earle, Alice Morse. *Costume of Colonial Times.* Scribner's, 1894.
25. Eberlein, H. D. and McClure, A. *The Practical Book of Early American Arts and Crafts.* J. P. Lippincott, 1916.
26. *European Printed Textiles.* Victoria and Albert Museum, British Information Services, 1949.
27. Glazier, Richard. *Historic Textile Fabrics.* London: B. T. Batsford, Ltd., 1923.
28. Gottesman, Rita Susswein. *Arts and Crafts in New York*, Vol. I 1726-1776, Vol. II 1777-1799, Vol. III 1800-1804. New York: New York Historical Society, 1938, 1954, 1965.
29. Gunsaulus, Helen C. *Japanese Textiles.* New York: Japan Society of New York, 1941.
30. Halsey and Tower. *The Homes of our Ancestors.* New York: Garden City, 1926.
31. *History of the State of Rhode Island*, 1636-1878. Philadelphia: Hoag, Wade & Co., 1878.
32. Hunter, George Leland. *Decorative Textiles.* J. B. Lippincott, 1919.
33. Langdon, William Chauncy. *Everyday Things in American Life 1607-1776.* Scribner's, 1937.
34. Lawrie, L. G. *A Bibliography of Dyeing and Textile Printing.* London: Chapman and Hall, 1949.

35. Lewis, Ethel. *The Romance of Textiles*, Macmillan, 1937.

36. Lewis, Frank. *English Chintz from Earliest Times Until the Present Day*. Essex, England: 1935.

37. Little, Frances. *Early American Textiles*. New York: Century Co., 1931.

38. Little, Nina Fletcher. *American Decorative Wall Paintings 1700-1850*. Studio Publications, 1952.

39. Lynes, Russell. *The Tastemakers*. New York: Harper, 1954.

40. McClellan, Elisabeth. *History of American Costume*. New York: Tudor Publishing Co., 1937.

41. McClelland, Nancy. *Historic Wallpapers*. J. B. Lippincott, 1924.

42. Montgomery, Florence. *Printed Textiles: English and American Cottons and Linens, 1700-1850*. New York: The Viking Press, 1969.

43. Parnell, E. A. *Dyeing and Calico Printing*. MacFarlane, 1860.

44. Peel & Yates Factory, *Pattern Book* c. 1780: Bury, Lancashire, England. Metropolitan Museum of Art Textile Study Room only.

45. Percival, MacIver, *The Chintz Book*. New York: Frederick A. Stokes Co., Inc., 1923.

46. Peto, Florence. *American Quilts and Coverlets*. New York: Chanticleer Press, 1949.

47. Ross, Ishbel. *Proud Kate*. New York: Harper, 1953.

48. Spears, W. F. *History of North Adams, Mass., 1749-1885*. North Adams, Mass.: Hoosic Valley News Printing House, 1885.

49. Stephenson, Jessie Banes. *From Old Stencils to Silk Screening*. Scribner's, 1953.

50. Stern, Madeleine B. *We, the Women*. New York: Schulte Publishing Co., 1963.

51. Tennent, J. Emerson. *A Treatise on the Copyright of Designs for Printed Fabrics*. London: Smith, Elder & Co., 1841.

52. Turnbull, Geoffrey. *A History of the Calico Printing Industry of Great Britain*. Sherratt, England: 1951.

53. Vaillant, G. C. *Indian Arts of North America*. New York: Harper, 1939.

54. Ware, Caroline Farrar. *The Early New England Cotton Manufacture — A Study in Industrial Beginnings*. New York: Russell & Russell, 1931.

55. White, George S. *Memoir of Samuel Slater*. Philadelphia, 1836.

PERIODICALS

56. *American Collector*. November 14, 1935, p. 7: "The Charm of Old Cotton Prints" by Rita Susswein.

57. *Antiques*. March, 1925: "Fire Sacks and Fire Pockets" by Howard M. Chapin.

58. *Antiques*. January, 1928, p. 38: "Early Cotton Printing in America" by Frances Little.

59. *Antiques*. April, 1928, p. 285: "Some Early Pattern Blocks" by Theo Merrill Fisher (and cover illustration).

60. *Antiques*. October, 1929, p. 286: "A Block-Printed Counterpane" by Florence Thompson Howe.

61. *Antiques*. February, 1930, p. 114: Block Printing Kit.

62. *Antiques*. April, 1930, p. 311: "Come, Gentle Spring" (Toiles de Jouy) by Elizabeth Merrill.

63. *Antiques*. April, 1931, p. 298: "Some Colonial and Early American Decorative Floors" by Esther S. Frazer (Brazer).

64. *Antiques*. September, 1931, p. 162: "Paintings on Velvet" by Louise Karr.

65. *Antiques*. November, 1937, p. 229: "Printed Calico trimmings made by the Merrimack Co., 1876".

66. *Antiques*. December, 1939: "A Cotton Travelogue" by Esther Lewittes. "Painted Window Shades" by Edgar Weld King.

67. *Antiques*. March, 1940, p. 119: Block Printed Coverlet; p. 122: "Three Stenciled Counterpanes" by Florence Thompson Howe.

68. *Antiques*. April, 1940, p. 192: "Stumbling Blocks, a Puzzle In Patterns" by Lawrence B. Romaine.

69. *Antiques*. January, 1941, p. 28: "Cloth of Colonial America" by Cedric Larsen.

70. *Antiques*. October, 1941, p. 212: "The Mexican War on Printed Cottons" by Esther Lewittes.

71. *Antiques*. May, 1948, p. 349: "Resist Printing Yesterday and Today" by Franco Scalamandre.

72. *Antiques*. August, 1953, p. 121: "A Textile Discovery" (Hewson print) by Florence Peto.

73. *Antiques*. September, 1955, p. 257: "Stenciled Fabrics from Old Sturbridge Village."

74. *Antiques*. May, 1956, p. 422: "Printed Textiles in America" by Jean Mailey.

75. *Antiques*. January, 1958, p. 69: Painted Floor Cloths."

76. *Antiques.* October, 1968, p. 536: "Textile Printing in 18th Century America" by Florence Montgomery.
77. *Burlington Magazine.* Vol. 97, No. 625, April, 1955, pp. 106-114: "Origins of the Oriental Style in English Decorative Art" by J. Irwin.
78. *Chronicle* of the Museum for the Arts of Decoration of the Cooper Union, June, 1953, Vol. 2, No. 5: "Indian Textiles in the Museum's Collections" by Jean Mailey.
79. *Chronicle* of the Museum for the Arts of Decoration of the Cooper Union. October, 1963, Vol. 13, No. 5: "Printed Textiles in the Museum's Collections" by Alice B. Beer.
80. *Ciba Review* #3 — November, 1937: Wall Coverings
81. *Ciba Review* #12 — August, 1938: Weaving and Dyeing in Ancient Egypt and Babylon.
82. *Ciba Review* #26 — October, 1939: Mediaeval Cloth Printing in Europe.
83. *Ciba Review* #31 — March, 1940: Textile Printing in 18th Century France.
84. *Ciba Review* #37 — January, 1941: Textile Ornament.
85. *Ciba Review* #58 — July, 1947: Batiks.
86. *Ciba Review* #70 — September, 1948: Textile Art in Ancient Mexico.
87. *Ciba Review* #76 — October, 1949: Early American Textiles.
88. *Ciba Review* #85 — April, 1951: Indigo.
89. *Ciba Review* #90 — February, 1952: Textile Arts of the North American Indians.
90. *Ciba Review* #105 — August, 1954: Textile Printing in Switzerland.
91. *Ciba Review* #135 — December, 1959: Rouen, French Textile Centre.
92. *Ciba Review* 1962/2 — Manchester — the Origins of Cottonopolis.
93. *Ciba Review* 1968/2 — Textiles in Biblical Times.
94. *The Connoisseur.* July 19, 1917: "Printed Cottons" by Celia Hemming.
95. *The Connoisseur.* May, 1919, p. 13: "How Cottons were Printed in the 18th Century" by MacIver Percival.
96. *Journal of Indian Textile History.* No. 1, 1955: "Indian Textile Trade in 17th Century Western India" by John Irwin.
96A. *Journal of Indian Textile History.* No. 1, 1955: "An English Source of Indian Chintz Designs" by K. B. Brett.
97. *Journal of Indian Textile History.* No. 3, 1957: "The Flowering Tree in Indian Chintz" by K. B. Brett.
98. *Journal of the Society of Dyers and Colourists.* May, 1960, pp. 425-435: "The Origins of English Calico Printing" by Peter Floud.
99. *Journal of the Society of Dyers and Colourists.* June, 1960, pp. 344-349: "The English Contribution to the Early History of Indigo Printing" by Peter Floud.
100. *Journal of the Society of Dyers and Colourists.* July, 1960, pp. 425-434: "The English Contribution to the Development of Copperplate Printing" by Peter Floud.
101. *Needle and Bobbin Club Bulletin.* Vol. 15: "Ikat Technique" by Iklé.
102. *Needle and Bobbin Club Bulletin.* Vol. 18: "Batik in Java" by Adam.
103. *Pennsylvania Magazine of History and Biography.* Vol. LII, No. 2, 1928: "Calico Printing and Linen Printing in Philadelphia" by Harold E. Gillingham.

BIBLIOGRAPHY ON BLUE RESIST PRINTING

Berthoud, Dorette, *Les Indiennes Neuchâteloises.* Boudry, Baconnière, 1951.
Dollfuss-Aysset, Daniel. *Materiaux pour la Coloration des Étoffes.* 2 vols. Paris: Savy, 1865.
Forrer, R. *Die Kunst des Zeugdruck vom Mittelalter biz zur Emperezeit.* Strassburg i Els., Schlesier & Schweikhardt, 1898.
Pageant of Japanese Art. Edited by the staff of the Tokyo Museum. Vol. V. Toyo Bunka Co., Ltd., Tokyo.

Pfister, R. *Les Toiles Imprimées de Fostat et l'Hindoustan.* Paris: Editions d'Art et d'Histoire.
Roy, Bernard. *Une Capitale de l'Indiennage: Nantes.* Nantes, Musée des Salorges, 1948.
Ryhiner, Jean. *Mss.* Traité sur la Fabrication et le Commerce des Toiles Peintes, 1766. Societé Industrielle de Mulhouse.
Vydra, Josef. *Indigo Blue Print in Slovak Folk Art.* Artia: Prague, 1954.

INDEX